IN THE HEART
OF THE CANADIAN ROCKIES

IES

D0760137

IN THE HEART
OF THE CANADIAN ROCKIES

:~

James Outram

"Mountains are the beginning and end of all natural scenery."
—Ruskin.

Foreword by Chic Scott

Rocky
Mountain Books

VANCOUVER · VICTORIA · CALGARY

Thompson-Nicola Regional District
Library System
300-465 VICTORIA STREET
KAMLOOPS, BC   V2C 2A9

Rocky Mountain Books   Rocky Mountain Books
#108 – 17665 66A Avenue   PO Box 468
Surrey, BC V3S 2A7   Custer, WA
www.rmbooks.com   98240-0468

Library and Archives Canada Cataloguing in Publication
In the heart of the Canadian Rockies / Sir James Outram ;
Chic Scott, foreword. Outram, James, Sir, 1864-1925.

(Mountain classics collection ; 3)
Previous ed. published in 1923.
ISBN 978-1-894765-96-1

1. Outram, James, Sir, 1864-1925. 2. Rocky Mountains, Canadian (B.C. and Alta.)—
Description and travel. 3. British Columbia—Description and travel. 4. Alberta—
Description and travel. 5. Mountaineering—Rocky Mountains, Canadian (B.C. and Alta.)—
History. 6. Mountaineers—Great Britain—Biography. I. Title. II. Series.

FC219.O98 2007   917.1104'3   C2007-902917-5

Library of Congress Control Number: 2007931978

Edited by Joe Wilderson
Cover design by Frances Hunter
Front cover photo is of Mount Assiniboine and Lake Magog, Alberta. (Glenbow Archive PA-3689-463)

Printed in Canada

Rocky Mountain Books acknowledges the financial support for its publishing program from the Government of Canada through the Book Publishing Industry Development Program (BPIDP), Canada Council for the Arts, and the province of British Columbia through the British Columbia Arts Council and the Book Publishing Tax Credit.

This book has been produced on 100% post-consumer recycled paper, processed chlorine free and printed with vegetable-based dyes.

FOREWORD

James Outram was a mountaineer's mountaineer. Although he passionately loved the cool forest, the alpine flowers and the mountain torrent, the place where he really wanted to be was high on the peak itself. He felt best balanced up there on the narrow crest, the wind lashing his face and the void only a small slip away. "The spell is upon us," he wrote, "—not of wonder only or of awe, or even love that can be satisfied with distance. A closer, fuller intimacy must be ours . . ."

Outram was born in 1864 in London, England, and educated at Cambridge. He was ordained in the Church of England in 1889, and over the next ten years held several cures. He came to Canada in 1900 with his brother William to recover from a "brain collapse from overwork." Here in the Rocky Mountains he found "the long-sought sanctuary of the storm-tossed soul." For the next three years he plundered the store of first ascents in the Canadian Rockies, making 32 first ascents, 20 of them peaks over 10,000 feet (3,050 metres). Many of Outram's first ascents were of the most difficult peaks. He wrote of the mountaineer: "No toil is too arduous for him to undergo; the very difficulties constitute an added charm . . ."

After his three great climbing seasons (1900–1902), he chose to call Canada home, and lived in Alberta for the rest of his life, in Vermilion and Calgary. In 1912 he inherited the title of baronet that had been bestowed upon his grandfather. Although he was never again an aggressive climber, he continued to attend annual camps of the Apine Club of Canada, where he was a prominent figure. He died in 1925 at Victoria, B.C.

This book is an account of Outram's own climbs as well as a history of the climbs and explorations of previous pioneer alpinists.

v

It is organized geographically (from Mount Assiniboine in the south to the peaks of the Columbia Icefield in the north) rather than chronologically, so it can be confusing to follow Outram's odyssey through the Rockies. The adventures begin with his climb of Cascade Mountain in 1900, where he got his first glimpse of Mount Assiniboine. The great peak, gleaming in the distance and reputed to be inaccessible, fascinated him. "Little did I dream, though it then stirred every mountaineering impulse in my being (and there is a considerable number of them there), that twelve months later I should have the opportunity of disproving the truth of this distinguished reputation, and not only visiting the famous mountain, but standing on its topmost pinnacle."

With chapter 3 and the story of the Mount Assiniboine climb, the incredible dynamo that was James Outram is revealed. In only five days and five hours, accompanied by his packer, Bill Peyto, and his two Swiss guides, Christian Häsler and Christian Bohren, he made his way from Banff to the base of Mount Assiniboine, made an unsuccessful attempt on the peak reaching the summit of Lunette Peak, then the following day climbed the mountain, and on the fifth day returned 50 km back to Banff. Standing on the summit of Assiniboine, Outram had revealed his secret plan to his guides—he wanted to traverse the mountain. They had just climbed the south side of the peak, but Outram wanted to descend the steep and untried north ridge. Although the guides were reluctant, they acquiesced, and by nightfall they were safely back in camp, the perilous descent behind them.

It was a characteristic of Outram that he always pushed his guides, demanding more and more of them. But he pushed himself even harder. The distances he travelled on his long legs are astounding— climbing to Abbot Pass in only four hours from the shore of Lake Louise, and traversing from the head of the Yoho Valley over Balfour Pass, descending to Hector Lake, then continuing along the Bow Valley to the train station at Laggan in one long day.

Outram's descriptions of the natural beauties of the Canadian

Rockies are a bit florid, but when he comes to writing about the climbing he is brilliant. On his first attempt on Mount Assiniboine he finds himself alone on a small ledge, and muses, "Here for some moments I stood in solemn awe, perched like a statue in a lofty niche, cut in the topmost angle of a vast, titanic temple, with space in front, on either side, above, below, the yawning depths lost in the wreathing mists that wrapped the mountain's base." Chapter 14, the story of the ascent of Mount Bryce, opens: "Darkness was gathering apace. The sun had set nearly an hour ago. A piercing wind from a world of glaciers was whistling by on its wild course; and the rising moon, shining feebly athwart a mist of clouds, revealed two shivering human forms silhouetted upon the sky-line of a rocky ridge 10,000 feet above the sea."

Outram also gives us a fresh and lively window on life in the Rockies at the start of the 20th century. We discover the fledgling communities of Banff and Lake Louise and settle in at Mount Stephen House, the Canadian Pacific hotel at Field, and meet its manager, Miss Mollison. We share a rope with many of the Swiss Guides and get to know the Canadian outfitters. And we relax around the campfire with Outram and his companions: "One of the chief delights of camp life is the fire. Its cheerful blaze and lusty crackling logs lure everyone to its vicinity and invite the greatest sociability. It is a democratic institution of the most powerful and valuable type. All are equals under its potent influence, and conversation flows apace .... Tales of the mountains of this and other lands, of hunting experiences and cowboy episodes; tales of the gold fields mingle with the stirring themes of war, and adventures, grim and gay, by land and sea, in almost every clime, contribute to the nightly entertainment and while away the passing hour."

The high point of the book is Outram's great summer of 1902, when, with Christian Kaufmann and outfitters Jim Simpson and Fred Ballard, he ventured north of Lake Louise, along what is now the Icefields Parkway. In eight weeks he made an incredible ten first ascents of major peaks high up on the Great Divide. The first was

Mount Columbia, the second-highest summit in the Rockies, which he and Kaufmann climbed in a 22-hour marathon from the Castleguard River across the Columbia Icefield. The last climb, Mount Bryce, was the best and is the climax of the book. Long and complex with plenty of difficult climbing, the crux came on the descent when they were forced to downclimb a steep rock wall in darkness, where a slip would have meant death for both of them. Outram brilliantly describes the tension and suspense of this descent in the dark, with the wind whistling and stones rattling into the abyss.

Although Outram retired from serious climbing after only three years, he accomplished more than any other early Canadian climber (apart from the professional guides). Many of his first ascents are still major prizes for 21st century mountaineers and are rarely climbed. In this book he shares his story of adventure, takes us through a magical world, and invites us to follow.

Chic Scott

APOLOGY

THE WRITER OWES AND MOST sincerely offers an apology for the existence of this book. Its inception was due to kindly pressure, only yielded to with great reluctance, and its completion has been effected under serious difficulties. The brain collapse from overwork, which first impelled him to the mountain heights for mental rest and physical recuperation, has throughout hampered clear thought and steady composition. A basis of a few magazine articles has been built upon by scraps of work at odd half-hours, and thrown together without the opportunity either to weld the fragments into literary form or polish the resultant in a manner that would justify its presentation to the public.

As there is no pretence to literary merit, so there is no attempt at a scientific treatment of any of the geological, zoological, or botanical features met with in the Canadian Rockies, interesting as each undoubtedly is and deserving of attention of specialists. These characteristics are dealt with merely *en passant* as they strike a very ordinary mortal, with less than an elementary acquaintance with these sciences.

The only claims to consideration the writer can put forward are those of an enthusiast: first, as a lover of Nature and her infinite Creator, who has had the privilege, during a long period of compulsory abandonment of all his wonted mental occupations, to spend a part of three summers in the most attractive region it has been his lot to visit; and, secondly, as a mountaineer, to whom, as to *Childe Harold*, "high mountains are a feeling," and who can say with him,

"Where rose the mountains, there to him were friends."

His endeavour has been to combine some of the most striking narratives of others with a considerable fund of new experiences, gained in the exploration of hitherto untrodden peaks and passes, and, from an intimate acquaintance with almost all of the loftiest mountains and most lovely scenery along the chain of the Divide, from Mt. Assiniboine to Mt. Columbia,—the highest peak in the Dominion as yet conquered by the mountaineer,—to present some account of all the more notable "First Ascents," together with a description of the chief points of interest and beauty massed in the mountain fastnesses.

Thanks are most heartily given to the publishers of *The Century Magazine, Outing, Leslie's Monthly, The English Illustrated Magazine,* and *Appalachia* for permission to incorporate articles which have already appeared. Also to Professor C.E. Fay, editor, for kind permission to make extracts from numerous papers published in *Appalachia,* amongst which his own are most valuable: to Mr. W.D. Wilcox for permission to quote and refer to his delightful book, "The Rockies of Canada," and to Messrs. Stutfield and Collie for similar favours in connection with their work, "Climbs and Exploration in the Canadian Rockies." The writer would also express his indebtedness to the following gentlemen for permission to use photographs: Messrs. A.H. Cowan (4), H.W. DuBois, C.E. Fay, J. Habel, I. Langmuir, H.C. Parker, E.R. Shepard, and W.D. Wilcox, and the Detroit Photographic Company; to Mr. E. Deville, Surveyor-General of Canada, for maps published by the Dominion Land Survey, and to the Royal Geographical Society and Professor J.N. Collie for the latter's valuable map, which has been almost exactly reproduced, with an extension from Mr. W.D. Wilcox's map. For any variations from these originals the writer is solely responsible.

Finally, the writer desires to express his special thanks to his friend, Mr. Harrington Putnam, for most valuable advice and assistance during the progress of this volume through the press; and earnestly hopes that some of the readers of its pages may not only while away a passing hour pleasantly, but be drawn into a new or closer intimacy with the mountains, which may enrich their lives in future years.

THE MOUNTAINS AND THEIR HISTORY

"Westward the course of Empire takes its way"

THERE IS A WONDERFUL FASCINATION about mountains. Their massive grandeur, majesty of lofty height, splendour of striking outline —crag and pinnacle and precipice—seem to appeal both to the intellect and to the inmost soul of man, and to compel a mingled reverence and love.

More especially is this the case where snow and glacier combine to add a hundredfold to all the other charms and glories of the peaks. Their inspiration almost overwhelms one as he gazes on their

"Stainless ramps, …
Ranged in white ranks against the blue—untrod,
Infinite, wonderful—whose uplands vast
And lifted universe of crest and crag,
Shoulder and shelf, green slope and icy horn,
Led climbing thought higher and higher, until
It seemed to stand in heaven and speak with gods."

Who can wander unmoved in the calm shelter of some verdant valley, a foaming torrent swirling tumultuously at his feet, or beside the placid waters of a mountain lake, reflecting mirror-like the darkly sombre slopes of pine that lead us onward, upward to those

"Palaces of Nature, whose vast walls
Have pinnacled in clouds their snowy scalps,
And throned eternity in icy halls
Of cold sublimity; where forms and falls
The avalanche—the thunderbolt of snow!
All that expands the spirit yet appals
Gathers around these summits, as to show
How earth may pierce to heaven, yet leave vain man below."

But the fascination of the peaks permits no quiet acquiescence in this suggestion to remain in passive admiration at their base The spell is on us—not of wonder only or of awe, or even love that can be satisfied with distance. A closer, fuller intimacy must be ours; gained by a reverent study of their character and form and nature, penetrating their reserve, breaking down barriers, till from point to point we pass to learn the fullness of their being, and on each soaring crest learn from itself and its environment new glories and fresh beauties in the world and its Creator.

Such is the spirit of the mountaineer, and to gain this is at once his keen endeavour and his highest joy. No toil is too arduous for him to undergo; the very difficulties constitute an added charm; it is a science, loved and studied long and patiently, which in pursuit and ultimate achievement brings invariably a full reward.

The tiny land of Switzerland is famed throughout the civilized world for the splendour of its mountain scenery. In the tremendous effects of absolute elevation and extent, wild desolation and rugged immensity, it cannot, of course, compare with the huge chain of the Andes or the vast summits of the Himalayas, but for variety and charm, as well as accessibility, it has well-grounded claims to the title of "The Prince of Playgrounds." The rich valleys, threaded by icy torrents, adorned by frequent waterfalls, clothed with dark, sheltering forests, or brightened by cultivated fields and vineyards, dotted with picturesque chalets, and eloquent of peaceful, healthful home-life, are invaluable complements to the magnificent lakes, the towering cliffs, majestic glaciers, and stupendous, ice-clad peaks, which form the crowning glory of that favoured country unique in scenic grandeur as in history.

But though its scenery is unchangingly beautiful and the familiar Alpine monarchs retain forever the affection the mountaineer, yet his soul will crave—and rightly so—the chief joy of the climber's ambition, a "first ascent." He turns most naturally, therefore, to the great Continent of America, where he expects to find plenty of new things and generally finds them on the largest scale. The United States, with its enormous area and limitless array of Nature's mightiest works and treasures, might well expect to possess some counterpart to Europe's pleasure-ground. But, hunt as we may amid upland solitudes of Colorado's sea of lofty mountains, the noble peaks and canyons of the Californian Sierras, or the icy fastnesses of Mt. Shasta and the Cascade Range, the more closely they are studied, the more intrinsically are they found to differ from Switzerland. Each contains some of the splendid features that are all combined within the scanty limits of the little European Republic, but the wondrous glacial fields, the massing of majestic ranges, the striking individuality of each great peak, the forest areas, green pasture lands, clear lakes, and peaceful valleys, are nowhere found harmoniously blended on the western continent until the traveller visits that section of the Rocky Mountains which lies within the wide domain of Canada.

Following the Continental watershed from Colorado northward, the ranges of Montana begin to display the characteristic features which culminate in the Switzerland of the Western Hemisphere. The rounded or gabled summits here give place to broken pinnacles, precipices rise in frequent grandeur, enormous seas of ice sweep from the alpine heights into the verdant heart of pine- and spruce-clad valleys, gemmed with emerald and turquoise lakelets, and silvery waterfalls, and sparkling rivulets unite in producing a series of absolutely perfect mountain pictures.

Two variations from the European prototype are certainly conspicuous. The one, that in this country of superlatives the ranges

3

and peaks are multiplied tenfold. The area is vastly larger and the mountains are more closely packed together; but, as a consequence, the individual peaks, with some notable exceptions, are scarcely so strikingly characteristic as their Helvetian relatives. The other obvious difference lies in the wildness of the Rocky Mountain region. Except where the railroad, with its intruding whirl of civilization, has caused the springing up of one or two small hamlets and an occasional section-house, even along the highway of transcontinental traffic there is but little sign of man. The graceful chalet, the climbing herd of cattle, the musical tinkle of whose bells chimes faintly through the distance, the sturdy toiling peasant, here are not. Nature alone holds sway, rugged and wild and beautiful. And yet the seeker of these temples of Nature, whether to worship from afar or to explore with strenuous foot the most recesses of the wooded valley or the topmost pinnacle of some white summit, whence a bewildering panorama of matchless mountain scenery is unfolded before his delighted gaze, need not endure a single privation or discomfort in his quest. In all the luxury of the modern sleeping car the traveller is rapidly transported into the very heart of the mountain world. Much of it may be enjoyed without passing from the sight and sound of the great railroad artery, where charming hotels and rustic chalets keep him in comfort during his stay, and combine with the unsurpassed scenery to lengthen the utmost limit.

But to view the grandest mountains and obtain the finest climbs, it is necessary to camp out for a short or long period, and as this mode of life is one of the most delightful of experiences, the necessity enhances the pleasure of one's holiday. It adds to all the varied charms of scenery a free and healthful life, long journeys through primeval forests, scented with the sweet fragrance of the balsam fir, the fording of great rivers, and the enjoyment of the numerous attractions, human as well, as scenic, of a roving life.

The Canadian Rocky Mountains form the northern portion of the great Cordilleran chain, which spans the Continent of North America from Mexico to the shores of the Arctic Ocean. The

4

characteristics of the range vary largely in its long-drawn sweep from sunny south to icy north; the structure and the scenery change from time to time as one passes from one section to another along its mighty length. The farther north the latitude, the more the mountains in general diminish until they die down into insignificance.

But, though the highest individual peaks and the greatest mean elevation are found south of the Canadian borderline, the general character becomes more abrupt and rugged, more alpine in its vast areas of glacier and striking grandeur of pinnacle and precipice, till, in the region between the 50th and 53rd parallels, the only real counterpart of the Alps is found. The culminating point is reached in the centre of this section, where, just north of 52° north latitude, the huge Columbia icefield, containing an area of about 200 square miles of solid ice, at a mean elevation of nearly 10,000 feet above the sea, forms the hydrographical centre of a quarter of the Continent, and supplies the headwaters of streams that flow to three different oceans: the Athabasca, via the Mackenzie River, finding its outlet in the Arctic Ocean; the Saskatchewan flowing into the Atlantic at Hudson's Bay; and the Bush River, a tributary of the Columbia, reaching the Pacific.

The Canadian Rockies are mainly composed of strata ranging in age from the Middle Cambrian to Lower Carboniferous, and having a minimum thickness of 20,000 feet. But few traces of igneous rocks are found, the outcrop in the Ice River Valley being the most important. The mountains rise abruptly from the great plateau that forms an approach more than 1,000 miles in extent, and form a series of parallel ranges, with deep intervening valleys, running in a general direction from southeast to northwest. East of the Divide, the Lower Carboniferous strata are often overlaid by beds of Lower Cretaceous, with so imperceptible a break that, in spite of the wide difference in age, they are frequently indistinguishable were it not for their fossils; demonstrating that prior to the last great upheaval, to which the present form is due, little disturbance and no folding or crumpling of rocks occurred to any appreciable extent. The later disturbing agencies produced, in the eastern parts, very regular but complex flexures, usually at high angles from the axis of the range and sometimes completely overturned, resulting in a general appearance of vertical cliffs and long, easy slopes. In the centre the strata are fractured and upheaved rather than bent, and present a massive, cubical aspect.

Two interesting features are specially noticeable. One, perhaps unique, where great longitudinal valleys divide the several ranges, running parallel to the main line of the watershed and forming the principal watercourses, which zigzag from one to the other through narrow defiles broken through the intervening mountains. The other is that the course of the watershed gets farther from the plain as it trends northward; the sources of the eastern rivers near the boundary being in the first range; the Kananaskis rises in the second; the Bow in the third; the North Saskatchewan in the fourth; and the Athabasca in the fifth; each in turn forcing its way through the remaining parallel ridges to the great plateau.

Another characteristic which strikes even the most cursory observer is the great wealth of glaciers,

"Those silent cataracts of frozen splendour
Singing the eternal praise of God,"

not only in the vast extent of certain icefields, such as the Waputik and the Columbia (perhaps the largest outside the fringe of Arctic territory), but also in their number, scarcely a peak 10,000 feet in altitude being without at least one, many possessing more than one, and sundry lower mountains also contributing their quota to the wonderful array.

The width of the Rocky Mountains proper averages about 60 miles, but the whole mountain system, often designated loosely by the same title, stretches from the plateau of the North-West Territories to the Pacific coast, a distance of nearly ten degrees of longitude. Included in this wider system are the Purcell and Selkirk Ranges (frequently referred to under the latter name alone), the Gold and the Coast Ranges, running roughly parallel to the line of the Divide.

The Selkirks, separated from the Rockies by the low-lying valley of the Columbia River, are wholly different in structure and considerably older. The rainfall is much greater, the vegetation richer, and their mineral capacity is considerable. Their elevation is somewhat lower than that of the Rockies, only two peaks over 11,000 feet being known, and Mt. Selwyn, near Glacier House, 11,038 feet, the highest accurately determined;

The highest peak known in the Rockies is Mt. Robson, near the 53d parallel of latitude, a short distance west of the Yellowhead Pass, estimated by the Dominion Land Survey at 13,500 feet. The Mt. Columbia section, 60 miles farther south, has, however, a higher mean elevation, and contains the grandest peaks and glaciers, forming the culmination of the chain; it is dominated by Mt. Columbia and Mt. Forbes, the former about 12,500 feet in altitude, the latter somewhat over 12,000 feet. Near the railroad the loftiest mountains range from 11,000 to nearly 12,000 feet and average almost 1,000 feet lower than the northern group. Still farther south, with the exception of Mt. Assiniboine, 11,860 feet (the highest summit south of Mt. Forbes), the mountains do not rise more than a bare 10,000 feet.

The line of the Divide, which marks the boundary between Alberta and British Columbia, is extraordinarily erratic during much of its explored length, and is broken by numerous deep and sharp-cut passes, which are remarkably low in comparison with the altitude of the peaks, which often tower 6,000 to 7,000 feet above; whilst from many of the valleys the summits lift their heads 1,000 to 1,500 feet more in almost sheer precipices.

The timber limit stands at about 7,000 feet, though in sheltered aspects and on the Pacific slopes fair-sized trees may be met with 500 feet higher. There is little variation from the jackpine, common spruce, and balsam fir, at an elevation of more than 5,000 feet, though in certain localities Lyall's larch, the cedar, and the hemlock will be found. Cottonwoods abound from 5,000 feet downward, alder and willow chiefly keeping them company in the upper valleys. Flowers are abundant and remarkable for the brilliancy and variety of their colouring. I collected over 70 kinds during a single summer in my wanderings, though never once hunting for them. Many of them can be gathered at any season through the year, excepting winter, by following upward the

"Living flowers that skirt the eternal frost,"

and late in September large and varied bouquets can be gathered in the higher altitudes.

The Canadian Rocky Mountains are not remarkable for a great profusion of animal life, though big game in abundance will reward the skilful hunter, provided he is accompanied by a guide who is acquainted with the habits and the habitat of the noble denizens of these grand mountain haunts. But unless hunting or research into their ways is the specific object of him who penetrates these wild recesses, few animals are likely to be seen. They are too shy and wary, as a rule, to allow human beings to get very close, and as the valleys are almost invariably thickly wooded in their lower portions, there is ample opportunity for effectual shelter. Most of them, therefore, are invisible unless some lucky chance enables the traveller to run across one near the water's edge or on the shingle flats that are characteristic of many of the riverbeds.

Their tracks, however, are of frequent occurrence and sometimes very recent. The mule deer, caribou, and occasionally moose, wander along these picturesque valleys and up their rugged sides, especially in the late fall, and fur-bearing animals are fairly plentiful. Bears in considerable quantities inhabit the woods: the grizzly and silvertip, as well as the black and brown and cinnamon, falling victims to the prowess of the hunter or the trapper's wiles. Mountain goats are still almost common, and on numerous occasions I have come across them singly or in small bunches, and once to the number of over 50 in one herd. The mountain sheep is much more rare and more restricted in his habitat.

Of smaller game the lynx, coyote, wolverine, muskrat and marten are most common. Few, if any, beaver now remain. Descending to the humbler walks of life, we find the marmot, whose whistle often breaks the stillness of the upland solitudes; the "fretful porcupine" is often met with waddling along in anxious haste to find a temporary refuge amongst the branches of a kindly spruce; a cheerful red squirrel, with bushy tail erect, a chipmunk, with its bright-striped coat, or a more soberly clad gopher will sometimes dash across the trail or make remarks from the security of a snug retreat.

A few ptarmigan and grouse (nicknamed "foolhens" locally) and a rare duck or two represent all that can be classed as game. Ordinary bird life is restricted to the whisky jack, a finch or two, and smaller birds (I once saw a golden-crested wren by the side of the Kicking Horse River). The whisky jack is the most familiar, especially to campers, as he is a regular camp follower, always looking out for scraps and seldom troubled by an excess of modesty. His name is a corruption of the Indian "ouiscachon," which passed from whisky john to the more familiar whisky jack. Fish eagles are by no means rare, as are fishhawks, and golden eagles, too, are sometimes seen.

Fish usually abound in the glacial streams and lakes, rainbow trout predominating, and they have been caught as large as six pounds in weight They are extremely good eating, as the flesh is firm, owing to the coldness of the water, and the flavour excellent.

From the grand rocky obelisk of Mt. Assiniboine, which has been styled the Matterhorn of North America, to the pure, snow-crowned heights of Mt. Columbia, it has been the writer's privilege to journey, skirting the lofty ridgepole of the Continent for about 200 miles, and making frequent ascents to the most prominent of the splendid summits that rise in all the majesty of glacier and precipice along the line of the Divide. Twenty of these climbs were "first ascents" of peaks over 10,000 feet and a dozen more of points slightly below that altitude; and it is of this region, the most beautiful as well as the most accessible portion of the Canadian Rockies, comprising all the loftiest known peaks, except Mt. Robson, that the present volume treats.

This territory may be divided into four chief groups, severed by low passes easily available for horses. The first and last of these groups are subdivided by higher passes, likewise possible for animals, but may be conveniently dealt with singly.

The southernmost is dominated by Mt. Assiniboine, and extends from the White Man Pass (6,807 feet) to the Vermilion Pass (5,265 feet), a distance of about 40 miles. Until Simpson Pass is reached (6,884 feet), no peak challenges notice, but beyond, Mt. Ball (10,900) and Storm Peak (10,330) introduce us to the mass of peaks that form the Bow or Laggan Group. This is not more than 20 miles in length, and is bounded on the northwest by Hector Pass, crossed by the Canadian Pacific Railway at an elevation of 5,296 feet above sea level. It includes the famous mountains of the Valley of the Ten Peaks and Lake Louise, the loftiest of which are Deltaform (10,905), Hungabee (11,305), Lefroy (11,290), and Victoria (11,400), on the Divide, and, higher than all, Mt. Temple (11,637), jutting eastward from the watershed. To the west, the mass of Cathedral Mountain and Mt. Stephen points to the Ottertail Group, well off the line of the Divide and most conspicuous with its three noble summits, Mt. Vaux (10,741), the Chancellor (10,780), and the magnificent triple-headed Mt. Goodsir, said to be nearly 12,000 feet in altitude.

Returning to the watershed, the area between Hector Pass and Howse Pass is occupied by the Waputik Range, the only one of the four main groups to bear an official title; but, whilst it contains vast icefields and numerous glaciers, no peak exceeds 11,000 feet, the loftiest being Howse Peak and Mt. Balfour, each about 10,800 feet, which are supreme in the northern and southern halves. At Howse Pass there is a sudden drop from Howse Peak to 4,800 feet, and a right-angled bend which brings us to the outposts of the culminating section of the Canadian Rockies. Here are combined the striking and lofty peaks that characterize the Laggan Group and the great snowfields that mark the Waputik; and both are on a vaster and a grander scale than heretofore.

Strange to say, this enormous area of mountains, more than 60 miles in length and containing nearly 20 peaks of very conspicuous elevation, has no distinctive name, and, except the section nearest to civilization, none of the subdivisions has been singled out for designation. The watershed is most eccentric, eight or nine sudden zigzags, often almost right-angled, marking its course from Howse Pass to the headwaters of the Athabasca River, and adding probably 50 per cent to the air-line distance.

Continuing from Howse Pass, we first come to the Freshfield Group, composed principally of peaks named after distinguished members of the Alpine Club. Beyond it, standing by itself, off the line of the Divide, is Mt. Forbes, a huge massif surmounted by a striking pyramid. Next comes what may be called the Lyell subdivision, taking in Mt. Lyell, Gable Peak, and Mt. Alexandra. These three sections combine to form the southern half of the great group, and Thompson Pass (6,800 feet) connects the deep valleys of the West Branch of the North Saskatchewan and the East Fork of Bush River, which cut the group in two. Mt. Bryce (11,750 feet) rises isolated to the west, projecting over the Bush Valley, whilst Mt. Saskatchewan (11,000 feet) is a conspicuous vis-à-vis on the eastern side. Thus we approach Mt. Columbia, the monarch of the region, from whence three ranges strike out: eastward, to the Dome (11,650) and Mt. Athabasca (11,900); northward, into the forks of the Athabasca River, where the Twins and Mt. Alberta may exceed 12,000 feet, and Mts. Stutfield and Woolley and Diadem Peak are very little lower; and to the northwest, along the curving watershed, a land as yet unknown in detail.

Such is a cursory survey of the chief features of this fascinating region, some of the interesting points of which are described particularly in the following pages.

In earlier days the glories of these mountains lay unnoticed or unknown. Stray bands of Indians passed along the wooded valleys and across the flower-strewn alps in search of the abundant game whose haunts were in these mountain fastnesses. But the peerless peaks that towered above, the lovely lakes enshrined amidst the rich forest growth, the sparkling cataracts and foaming streams, were unconsidered items of their wonted environment, useful alone as a habitat for their accustomed prey.

As time went on, the pioneer of Anglo-Saxon civilization, pushing his resistless western way, reached the great barrier of ice-clad peaks and penetrated here and there the lower passes that link the richer lands of the Atlantic and Pacific slopes, meeting and trading with the Indians at various points One of the most notable of these is the Kootanie Plain, near the headwaters of the North Saskatchewan, where something approaching to an annual fair was held.

In 1793, a dozen years before the famous Lewis and Clark expedition across the States, the first recorded journey from ocean to ocean was made by Alexander Mackenzie, whose name will always be perpetuated by the mighty river of the Great North-West. He crossed the Rocky Mountains at a point far to the north of the vast alpine world just described, travelling up the Peace River to its source and reaching the Divide in latitude 54°24' north, where the altitude was only 2,000 feet above the sea. Thence he proceeded to the coast, returning just two months later on his homeward march.

Sixteen years later, in 1809, Simon Fraser, Jules Quesnel, and John Stuart crossed the Rockies farther south, and voyaged down the Fraser River under the impression that it was the Columbia. In 1817, a most ill-fated expedition under the leadership of Ross Cox, consisting of 86 persons of various nationalities, journeyed up the Columbia River from Astoria and crossed the Athabasca Pass, 52°27' north latitude, many perishing of starvation on the way, and only a remnant escaping with their lives.

This same pass was crossed in the same direction in 1827 by David Douglas, the botanist after whom the Douglas fir is named, and his account of the two guardian mountains of the pass, called by him Mts. Brown and Hooker, and estimated at 16,000 to 17,000 feet in height, has brought these peaks, now shown to be no more than 9,000 to 10,000 feet, 70 long years of spurious fame, which still is hard to combat. Between the two peaks lies the famous "Committee's

Punchbowl," a little circular tarn about 20 yards in diameter, having an outlet at each end, one of which runs towards the Atlantic and the other to the Pacific. The reputation of the two mountains has been responsible for several expeditions in later days, and the conflicting accounts, which, however, were unanimous in steadily reducing the gigantic altitudes ascribed to them by Douglas, provoked the humorous prophecy that they would eventually be found to be only holes in the ground.

The earliest account of a journey across the range in the immediate neighbourhood of the present transcontinental highway, dates from 1841, when Sir George Simpson, in the course of the first overland journey round the world from east to west, traversed the pass that bears his name, a few miles west of Banff. His approach was by the Bow River, now the best-known route into the heart of the Canadian Rockies.

Then came the news of gold, and an immediate rush ensued from east to west to seek the treasures of the hills: both north and south of the great culminating mass of glacier-bearing peaks, passes were sought and conquered, and rough wagon trails constructed by the immigrants. This influx of inhabitants and the stir of gold excitement led to the expedition sent by the British Government in 1857, headed by Captain Palliser. His party, chief amongst whom was Dr. Hector, perhaps the best known of all the explorers of the Rockies, investigated five passes across the Continental watershed,—the Kootenay, Kananaskis, Vermilion, Kicking Horse (now called Hector), and Howse Passes,— besides three lesser passes between important valleys on the same side of the Divide,—Bow Pass and those from the headwaters of the Kootenay River to the Beaverfoot and the Columbia. An immense area of country amongst the mountains, in the foothills, and on the plains was also thoroughly explored.

Simultaneous with this expedition was Lord Southesk's visit to the Rockies, and a year or two later Viscount Milton and Dr. Cheadle made an extended journey through the mountains, sport being the main incentive in. these two latter trips.

Next came the Railroad, rendered a necessity by the formation of the Dominion of Canada in 1867, and the union of British Columbia with it four years later. The barrier of the mountains severed the newly admitted province so effectually from the rest of the Dominion that its only outlet for commerce was through the States, and self-interest must of necessity have driven the inhabitants, however loyal, from their allegiance, had not that far-sighted politician, Sir John A. Macdonald, recognized the inevitable result before it was too late, and promised a Government railroad across the Rockies to unite the interests and commerce of the entire Dominion. Numerous passes, etc., were surveyed, many of them new, and finally, in 1885, after the enterprise had been handed over to a corporation, the Canadian Pacific Railway Company, the route was constructed as at present.

The Dominion Land Survey and Geological Survey did most valuable work in the eighties; Dr. G.M. Dawson's expedition of 1885 and the work of Mr. J.J. McArthur being specially notable, and the latter was the pioneer of mountain climbing in the Rockies, his ascent of Mt. Stephen calling for particular commendation.

This paved the way for the exploitation of the mountains for their own sakes. The railway gave easy access to the hitherto unknown or far too distant peaks, glaciers, and valleys. These now became the opportunity for those in search of fresh fields and pastures new, in which to spend a pleasant and profitable vacation. The charm of the unknown, the fascination of the peaks, attracted the amateur explorer and the mountaineer.

No sport appeals to all the aspirations of complex manhood in so satisfying a degree as mountaineering, besides the great advantage it possesses in having practically no age limit. All the artistic instincts are aroused by the wondrous beauty and grandeur of such scenery as Switzerland or its American counterpart, the Canadian Rockies, so lavishly display. Hundreds of pictures, exquisite in form and composition, variety and colouring, charm the eye of the climber amidst the lofty ice-bound peaks, the jagged ruined crags, the glittering glaciers, the dense dark forests, flower-strewn meadows, sunny lakes and streams and waterfalls, that everywhere abound. The scientist finds in the structure of the mighty ranges and the fascinating phenomena of the desolate glaciers a constant source of interest. The botanist has his trees and shrubs and flowers, and a limitless and untried field before him. The fauna are fairly numerous and uncommon. The athlete, pure and simple, finds scope for all his energies and love of conquest in the battle against snow and ice, precipice and pinnacle, cornice and avalanche. The more formidable the foe, the greater is the joy of conflict; the more numerous and serious the difficulties, the greater the attraction for the true mountaineer and the more complete his satisfaction if skill and patience can surmount the obstacles and win a way to the desired goal. It is a vast mistake to think that danger *as danger* lends any enchantment to the climb: what the mountaineer delights in is bringing skill and science so to bear upon the difficulties that would be dangers to the less gifted or experienced, that their hazards are eliminated. Finally, the panoramas from the lofty summits are overwhelming in their comprehensiveness and sublimity. And, added to all, in Canada there still exists that chiefest charm of novelty and adventure, the thrill of climbing virgin peaks, of traversing untrodden valleys, of viewing regions never seen before by human eyes.

To the Selkirks belongs the honour of earliest alpine fame, and the names of the Revs. W.S. Green and H. Swanzy, members of the Alpine Club, head the roll of climbers, with the year 1888 standing out as the date of the birth of mountaineering in Canada; and the former's book "Among the Selkirk Glaciers" had much to do with the first awakening of interest in the American Switzerland. Two years later, Messrs. Huber and Sulzer, of the Swiss Alpine Club, made the first ascent of Mt. Sir Donald, the most conspicuous and noted peak of the Selkirk Range. The same summer two more, English members, Messrs. H. Topham and Forster, explored a portion of that district, but still the loftier Rocky Mountains proper remained untouched.

In 1893, however, Messrs. W.D. Wilcox and S.E.S. Allen, both Yale students, commenced the valuable series of explorations in the neighbourhood of the Divide, which opened up a vast area of new ground and introduced the rope and ice axe with conspicuous success. The splendid work of Mr. Wilcox during a number of years, from Fortress Lake in the north to the headwaters of the Kananaskis River in the south, and his charming book, place him in the forefront amongst those who have in modern days brought into prominence this magnificent mountain world, though he makes no claims to be a mountaineer.

The next year was signalized by the appearance of the members of the Appalachian Mountain Club, of Boston, headed by Professor Charles E. Fay, and to the Club, and preeminently to the Professor (just reelected to the Presidency for the fourth time, and the first President of the American Alpine Club), no tribute of praise and admiration can be too lavishly bestowed by all who love the peaks and other noble features of this wild home of Nature's grandest works. The names of Philip Abbot, C.S. Thompson, and G.M. Weed shine specially forth amongst the numerous members of the Club who have contributed to the long list of first ascents and new discoveries; and as pioneers, without previous alpine experience or the benefit of guides, the value of their achievements is enhanced tenfold.

1896 stands forth in melancholy prominence as the year that witnessed the first, and happily the last, fatal accident that tarnishes the otherwise singularly bright escutcheon of the record of Canadian mountaineering. The foremost climber fell in the hour of victory, amongst the peaks he loved so well, leaving a memory that has been an inspiration to many a climber since.

1897 also is conspicuous amongst the years of alpine chronology in Canada, by the arrival of the first professional Swiss guide to bring to bear upon the problems of Canadian peaks the experience and skill evolved in his native Alps. Peter Sarbach came over with Professor Dixon, Professor Collie and Mr. G.P. Baker, of the Alpine Club, and inaugurated the long series of successful climbs which has now grown to most imposing proportions.

The name of Professor J. Norman Collie is writ large upon the tablets of Canadian mountain exploration: no less than four times has he, in company with members of the Alpine Club, journeyed all the way to Canada from England, and he has opened out the splendid northern region to the world, his map being the only one in existence covering at all adequately that important section of the Rockies; and as a mountaineer he holds the foremost place.

Two other names there are which cannot be omitted in any résumé of mountain history, though many more deserve inclusion in the list The late Mr. Jean Habel, a veteran alpinist of Berlin, to whom is due the opening up of the Yoho Valley, amongst other useful explorations, was an enthusiast on the subject of the opportunities and the delights of the Canadian Rockies, and his untimely death in 1902 has been a blow to the cause of the peaks. Mr. Edward Whymper, another veteran of worldwide fame, spent six months in 1901 amongst these summits and returned to England full of enthusiasm and admiration for the immensity of the alpine area, the grandeur of the peaks, and the sublimity of the scenery throughout the entire region, and they have drawn him yet again across the ocean to pay another visit to their neighbourhood.[2]

Such is the great chain of the Divide, for a brief section of its long-drawn line; such is an incomplete and all too bald epitome of its history. The everlasting hills, the peerless valleys, which have fascinated thousands in the past and called them back time and again by their enchantments, remain to cast their wizard spell on countless thousands more. Year by year new beauties are still being discovered far and near, whilst yet more distant regions, with untrodden peaks and glaciers, await the enterprising traveller, who, with camping outfit and string of pack horses, plunges still farther into the unknown to enjoy the unspeakable de light of discovering for himself new scenes that in some future day thousands will be seeking beyond the limits of the present round of famed resorts.

Chapter II

BANFF THE BEAUTIFUL

THE USUAL APPROACH TO THE Canadian Rockies is from the east, and by a happy chance the great transcontinental route of the Canadian Pacific Railway, constructed along a line selected solely on engineering grounds, passes through by far the most attractive section of the mountains, both in the Rockies and the Selkirks. This has the double advantage of providing an infinitely finer outlook from the cars than any other transcontinental road and also enabling the traveller to visit the most exquisite mountain scenery in North America with the utmost comfort and convenience.

The Canadian Pacific Railway enjoys the distinction of owning more miles of line than any other railroad company in the world (upwards of 10,000), and of possessing the only trains which run from end to end of the Continent without a change of cars, 2,906 miles from Montreal to Vancouver, 500 miles being through a continuous panorama of the grandest mountain views visible from a railroad track.

The history of the Railway dates from the admission of British Columbia as a province of the Dominion in 1871. The work connected with the survey was tremendous. The rocks and lakes and rivers of the eastern portion, the unknown stretches of vast prairie land, and, most formidable of all, the barrier of the mountains, 500 miles across, presented difficulties almost insurmountable. But in 1875 the work of construction was begun as a Government enterprise. The Herculean nature of the undertaking, the difficulties occasioned by changes of ministries, and other causes of delay, resulted in the surrender of the work to a private company, and in 1881 the Canadian Pacific Railway

Company was organized: 1,920 miles remained to be constructed, and the Company agreed to complete the line within ten years. So marvellously rapid, however, was the progress made (the prairie section being built at an average daily rate of more than three miles), that on the 7th of November, 1885, considerably less than half the contracted period, the last spike was driven at Craigellachie, 351 miles from the western terminus, and the longest continuous line in the world was finished.

It is by this romantic route that we set out from Montreal on board the well-equipped "Imperial Limited," and for three days the constantly varied scenery holds our attention almost without a break even before we reach the crowning glory of the Rocky Mountains.

First the valley of the Ottawa River is traversed for upwards of 300 miles, mostly beside the broad waters of that noted lumber highway. Beyond, a wild territory of forests, lakes and rocks is entered, stretching to the shores of Lake Superior. For nearly 200 miles the waters of this huge inland sea are skirted, rock cuttings, viaducts and tunnels frequently occurring along the rugged indented coast. At its western end the enormous grain elevators of Fort William introduce us to a new realm and mark the gateway of the world's foremost granary. A picturesque country next succeeds, bold and rocky, a network of lakes and waterways, clothed with abundant timber, until the limits of Manitoba are entered on and the first prairie lands appear in sight.

Almost exactly halfway across the Continent stands Winnipeg, only a few short years ago no more than the little trading post of Fort Garry, but now the flourishing metropolis of the vast grain area of Western Canada. Numerous lines branch out in all directions across the rich wheat lands, bringing thousands of acres of grain into close connection with the markets of both hemispheres.

The train rolls on through miles and miles of almost unbroken fields of waving wheat, with neat and prosperous homesteads, gradually ascending the long steppes of the great North-West. Soon the farms become fewer, the wild, undulating expanse more and more free from signs of human encroachment. Far blue hills occasionally break the wide level range of the horizon. Herds of cattle dot the landscape, antelope scour the plain, a stray coyote lopes leisurely along, cranes, ducks, geese, prairie chickens, snipe and swans may be seen in this paradise of game. Here and there the smoke-stained cone of a tepee indicates the presence of the ancient owners of the soil, buffalo wallows and trails proclaim the numbers of the now departed millions that once ranged the limitless expanse, and the red coat of a member. of the North-West Mounted Police tells of the new *régime*.

Farther west the ranching region is approached. The winters are much milder than in the wheat belt, and the warm "Chinook" winds melt the snow at frequent intervals, enabling cattle and horses to forage for themselves. The Bow River traverses this territory and is now followed almost to its source in the heart of the Rocky Mountains, which already, in clear weather, may have been seen, white and distant on the horizon, as far away as Tilley, 150 miles from their base.

The prairies, wearily monotonous to many, have yet a fascination all their own and hold a potent sway over the lives of countless devotees. Whatever other claims they may possess, there is no question that if one has the good fortune en route to witness a characteristic prairie sunset, there will be few more lasting and entrancing memories in the most richly endowed experience.

At Calgary we enter the low foothills, the last stage of the 1,400 miles of gradually rising steppes; the snow-clad peaks rise closer and frowning precipices loom grand and lofty in a seemingly unbroken wall, rising abruptly 5,000 feet directly from the plain. The foaming river swirls beside the track, and suddenly we swing between the giant portals of a narrow gateway and are engulfed in a moment by the mountain mass. It is a fitting introduction to the superb scenery that holds one enthralled for the next 500 miles.

From the first moment of entrance striking peaks give earnest of the galaxy of kingly summits of the main continental range. Prominent on the left are Pigeon Mountain, Wind Mountain, and the effective group of the Three Sisters; right in front rises the majestic form of Cascade Mountain, 9,875 feet above the sea, 5,500 above the railroad track, though seeming in the clear air not more than half the height. At its base we turn sharply to the left, rounding the little insulated. Tunnel Mountain, and, passing a huge corral where a herd of buffalo is kept, besides antelope and other small game, we arrive at Banff, the first of the three mountain centres. of the Rockies at which it is imperative to stay.

We have now entered the first of the great National Parks, set apart by the Government to preserve and enhance the natural beauties and resources of these unrivalled mountain fastnesses. The Rocky Mountain Park stretches from the great wall that overhangs the foothills to the Divide, where it is joined by the almost equally extensive Yoho Park Reserve embracing a vast tract on the Pacific slope. The two contain upwards of 4,500 square miles, whilst in the Selkirks another smaller Park has also been reserved.

Banff the Beautiful is an alliteration that is not misapplied, and to appreciate the appropriateness of the title, Tunnel Mountain, a strangely isolated rocky mass 1,000 feet above the valley, should be ascended,—first ascent in the Canadian Rockies,—and the view will never be forgotten.

We are not yet in the land of giant peaks, only a single one in sight surpassing 10,000 feet, though square Mt. Massive has some alpine features.; but the restful beauty of the valley, gemmed by the ruddy waters of the Vermilion Lakes, threaded by the lazy river with its contrasted colouring of rich translucent green, and completely circled by a wall of sheltering peaks, strikes home to the heart and remains enshrined there as a joy forever. Mt. Rundle's overhanging precipices commemorate an early missionary, and from thence the eye travels past the deep wooded cleft of the Spray Valley to the Bourgeau Range and Mt. Massive, severed by Simpson Pass, across the Bow River to the serrated Sawback Mountains and the impressive mass of Cascade Mountain; then, turning eastward, the long line of the frontier ranges stretches as far as eye can reach beyond the placid waters of Lake Minnewanka, Mt. Aylmer, 10,333 feet in altitude, standing out preeminently.

At our feet the river, suddenly swerving to avoid the little mountain thrown across its path, forms a picturesquely foaming cataract—Bow Falls—and, again turning abruptly at its confluence with the Spray, cuts its way between the lofty cliffs of Tunnel Mountain and Mt. Rundle and swings round the latter's base towards the Rocky Mountain Gap and onward to the plains.

Banff is a place for leisure rather than the strenuous life. Pleasant drives and rides and walks abound; the river invites laziness in a canoe, and many a delightful hour may be spent amongst the shallow lakes or threading the narrow waterways amidst the trees and bushes. Weird little Sundance Canyon, the wooded valley of the Spray, Lake Minnewanka, and various minor altitudes can easily be reached by trail, and the Hot Springs demand a visit and a swim in the warm aerated depths.

For the aspiring mountaineer Banff offers but little immediate attraction except for training and an introduction to the topography of the Rockies, although it is the starting point for Mt. Assiniboine, one of the most famous and fascinating peaks in Canada.

Quite a little interesting rock work can be obtained upon Mt. Edith (9,154 feet), first climbed by Professor Collie and Fred Stephens in 1900, and likened by the former to the Little Dru from Montanvert in miniature. Up to the col[3] connecting Mt. Edith with the next peak to the north, the climbing, writes Professor Collie,[4] "was steep and somewhat rotten, but not very difficult. . . . On reaching the *col*, . . . it seemed impossible to climb direct to the summit; so, crossing the col to the western side, a series of, traverses and climbs through holes in the ridge were made: we next crossed some very sloping slabs overhanging dizzy precipices; then climbed up excessively rotten gullies, first one way then another but always getting higher, till we emerged quite unexpectedly onto the top."

My brother and I selected Cascade Mountain as our training ground, and the wearisome and arduous ascent gave us all the exercise we wanted for one day, although the climbing presented not one single difficulty. Marvellous tales were told the previous evening of its tremendous problems,—how even with a guide (a native,—not, of course, a Swiss guide) two days should be devoted to the task; how certain enthusiasts had dared to go alone and had got lost and wandered for I dare not say how many days and nights, till rescued by a search party, and so forth. Doubtless the main object of these harrowing stories was to secure for some lazy man a well-paid job on easy terms. If so, it failed entirely, and in spite of dire predictions we preferred to trust to our own estimate of the mountain's character and were most fully justified. Starting across the buffalo corral and up Forty-mile Creek, we traversed to the long main ridge of the peak and by it directly to the top. The descent was made right down the straight incline, across the creek and home over Stony Squaw Mountain in ample time for dinner, without the slightest hurry.

Out of condition, on a scorching August day, it was a toilsome undertaking, as the slope is long and tedious, encumbered by an *embarras de richesse* of loose rough stones. But it was well worthwhile enduring all for the sake of the view, our first extensive survey of the "Promised Land," and it was here that I obtained my first glimpse of Mt. Assiniboine, at that time the most talked-of peak in the Canadian Rockies, christened "the Matterhorn of North America," and deemed as inaccessible as its prototype was 40 years before.

Little did I dream, though it then stirred every mountaineering impulse in my being (and there is a considerable number of them there), that 12 months later I should have the opportunity of disproving the truth of this distinguished reputation, and not only visiting the famous mountain, but standing on its topmost pinnacle.

CHAPTER III

MOUNT ASSINIBOINE

THREE CHIEF CAUSES HAVE COMBINED to bring Mt. Assiniboine into special prominence among the peaks of Canada. First, its remarkable resemblance from certain aspects to the world-famed Matterhorn; though perhaps the Dent Blanche is more nearly its prototype in the better-known Swiss Alps. Secondly, the exquisite photographs and fascinating descriptions of Mr. W.D. Wilcox, the principal explorer of that region and the mountain's earliest biographer. And, lastly, the fact that it has repelled more assaults by mountain climbers than any other peak in the Canadian Rockies, and gained a reputation at one time of extreme difficulty or even inaccessibility.

Its massive pyramid forms a conspicuous landmark from almost every considerable eminence for scores of miles around, towering fully 1,500 feet above its neighbours, and by its isolation no less than by its splendid outline commanding attention and admiration.

It enjoys the proud distinction of being the loftiest mountain south of the railroad, 11,860 feet above sea level, and is situated on the Continental watershed; and its mighty mass, with five huge spurs, covers an area of some 30 square miles and harbours fully a dozen picturesque lakes within the shelter of its giant arms.

The peak is grandest from its northern side. It rises, like a monster tooth, from an entourage of dark cliff and gleaming glacier, 5,000 feet above the valley of approach; the magnificent triangular face, barred with horizontal belts of perpendicular cliff and glistening expanses of the purest snow and ice, which constitutes the chief glory of the mountain, soaring more than 3,000 feet directly from the glacier that sweeps its base. On the eastern and the southern sides the walls and buttresses are practically sheer precipices 5,000 to 6,000 feet in vertical height, but the contour and character of the grand northern face more than compensate for the less sheer and lofty precipices.

The mighty monolith was named in 1885 by Dr. G.M. Dawson, of the Dominion Geological Survey, from a tribe of Indians inhabiting the plains, but he and his party only viewed it from afar. The first white men to explore the immediate vicinity, so far as can be learned, were Messrs. R.L. Barrett and T.E. Wilson, who, in 1893, made an expedition to the mountain's base. The latter is a famous pioneer of the Canadian Rockies, with probably a greater knowledge of them than any man has ever yet possessed, and his store of yarns, drawn almost entirely from personal experience or that of his immediate associates, is as full of interest and valuable information as it is extensive. He and Mr. Barrett crossed the Simpson Pass and followed down the Simpson River to the mouth of a tributary flowing straight from the direction of Mt. Assiniboine. Ascending this with infinite difficulty, they crossed over to the North Fork of the Cross River and thence upward to their goal.

The ensuing summer Mr. S.E.S. Allen visited the northern side by the same route, and the next year both Mr. Allen and Mr. Barrett again succumbed to the fascinations of the neighbourhood and were found once more encamped under the shadow of the monarch of the southern Rockies. The latter traveller was accompanied by Mr. J.F. Porter and Mr. W.D. Wilcox, who made some careful observations for altitude, and has given us a charming and instructive description of his wanderings in his magnificently illustrated book, "The Rockies of Canada." Messrs. Barrett and Wilcox with Bill Peyto completed the circuit of the mountain on foot, a laborious but interesting undertaking which occupied them a fraction more than two days. Beautiful valleys, heading in glaciers and adorned with lakes, alternated with rough and precipitous intervening ridges, each in turn having to be crossed. A large portion of the first day was spent traversing a valley devastated by a huge forest fire, the denseness of the charred and fallen trunks, sometimes piled ten or 12 feet above the ground, rendered progress painfully slow and toilsome, and, on emerging "black as coal heavers from our long walk in the burnt timber, seeking a refuge in the rocky ledges of the mountains, and clad in uncouth garments torn and discoloured, we must," writes Mr. Wilcox, "have resembled the aboriginal savages of this wild region."[5] Finally, by following a tiny goat track, discovered on the face of a dangerous-looking ridge, they reached the valley of the North Fork of the Cross River, falling in with Messrs. Smith and Allen, encamped in that pleasant spot and bent on similar investigations, and early next morning regained their camp on the shore of Lake Assiniboine.

Amongst the many valuable results of this complete inspection of the massif from every point of the compass, much information appealing particularly to the mountaineer was obtained. The contour of the main peak was shown to be very different from the symmetrical cone anticipated by the view from the north; the previously hidden southern ridge was found to extend a considerable distance at a comparatively easy angle to an abrupt and absolutely vertical precipice, and broken only by a deep notch that transforms the southern extremity into a sharp subsidiary peak. The eastern face defies approach to the summit from that direction, as does the southern buttress, but the southwestern side developed a more practicable line of ascent and one that offered every prospect of success.

Not until 1899, however, was any attempt made to scale these attractive heights. That summer Mr. Wilcox returned to the neighbourhood accompanied by Mr. H.G. Bryant, of Philadelphia, well-known to those interested in Arctic exploration, and Mr. L.J. Steele, an Englishman. These two were the first to attack the formidable citadel, and narrowly escaped losing their lives in the attempt. They ascended the northwest arête[6] to an altitude of about 10,000 feet, when they were compelled to desist after several hours of hard climbing, an approaching storm assisting to hasten their descent. "They had just come to the top of the last ice slope, when Steele's foothold gave way, and he fell, dragging Bryant after him.

There was but one possible escape from a terrible fall. A projecting rock of considerable size appeared not far below, and Steele, with a skilful lunge of his ice axe, swung round to it and anchored himself in a narrow crevice, where the snow had melted away. No sooner had he come to a stop than Bryant shot over him from above and likewise found safety. Otherwise they would have fallen about 600 feet, with serious, if not fatal, results."[7]

Another year went by, and a far more serious climbing expedition was fitted out to try to conquer the now famous mountain. Two brothers, the Messrs. Walling, of Chicago, with larger enthusiasm than experience in matters mountaineering, took with them three Swiss guides to force a way to the tantalizing summit. Camping, as usual, by the side of Lake Assiniboine, they followed Steele and Bryant's route to the northern glacier, ascending thence directly towards the apex by rock outcrops and snow slopes. So far so good, though progress was extremely slow even on such an easy task; but when they came to the lowest belt of vertical cliffs the retreat was sounded and for the second time victory rested with Mt. Assiniboine.

On the return to Banff the shortest route (geographically) was taken, by White Man Pass and down the Spray Valley, but through some mismanagement or worse, the guides went on ahead, the Wallings were lost and, so the story goes, reduced to slaying a horse for sustenance before they were discovered by a search party. But the whole proceedings of the climb and the return were never very fully given to the public.

Thus far the northwest arête and the north face had been unsuccessfully approached, but Mr. Wilcox, mindful of the easier appearance of the southwestern side, in 1901 made a determined effort to achieve victory from that direction. Mr. Bryant and two Swiss guides, E. Feuz and F. Michel, completed the party.

The main difficulty of this route was the approach to the mountain's base with a camping outfit, my more recent plan of access never having been deemed worthy of consideration as even entering the region of practicability. So eventually, after a long and toilsome march, they found themselves encamped in the deep gorge beneath the huge steep mass of the great peak. I shall have more to say concerning this side and their line of ascent later; suffice it now briefly to chronicle that, after attaining an altitude of 10,850 feet (just 1,000 feet below the top), the avalanching appearance of the snow, the difficulties beyond, the lateness of the hour, and the overburdening of Feuz (Michel having had an accident an the way out), combined to drive them back.

Thus the fortress still remained inviolate; the eastern side a precipice, the southern equally impossible, the northern and southwestern faces, if possibly accessible, yet strongly guarded, each holding a record of an attack repelled. The glacis had proved too much for the first party of assailants, the solid rampart of the first line of fortifications beat back the next assault, and on the opener, more vulnerable side, alpine artillery had to be brought into play in order to defeat the last attempt. Who should be the next to storm the citadel and what the outcome?

This question was uppermost in many minds when the disappointing news of the last failure became known, and the pros and cons were most exhaustively debated around Mr. Whymper's campfire in the upper Yoho Valley, where I was having a glorious time amongst the untrodden peaks and glaciers of that delightful region. Peyto, our outfitter, Mr. Wilcox's companion on the circuit of Mt. Assiniboine six years before, added much fuel to the already consuming desire to examine and if possible ascend the mountain, but the distance and expense placed the enterprise beyond my reach, and I had sadly given up the whole idea when Peyto, asserting that for experienced mountaineers there was absolutely no question of a failure, pledged himself that if I would go and see and conquer he would undertake to get me there within two days from Banff and bring me back in less; and he proved even better than his word, although the journey had never previously been made in less than three days.

At the end of August, therefore, the weather being fine, though showing indications of the inevitable break which comes each year about this date, bringing a snowstorm to usher in the Indian summer of September, the opportunity arrived. It was "now or never" for this season, so I resolved to make a dash for the peak before the snow should render it impossible, and, Peyto being ready, a start upon the 31st was hastily arranged.

Thanks to the ready and able cooperation of Miss Mollison, the incomparable manager of the Hotel at Field, provisions, blankets, etc., were rapidly collected, and on the afternoon of the 30th Christian Häsler, Christian Bohren and I were in the train bound for Banff. Here we were met by Peyto and conducted to our tent pitched amongst the bushes near the bank of the Bow River. Our object was kept entirely secret, and scarcely a soul knew of the starting of the expedition at all.

The next morning was occupied in final arrangements, making up the packs and loading up, and eventually at half-past one the procession set out First the cavalry; Bill Peyto, picturesque and workmanlike, led the way upon his trusty mare, then followed four pack horses, the fastest and most reliable of Peyto's bunch, laden with tents, provisions, and our miscellaneous impedimenta; and Jack Sinclair, our assistant packer, also mounted, brought up the rear, to stimulate laggards and maintain the pace. Then came the infantry, comprising the two Christians and myself. Both the guides were tried companions, especially Häsler, who had already made several first ascents with me.

Mt. Assiniboine is only distant from Banff 20 miles in an air-line, yet by the shortest route it cannot be reached in twice that length of march; the trails are rough and often blocked with fallen timber, and no small amount of climbing is involved. But all of us were keen and determined each to do his best to make the journey to the base a record and the expedition a success.

The afternoon was sultry, with a haze about the summits and a look towards the west that boded rain; but the barometer stood well and hope was high.

At first we passed along the dusty road, with the cool, peaceful Bow eddying alongside, hemmed in by green banks, with overhanging branches dipping lazily in the current. Then we turned off into a winding trail that meandered among alders and small timber, with fallen logs and an occasional morass to vary the monotony. Close by, an eagle's nest hung in the branches of an isolated tree, the memorial of a domestic tragedy. Earlier in the summer Mr. Whymper had discovered it, had the two fine parent birds shot as specimens, each measuring over six feet from tip to tip of wing, and sent the baby to the aviary at Vancouver.

Behind us rose the impressive walls of Cascade Mountain; on our right, across the valley, the sharp pinnacles of Mt. Edith pierced the sky; and wooded slopes flanked us on the left and rose to the fine summit of Mt. Massive right in front.

Soon we reached Healy Creek where it emerges from a narrow gorge, and crossed its double stream, the pedestrians having to clamber up behind the horsemen to make the passage dryshod. Leaving the broad, level valley of the Bow, and with it every trace of civilization for some days to come, we plunged into the ravine beside the swift, translucent river, until we mounted a very steep trail through thick forest and emerged high above the creek in a fine valley whence the retrospective views were very beautiful.

Our path led through a tract of burned and fallen timber to more open ground, trending steadily towards Simpson Pass, above which stood a gabled mountain, with a small glacier cradled on its bosom, against a gloomy, ominous background of dark and lurid clouds. The valley narrowed before us, well wooded near the torrent bed. On one side rugged summits rose abruptly from the thickly timbered slopes; on the other, the more open alps, interspersed with belts and groves of trees, bare cliffs and rocky terraces, merged into castellated peaks, the topmost crowned with snow.

As the evening shadows lengthened, before our camping ground was reached, strong gusts of wind came sweeping down the gorge, with driving rain, beating pitilessly in our faces, but we pressed on until we found a pretty and fairly sheltered spot among the woods, where we pitched our tents.

A busy scene ensues. Peyto and Sinclair unload and attend to the horses; the guides are energetically employed cutting and collecting fuel; fire and water, the opening of boxes and unpacking necessaries are my allotted share. In an incredibly short space of time the tents are up, the packs made snug, supper is ready, and we are all gathered round the blazing fire fully prepared to do ample justice to the bannocks and bacon and the huge saucepan full of steaming tea, under the black canopy of pines and almost darker sky.

Next morning we were off at half-past seven, in fair weather, though the trees and undergrowth were dripping. We crossed the stream and, after 20 minutes' gradual ascent, diverged from the main trail to Simpson Pass and followed a steep pathway to the south through thick firs up a narrow rocky canyon till we arrived in a beautiful open park. The carpet of luxuriant grass and mossy turf was sprinkled gayly, although September was upon us, with a wealth of flowers, dark groups of trees bordered the rich expanse and crowned the knolls that broke its surface here and there, and, on either hand, the green slopes, broken by picturesque rock outcrops, culminated in a line of rugged pinnacles.

The timberline is passed soon after, and we mount steadily to a breezy, undulating alp, green and flower-strewn, skirting the Continental watershed, and bearing frequent pretty lakelets in the sheltered hollows. Ever and anon a deep gorge dips sharply towards the east or west, giving a glimpse of larger, wooded valleys, where Healy Creek and Simpson River run to join the Bow and Kootenay, and finally sink to rest in the waters of the rival oceans.

This upland route was taken by Mr. Wilcox on his second journey to Mt. Assiniboine, and it is undoubtedly the finest way as well as probably the easiest and quickest, in spite of a terrific 1,500 feet of descent to the source of the Simpson River.

About ten o'clock, from a lofty ridge some 2,000 feet above our camp, we caught our first glimpse of our objective peak, bearing from this point a remarkable resemblance to the Swiss Dent Blanche as it loomed through the slight haze, 14 or 15 miles away, dwarfing all the other points and ranges. An hour later, from the highest point upon our highland trail, about 7,700 feet above the sea, we obtained a still better view of the noble pyramid, towering above a blue-black ridge hung with white glaciers, which lay between us and its base.

Crossing and recrossing the "backbone of the Continent," we skirted the walls of an imposing natural fortification, fully 2,000, feet in height, and, passing under its frowning ramparts close to the shores of two or three small lakes, halted for lunch near a round pond, from which some ducks flew off at our approach, and which, from the numerous tracks leading into and out of it, we christened "The Bears' Bathtub."

All this time the going had been good, and Peyto made the most of it, leading at a tremendous rate, with Sinclair driving on the pack animals, we poor two-legged tramps having to do our utmost to keep pace with them.

After lunch a new experience began, where we in turn had a conspicuous advantage,—a tremendous drop (1,500 feet in 55 minutes, pack horse time) into an extraordinarily steep, weird valley, narrow and fire-swept, its serried ranks of bare and ghostly poles backed by slopes of scanty grass and a tumultuous expanse of rough gray rocks and tongues of scree. Towards the lower end an intricate maze of fallen logs was encountered, through which Peyto steered the horses with marvellous skill and rapidity, until we gained the valley of the chief source of the Simpson River, barren and boulder strewn, divided into rugged sections by great ridges traversing it from side to side. Bare, burned trees reared their gaunt stems about us, or, fallen, littered the valley bed, where strawberries and raspberries, gooseberries and blueberries, grew in wild profusion.

Crossing several of the strange barrier ridges, we soon arrived at the head of the valley, a cul-de-sac, with a grand amphitheatre of precipices and abrupt acclivities, 300 feet or more in height, blocking our way and towering above the rich green flat, on which we halted for a brief well-earned rest beside a tree-girt lakelet, fed by a fine cascade that leaped from the rim of the great cirque above.

A zigzag track conducted us to the lowest point of this imposing barrier, and a scene of indescribable bleakness burst upon our gaze. The sun was hidden by the gathering clouds and the, leaden sky formed a fit background for the rock-bound basin at our feet, hemmed in by gray, ruined towers, from which wide belts and tapering tongues of tumbled scree streamed down among the bare poles of the stricken pines, with a tiny tarn, sombre and forbidding, in its depths.

It was a fitting prelude to the long valley on which we now entered. Here was the acme of sheer desolation. Green-gray rocks and stones were strewn and piled in wild confusion amid sparse, stunted pines and firs; crumbling, drab-coloured sidehills were lost in jagged, broken ridges and shattered pinnacles, that loomed in sullen dullness against the mournful sky, while a light drizzle bathed the scene in gloomy haze. Here and everywhere along the route the dreary silence and the strange scarcity of living things—notable characteristic of the Canadian Cordilleras—were very striking. The whistle of the marmot, the rare whir of grouse, a hawk or eagle, and a little bird or two, with the occasional tracks of bear or deer, marten or mountain goat, alone betrayed that the region is not quite bereft of life.

Thus we swung on mile after mile, till the melancholy conditions began to change: grass and light undergrowth appeared, the clouds broke, and, as we neared a rocky lake, Mt. Assiniboine came into view once more, about five miles ahead, grander than ever, and, in spite of evening gloom, showing some detail of its horizontal belts of cliff and smooth, shining, icy slopes.

Then came park country, rich green pasturage and dark forest belts, with a winding coal-black streambed meandering in the most abandoned manner through it all; and above, on either side, sharp, serrated ridges, severed by wide passes to the Spray and Cross Rivers, converged in the mass of Mt. Assiniboine.

Still on we tramp, weary but buoyed up by the knowledge that the goal is near. Darkness falls apace and

"Far along
From peak to peak, the rattling crags among,
Leaps the live thunder! Not from one lone cloud,
But every mountain now hath found a tongue."

A most impressive welcome from the still unconquered mountain, but more sinister than those whose hopes depended on fine weather quite appreciated.

At length, at 7:20, our chosen camping ground was reached, sheltered by a grove of trees, beside a trickling rivulet with the dark waters of Lake Assiniboine just visible beyond.

This lake, one of a dozen or more that nestle close under the precipices of the giant peak, is nearly two miles long, and, like many others in the neighbourhood, is without a visible outlet. The waters seem to drain away through the loose limestone strata, and in some valley far below suddenly burst forth from a mysterious subterranean cavern, a full-grown stream. This we were able to observe for ourselves at the source of the main Simpson River, at the head of the cul de sac, some miles from the nearest body of water at a higher altitude sufficient to produce so large a flow.

The night was none too promising—warm and cloudy, with light showers at intervals and distant muttering thunder; and, although later on the stars came out, ominous clouds still hung heavy round the horizon The silence was broken again and again by the rumble and crash of falling ice and stones from the glacier a mile away, which aided the anxiety concerning weather prospects to drive the slumber from our wearied frames.

Nevertheless we were early astir. The moon was shining fitfully athwart the clouds and lighting up our noble peak with silvery brightness. As the sun rose, we had an opportunity of studying the mountain. Our camp, at an elevation of about 7,200 feet, lay near the shore of the lake, a long mile from the cliff over which the northern glaciers of Mt. Assiniboine descend abruptly; 3,000 feet above the glacier rises the mighty monolith, a relic of the Carboniferous age.

Two jagged ridges trend sharply upward from the outlying spurs, until they meet in a dark rocky apex just below the glistening, snowy; summit; between them lies the formidable northern face, set at a fearsome angle, and banded with almost horizontal strata, which form an impressive alternation of perpendicular cliff belts and glassy slopes of ice. The lowest band is specially remarkable—a spectacular, striated wall of brilliant red and yellow rock, running apparently entirely round the mountain, and particularly striking where the erosion and disintegration of the ridges leave a succession of coloured spires and pinnacles, radiant in the glowing sunshine.

By the advice of Peyto, the only member of the party who had ever been near the peak before, we determined to make our attempt from the southwestern side; but, instead of taking the horses by the long and arduous route adopted by Mr. Wilcox and Mr. Bryant on the occasion of their last attack, I conceived the plan of crossing the outlying spurs at a high altitude on foot from the usual base camp, believing that some way, for practised mountaineers at least, could be discovered whereby the farther side might be reached and an open bivouac be made a starting point next morning, if it proved too long or difficult a task to gain the summit in a single day.

Being wholly unaware of the character of the mountain on the hidden side, and anticipating considerable difficulty in getting to the southwestern ridge, by which we hoped to reach the point where the last climbers were compelled to halt, we had little expectation of being successful on the first day, particularly as the nights were closing in at a comparatively early hour. So off we started at six o'clock,—Peyto, Häsler, Bohren and I,—laden with two days' provisions, minor changes of raiment, blankets, and a light tent for the night, besides the usual camera and sundry other paraphernalia.

Twenty minutes' walk along the green flat brought us to the first snow, and a steep pull up hard snow slopes and a craggy wall of rock, followed by an awkward scramble over loose debris, landed us at half-past seven on the ice above. The glacier, covered with congealed snow and thin moraine, stretched away before us at an easy angle, with the great peak towering aloft upon our left. As we moved rapidly along I took the opportunity to scan with interest and curiosity the peculiar characteristics of that remarkable face, but the result of my observations was locked securely in my breast, and not revealed until, on the following afternoon, we stood upon the crest above.

Forty minutes of quick walking took us to the summit of the sharp ridge which forms the skyline to the west and merges in the main northwestern arête. Two hundred feet below us lay another glacier, and away to our left a second pass, at the base of the great western ridge. Dropping down to the ice, we followed up the glacier, zigzagging to avoid the large crevasses,[8] to the narrow little pass, which we reached at nine o'clock and found ourselves about 9,600 feet above the sea and 2,400 feet above the camp.

From this point the lower portion of the unknown side of our mountain lay in full view, and, to our joy, we saw that the anticipated difficulties were non-existent. A comparatively easy traverse, along narrow but ample ledges covered with snow and debris, across the ribs and stony gullies which seamed the southwestern face, would bring us, with scarcely any loss of elevation, to the southwest ridge, whence the climb proper was expected to begin. Each of the gullies seemed to be a much-used channel for stones and ice and snow, and was of excessive steepness, so no inducement was offered to try an upward route nearer than the line that Mr. Wilcox took in his ascent from the valley. Below the horizontal ledge of the proposed traverse the mountain shelved steeply down in long expanses of loose stones and snow, with not a little ice, into the depths of the contracted valley far beneath, containing the inevitable lakelet.

To counteract, however, this piece of unexpected good fortune, the light fleecy clouds, which had been hovering over the lower western peaks and growing larger and denser every hour, were blotting out the view and soon enveloped us in their chill embrace. With little hope of a successful ascent, we nevertheless made our way to the ridge, where we cached[9] our blankets, tent, and the bulk of the provisions, and, after a second breakfast, continued our upward progress at about half-past ten.

Our circle of vision dwindled from 100 yards to 50 at the most; a steady drizzle, mingled with sleet, began to fall as we climbed cliff and ledge and gully, loose rocks and slopes of debris, as each appeared through the mists in front of us; and every few yards we built a little pile of stones to guide us in returning.

At length, at about 10,750 feet altitude, out of the gloom a mighty wall, 70 or 80 feet in height, loomed before us, its top lost in the clouds. The face seemed sheer, and actually overhung in places. None of us had ever seen this side of Mt. Assiniboine, excepting Peyto, who had left us a short distance below to prospect for minerals, and we knew not where the summit lay. Of course we went first in the wrong direction. Imagining that this belt was as unbroken here as on the northern face, we sought a cleft up which to clamber and skirted the base to the right till we were brought up by a tremendous precipice some 6,000 feet in depth. We had suddenly reached the edge of a gigantic buttress, where its converging sides met at an abrupt angle. Before us, and on either hand, was empty space and at our feet a seemingly unbroken drop thousands of feet deep.

Behind rose the sharp edge of rock like polished masonry. Below the stony ledge by which we had approached, the mountainside shelved to the south in rugged steepness into far-distant gloom; and as we peered with caution round the angle, the farther side disclosed a most appalling face of black, forbidding precipice, one of the finest and most perpendicular it has been my lot to see.

Here for some moments I stood in solemn awe, perched like a statue in a lofty niche, cut in the topmost angle of a vast, titanic temple, with space in front, on either side, above, below, the yawning depths lost in the wreathing mists that wrapped the mountain's base.

Our progress in this direction barred, we now retraced our steps and spied a little rift by which, in spite of a fair overhang for the first 12 or 15 feet, thanks to firm hand and foot holds, we were enabled to scramble to the summit of the cliff. Working to the left by a steep succession of ledges and clefts, we reached a narrow, broken ridge running upward from the west, with a sheer drop upon the farther side. We thought that we had struck the main western arête (for it is very difficult to locate one's self in a dense mist, especially upon an unknown mountain which we expected to find a regular three-sided cone) and followed its lead, till in ten minutes, to our great amazement, we found ourselves upon a *peak*! Narrow ridges descended to the east and west, the steep face of our ascent lay to the south, while upon the northern side a mighty precipice fell away virtually perpendicularly for thousands of feet, broken only by a short buttress, with equally sheer walls and edged with jagged pinnacles.

This "Lost Peak" was to us most mysterious. It seemed a genuine summit, narrow and pointed though it was, in altitude a trifle over 11,000 feet. Yet where upon the mass of Mt. Assiniboine was such a peak? We had imagined that the giant tooth rose more or less symmetrically on every side and judged the back ridge by the two that we had seen. Häsler at first insisted that we were on the veritable summit, but the elevation and configuration of our whole environment demolished such a theory. We strained our eyes; but, though the breeze kept the thick clouds in constant motion, we could not see more than about a hundred yards ahead. We shouted in this direction and in that; but our voices died away into space until at last held by some loftier mass, which echoed back an answer from the direction whence we had just come! Then we knew that we were standing upon the southeastern ridge, which must be longer and less steep, at any rate in its upper portion, than any of the others, and possess a distinct minor peak, separated from the main summit by a considerable break.

Such proved to be the case. After an hour spent in the cold and wet, striving to pierce the clouds, hoping some stronger current of wind might waft them off, and thus enable us to see the top and give us some idea of its character and how we might approach it, we built a "stone man" to commemorate our visit, and, at half-past one, returned along the west arête until a chasm yawned beneath our feet—how deep we could not tell (it proved about 200 feet)—and forced us to descend by our cliff route and down the crack to the base of the big wall. A few minutes' going in the opposite direction brought us to a broad snow couloir,[10] where the cliff receded and trended upward to the gap into which we had been gazing from above not long before, and away upon our left stretched the steep face of the great peak itself.

It was now too late, to think of climbing farther, so we descended rapidly and rejoined Peyto near the cache. Here, during a meal, we held a council of war, and came to the unanimous determination to shoulder our packs and return to camp; feeling that, if the morrow were wet, we should be better off there, and if fine, it would take but little longer to come round in light marching order from the north than to make the ascent thus far with heavy packs from the tree line. In spite of a very speedy return, night fell upon us before we had quite descended the cliff wall below the northern glacier, and we stumbled into camp in black darkness about a quarter-past eight.

The clouds had begun to dissipate towards sunset: later on the moon rose in a clear, star-spangled sky; and the chill of frost augured favourably for our second campaign.

September 3rd, a notable date for us and Mt. Assiniboine, dawned brilliantly. At ten minutes past six our little party of three set out from camp in the best of spirits, encouraged by the hearty good wishes of the packers, and made rapid progress by the route of the previous day. In two and a half hours we were on the second pass, enjoying this time a wide view to the south and the northwest of an expanse of indented mountain ranges and deep yawning valleys, with a little lake far below in every gorge. A brief halt here, and then on to the southwestern ridge, reaching the cache three and a quarter hours from the start. Upward, past the coloured belt, to our great cliff of yesterday. There, at half-past ten, we turned off to the left and crossed the couloir, full of deep snow upon an icy basis.

Beyond it lay the final 1,000 feet of the great mountain, its steep and rugged face a series of escarpments broken by tiny ledges and occasional sharp pinnacles, and rent at distant intervals by clefts and crevices nearly vertical. Slopes of solid ice or ice-hard snow, demanding arduous step-cutting, intervened below each wall and ledge and filled each cavity. The rocks were very brittle and extremely insecure, and to the ordinary difficulties there was added that abomination of the mountaineer, verglas, the thin coating of ice upon the rocks from the night's frost after the rain and sleet of yesterday.

The general line was diagonally across the face, but frequent minor consultations were required, the problems of immediate procedure being numerous.

Steadily onward the little party made its cautious way across these difficult approaches: ever on the alert, hand and foot alike pressed into service; each hold fully tested before the weight was trusted to it. A slippery ledge demanded an ignominious crawl; a series of gymnastic efforts were required to surmount some of the straight-up rocks and buttresses, where holds were few and far between. Detours were frequent to avoid impossible conditions; all sorts of cracks and crevices had to be utilized; and icy rifts were sometimes the only avenues of access to the tops of smooth, unbroken cliffs.

Thus step by step the advance continued, till, after a final scramble up a gully lined with solid ice and almost as steep and narrow as a chimney, we stood triumphantly upon the south arête, the summit in full view not more than 300 feet above, reached by an easy ridge of snow, and Mt. Assiniboine we knew was ours.

The strangest feature of the ascent lay in the fact that now for the first time we saw the actual summit, as the cliffs rose so steeply during our approach that we could never see more than a short distance beyond us.

White, vaporous clouds had been slowly drifting up for the last hour, and, fearing a repetition of the previous day's experience and the loss of the view, we hurried to the top, pausing only for a few moments to enjoy the panorama, to renew our acquaintance with our "Lost Peak," now 500 feet below us, and to take a picture through the mist of the white summit, with its splendid eastern precipice.

A quarter of an hour sufficed to complete our victory, and at half-past 12 we stood as conquerors 11,860 feet above the sea (Government survey altitude from distant bases), on the loftiest spot in Canada on which a human foot had then been planted.

The summit is a double one, crowned with ice and snow, the two points rising from the extremities of an almost level and very narrow ridge 150 feet in length, at the apex of the sharp arêtes from north and south. On the western side snow slopes tilted downward at a very acute angle, while on the east a stupendous precipice was overhung by a magnificent succession of enormous cornices[11] from which a fringe of massive icicles depended.

One at a time—the other two securely anchored—we crawled with the utmost caution to the actual highest point, and peeped over the edge of the huge, overhanging crest, down the sheer wall to a great, shining glacier 6,000 feet or more below.

The view on all sides was remarkable, although the atmosphere was somewhat hazy and unsuitable for panoramic photography. Perched high upon our isolated pinnacle, fully 1,500 feet above the loftiest peak for many miles around, below us lay unfolded range after range of brown-gray mountains, patched with snow and sometimes glacier-hung, intersected by deep chasms or broader wooded valleys. A dozen lakes were counted, nestling between the outlying ridges of our peak, which proudly stands upon the backbone of the Continent, and supplies the headwaters of three rivers,—the Cross, the Simpson, and the Spray.

Far away to the northwest, beyond Mt. Ball and the Vermilion Range, we could descry many an old friend among the mountains of the railway belt,—Mt. Goodsir and the Ottertails, Mt. Stephen and Mt. Temple, with the giants of the Divide, Mts. Victoria, Lefroy, Hungabee, and a host of others; a noble group of striking points and glistening glaciers.

The main ridge northward, after a sharp descent of 50 feet, falls gently for a hundred yards or so, and then makes a wild pitch down to the glaciers at the mountain's base. When we arrived at this point (only through my most strenuous insistence, for the guides were anxious to return at once by the way we came), we looked down on the imposing face that is perhaps Assiniboine's most characteristic feature.

On the right the drop is perpendicular, a mighty wall with frequent overhanging strata and a pure snow curtain hanging vertically beneath the crowning cornice. But the north face, though not so sheer or awesome, is perhaps still more striking and unique. The shining steeps of purest ice, the encircling belts of time-eroded cliffs, sweep downward with tremendous majesty. Between the two a ragged ridge is formed, narrow and broken, like a series of roughly fractured wall ends.

As we gazed, the scheme that had been simmering in my brain since I looked upward to these heights the previous morning, seemed more than ever practicable and at last found utterance: "Could we not manage to get down this way?" and the hope of crowning the triumph by a traverse of the mountain, conquering its reputed inaccessible ramparts (and that, too, in a descent), together with the prospect of an absolutely first-class climb, decided the reply in the affirmative. True, at least three great bands of rock lay there below us, any one of which might prove an insurmountable obstacle and necessitate a retracing of our footsteps, with the probable consequence of a night out, at a considerable altitude, among the icy fastnesses; but we had found *some* crack or cranny heretofore in their courses on the farther side, and—well, we would try to find an equally convenient right of way on this face, too.

So, after a halt of nearly two hours, at 1:40 we embarked upon our final essay.

Well roped and moving generally one at a time, we clambered downward foot by foot, now balancing upon the narrow ridge, 5,000 feet of space at our right hand; then scrambling down a broken wall end, the rocks so friable that handhold after handhold had to be abandoned, and often half a dozen tested before a safe one could be found; now, when the ridge became too jagged or too sheer, making our cautious way along a tiny ledge or down the face itself, clinging to the cold buttresses, our fingers tightly clutching the scant projection of some icy knob, or digging into small interstices between the rocks; anon, an ice-slope had to be negotiated with laborious cutting of steps in the hard wall-like surface; and again, cliff after cliff must be reconnoitred, its slippery upper rim traversed until a cleft was found and a gymnastic descent effected to the icebound declivity that fell away beneath its base.

For close upon 2,000 feet the utmost skill and care were imperative at every step; for scarcely half a dozen could be taken in that distance where an unroped man who slipped would not inevitably have followed the rejected handholds and debris, that hurtled down in leaps and bounds to crash in fragments on the rocks and boulders far below.

But with a rope a careful party of experienced mountaineers is absolutely free from danger; and, though it took our usually rapid trio three and a half hours to descend some 1,800 feet, our confidence was fully vindicated, for nothing insurmountable obstructed our advance, and, after a brief halt below the last cliff wall (where sundry relics of the Walling expedition were observed), a gay descent, on snow that needed no step-cutting, brought us soon after six o'clock to easier, continuous rocks, where we unroped.

A speedy spell swinging down rocks, with an occasional glissade, landed us on the glacier in 40 minutes, and an hour later, in the gathering darkness, we approached the camp, after an absence of 13 hours and a half, greeted by shouts of welcome and congratulation from Peyto and Sinclair (who had seen us on the summit) and strains of martial music from the latter's violin.

Before turning in, we took a last look at the splendid obelisk above us, radiant in the moonlight against the dark star-strewn canopy of heaven. A last look it proved; for next morning we awoke to a white world, with nothing visible of Mt. Assiniboine but an occasional glimpse, through sweeping, leaden clouds, of its steep flanks deeply covered with the freshly fallen snow.

The return journey was begun at one o'clock that afternoon,

and Desolation Valley was traversed in the snow and rain, our chill encampment being made in the flat pasture at the head of Simpson Valley.

Next day we made a most tremendous march in the teeth of a driving snowstorm. The valley, with its gaunt, spectral tree trunks, was drearier and more weird than ever, the blackened timber, outlined against the dazzling snow, showed in a mazy network; the bushes, with their load of fruit, peeped out forlornly amid their wintry environment, and every flower bore a tiny burden on its drooping head. The steep ascent of 1,500 feet was made in ever deepening snow, and on the alp above we met the fierce blasts of the keen north wind, sweeping across the unprotected uplands. Wearied with our forced marches and two long days of arduous climbing, the tramping through soft, drifting snow, the steady upward trend of our advance and the hard conflict with the driving storm, it was with deep relief that we crossed the final ridge and could descend to calmer regions through the dark, snow-laden pines. Still on we went, down Healy Creek to the Bow Valley, where the packers camped with their tired horses, and the guides and I tramped on two hours more to Banff, arriving there just five days and five hours from the time of our departure.

Our toils were over. In spite of adverse weather conditions, the expedition had been intensely interesting from start to finish, and more than a success from a climber's point of view; and the fact that the ascent was made upon the last possible day the weather would permit that season gave a dramatic touch that added an extra spice of satisfaction to the accomplishment of a mountaineering feat, perhaps the most sensational then achieved in North America.

Note.—In July, 1903, another Scotsman, Mr. W. Douglas, of Edinburgh, with Christian Häsler and Christian Kaufmann, made the second ascent, this time by the north face, along the line of our descent, returning by the same route. Considerable quantities of snow, in excellent condition, facilitated climbing immensely where glare ice had called for strenuous step-cutting on the first occasion, and no special difficulties were encountered.

Chapter iv

LAKE LOUISE

"I HAVE TRAVELLED IN ALMOST every country under heaven, yet I have never seen so perfect a picture in the vast gallery of Nature's masterpieces as you have brought me to this afternoon." Such was the final verdict of a close observer of nature and enthusiastic lover of the picturesque, as we emerged from the shelter of the forest pathway, where the glistening waters of peerless Lake Louise suddenly burst upon the view, and we stood fascinated by the enchanting scene.

As a gem of composition and of colouring it is perhaps unrivalled anywhere. To those who have not seen it words must fail to conjure up the glories of that

> "Haunted Lake among the pine-clad mountains,
> Forever smiling upward to the skies."

A master's hand indeed, has painted all its beauties; the turquoise surface, quivering with fleeting ripples, beyond the flower-strewn sweep of grassy shore; the darkening mass of tapering spruce and pine trees, mantling heavily the swiftly rising slopes, that culminate in rugged steeps and beetling precipices, soaring aloft into the sun-kissed air on either side; and there, beyond the painted portals of the narrowing valley, rich with the hues of royal purple and of sunset reds, the enraptured gaze is lifted to a climax of superb effects, as the black walls of Mt. Lefroy, surmounted by their dazzling canopy of hanging glaciers, and the wide gable-sweep of Mt. Victoria, resplendent with its spotless covering of eternal snow, crown the matchless scene. The azure dome of heaven, flecked with bright, fleecy clouds like angels' wings, completes the picture, which not only charms the eye but lifts the soul to closer contact with the Divine Creator, Whose eternal love has given us these wondrous beauties to enjoy.

At every season, every hour, it is wonderful. Whether in winter, icebound and snow-beset, sparkling in all the brilliancy of countless myriads of diamond rays, or, suddenly bereft of sunshine, a weird expanse of mystic white, whose still death pallor strikes to the heart with solemn awe. Or in the springtime, when the bright glints of emerald leaves and buds illuminate the scene with fresh-won life; or, under the spell of autumn's magic touch, when changing hues of crimson and of gold, with an attendant train of countless interwoven tints scarcely less regal in their richness, mingle with the sombre evergreens, and the peaceful lakelet flashes back the glory of their radiance.

It may be in the early dawning, with the long shadow sweeping across the slumbering waters, and the ruddy gleam of bright Aurora flaming full upon the snowy crests of the far peaks; or, later, under the noontide brilliance, when every pinnacle and fissure of the uplifted crags and every bough and feathery tip of fir stands out in clearest detail, emphasized by the marvellous effects of light and shade; or, later still, when twilight steals upon us, draping the foreground and the middle distance in soft, tenuous mystery, while the snow summits blush beneath the roseate embrace of the departing day, and the ethereal skies whisper of God and heaven: then the glow fades, the stars shine forth, first one by one, then in advancing squadrons, till their hosts, in the pure atmosphere, blaze forth from the dark vault with an unearthly splendour that gives new character to lake and cliff, mountain and glacier.

By night or day, in storm or sunshine, peaceful or tempest-tost, in smiling innocence or swaying with fiercest passion and the forces of omnipotence let loose, the lake enthralls with a spell that is irresistible; and above God reigns supreme. His "everlasting hills" attest His might, His hand gives life and colouring to leaf and rock and flower, and we, to whom He gives it richly to enjoy, dare not lift up our eyes upon His world and yet withhold our wonder, our worship, and our love.

> "O, watched by silence and the night,
> And folded in the strong embrace
> Of the great mountains, with the light
> Of the sweet heavens upon thy face—
> Lake of the Northland! keep thy dower
> Of beauty still, and, while above
> Thy silent mountains speak of power,
> Be thou the mirror of God's love."

This delightful resort, three miles from the railroad, was one of the earliest discovered of the many beauty spots along the line of the Canadian Pacific Railway, whose names are household words amongst lovers of the picturesque. The lake was named for the Princess Louise, wife of the Governor-General of Canada at that date, the Marquess of Lorne.

In the eighties a small log cabin served as an inn for the few travellers who turned aside at Laggan to visit the lake and its surrounding scenery. In 1891 Mr. S.E.S. Allen spent a few days there and returned in 1893 with Mr. W.D. Wilcox, of Washington, for a brief sojourn. The following summer both were lured back again, and the party was increased by the advent of Messrs. Y. Henderson and L. Frissell. They thoroughly explored the neighbourhood. Mt. Temple and Mt. Aberdeen, with sundry minor peaks, were climbed, and the accounts of these expeditions, published by Mr. Wilcox in his book, and by Mr. Allen in the *Alpine Journal* did much to bring the district into early prominence.

Continuing our journey from our first halting place at Banff, the train traverses the green valley of the Bow, ascending steadily beside the swiftly flowing stream. Swinging round the end of the serrated Sawback Range, we enter a long stretch that runs at right angles to our recent course and parallels the watershed for 70 miles to the most distant source of the Bow River at Bow Pass. The railroad follows this for half the distance before turning again at a right angle to cross the Great Divide.

At the first bend Healy Creek comes in from the south and points the way to Mt. Assiniboine. Farther on, beyond the ramparts of Mt. Massive and Storm Peak, the low, forest-clad Vermilion Pass opens to the left. Meanwhile two dominating mountains have been looming ever larger and more imposing as we speed along. First, on the right, the towering battlements of Castle Mountain, like a gigantic medieval fortress, a vast mass of rocky walls and turrets. Then, beyond it on the other side, great helmet-shaped Mt. Temple rears its lofty brow, crowned with a diadem of glacier, the highest summit seen from the railroad track, and nearly 7,000 feet above it.[12]

To the left of the precipices of this splendid peak, utterly inaccessible from any point within out range of vision, lies the weirdly attractive Valley of the Ten Peaks, beyond the forest slopes that flank the stream locked in their adamant embrace, the pyramid of Deltaform conspicuous amongst the jagged summits. Sweeping round Mt. Temple's base, just as Mt. Lefroy and Mt. Victoria in icy splendour come to view, the train stops and we find ourselves at Laggan, the station for the "Lakes in the Clouds."

A walk or ride of three and a half miles leads to the comfortable hotel on the shores of Lake Louise. By all means walk if you can manage it. There is an upward tilt about the road as it mounts 600 feet to reach the lake, but there are so many excellent excuses to rest upon the way and to enjoy the exquisite peeps and vistas, as we stroll along the forest track, that the end comes all too soon. The dancing waters of the tumbling rivulet are chattering amongst the boulders as they go "to join the brimming river"; high peaks are reared into the heavens above the feathered pines and spruces, draped with "old man's beard," that close us in; whilst the luxuriant undergrowth and countless flowers fill the tale of brilliancy and beauty.

Ere long a glimpse of gleaming silver strikes athwart the trees, the lofty crest of Mt. Victoria appears beyond, we turn a corner, and the peerless panorama bursts with startling suddenness upon our gaze.

The old-time "chalet," with its dozen guests when fully crowded, is now no longer recognizable in the enlarged and well-equipped hotel that can provide accommodation for above a hundred. But the most cherished memories linger around the little building, with its one public room, looking out upon the lake and made so cozy in the cool evenings by the blaze of four-foot logs on the gigantic hearth.

In the sultry haze of summer heat, and in the deep snows of winter's mantle, it is alike good to wander by the lake shore, climb the steep woodland paths to little Mirror Lake (900 feet above), a lustrous circle of unruffled sheen, to lofty Agnes Lake (6,820 feet above the sea), cliff-girt and overhung with towering pinnacles; or higher still to the quaint Beehive, than which no spot was ever more aptly named, or Mt. St. Piran, with the most glorious view of all.

Across the ridge the Cataract Valley can be reached by rugged climbing, and mountain goats still give the hunter opportunity for plenty of arduous exercise and, possibly, a far-off shot or two.

On the opposing shore Mt. Fairview affords a rival panorama, with Mt. Temple's massive wall and little hanging glacier rising 6,000 feet above the deep-cut trench of Paradise Valley, which gleams bright and verdant at the base of grim Mt. Sheol, a quaint juxtaposition of nomenclature. As we roam among the rocky heights, the whistle of the marmot frequently breaks in upon the otherwise insistent silence characteristic of the region. Often, when alone, I have been almost startled by its human tone and turned involuntarily to see who could be sharing the quietude I thought mine alone. Sometimes they are seen perched on a big boulder or a pile of rocks, and even permit, at times, prolonged and close observation, and, on a rare occasion, photographic portraiture. Fine, fat fellows usually, with handsome gray fur coats and abundant tails, and, if one could so far steel his heart as to deprive them of their right to live, their pelts would make up into splendid rugs.

Two peaks stand out above all others here at Lake Louise to

lure the mountaineer: the one, Mt. Victoria, the other, Mt. Lefroy. The latter, conquered first by two days' interval, demands a chapter to itself, since to it pertains the melancholy notoriety of being the one mountain in the Canadian Rockies that has a fatal accident connected with its alpine history.

The scaling of Mt. Victoria was undertaken on the 5th of August, 1897 (most appropriately the year of Queen Victoria's Diamond Jubilee), by Professor J.N. Collie, Professor C.E. Fay (men who have in different ways done more than any others to investigate and popularize the glories of the Rockies as an ideal haunt for mountaineering, one in England, the other in America), Professor A. Michael, of Boston, and the Swiss guide Peter Sarbach, from St. Niklaus. At 3:45 they stole out into the darkness from the comfortable chalet, and embarked upon the lake to row to the upper end. Thence to the glacier, which was ascended to Abbot Pass in four hours from the start.

With Professor Collie in the lead the bold wall to the north of the pass was soon surmounted, and proved by no means so formidable as it looked, its rottenness being its main difficulty. Then, after a second breakfast, the rocks gave place to snow in the ascent, and the story must be told from the narrative of Professor Fay.[13]

"The skyline of Mt. Victoria as seen from the lower end of Lake Louise gives the impression of a very gradually ascending snowy ridge. A more careful study, however, brings out two features which break this reposeful monotony: the first, a sag not far to the right of where the profile of our mountain vanishes behind the icy helmet of Lefroy; the other, an inconspicuous stretch of rock wall about midway between this depression and the main summit, where for a space its dusky hue interrupts the white at the meeting of mountain and sky. In reality this sag separates from the principal mass of Victoria a portion almost individual enough to have a name of its own. It was upon the southern end of this portion that we were pausing for our luncheon. ... we were about to pass over the dome of snow to the left of the sag and as we supposed directly upon the skyline. To our surprise, as we approached its summit, we found an entirely different situation from what was anticipated. The true crest of this mass is a palisade of rock lying a little back of the visible snowy one. This latter sweeps gently over to its base.

"It was while passing along under this wall that there was prepared for us the most dramatic surprise that I ever experienced on a mountain. Without a moment's warning we found ourselves opposite a breach perhaps 50 feet in width straight through this Titan wall, and our vision, as if suddenly released from bonds, leaped forth into the west over range after range to rest at last upon the grand triple pyramid of Goodsir. Its imposing mass was perfectly framed between the vertical sides of the breach. Four distinct ranges lay between us and it; and what a tremendous gulf between ourselves and the first of these! The snow on which we were standing swept downward at an angle of 45 degrees, ending in a clear-cut line at the outer face of the palisade. Beyond it lay a depth of air; and then, a half mile away, the dark wall of Mt. Yukness. ... Never, not even on Mt. Hector, did I experience such an impression of profundity.

"Passing on we reached the point from which the descent is made into the sag. ... From here the subordinate peak called Mt. Huber is in full view. ... But still more did the peak of Victoria itself challenge our attention. Our way to it was now revealed to us; but how different from the easy grade we had been led to expect! How little like 'a wall of uniform height'! It towered a graceful pyramidal spire before us. Our line of sight being parallel to the axis of the mountain, we saw in profile the snowy slope that faces Lake Louise.

It swept rapidly up from the, top of the cliffs at an angle of 40 to 60 degrees, steepening yet more as it approached the clearly defined pinnacle. 'Hot plates' broke its surface at frequent intervals, with suggestions of imminent avalanches, which will always defend any approach to its icy citadel from this side. ...

"The climb of the long arête soon depleted any stock of exuberance the lively descent [to the bottom of the sag] had developed. At every step we sank to the knee, at many a one much deeper. Gratitude to Collie for the pioneer work he was putting in at the head of the line mingled with admiration for his endurance as we 'entered into his labors.' It was with a decided sense of relief that we at last reached the base of the parapet and found what we had hoped, a point where it could be scaled. Its crest proved to be exceedingly narrow, in places not over a foot wide, and rapidly weathering; nevertheless, it offered a line of rapid advance—the sooner, therefore, to come to an end and compel us once more to take to the snow. We were now (about 11 o'clock) at the base of the final peak. From here to the summit we were to move—as indeed we had been doing much of the time hitherto—along the very ridgepole of the North American continent. . . . Stride on, O Collie, we are right after you. . . .

"At last! But why does he not stop? Now that our eyes get level with where his thighs wallow out of the snow, we see we were too sanguine; the highest summit is that hillock, still beyond. One final push, and at 11:45 'the great white peak' is conquered.

"The summit [11,400 feet above the sea level] is an ideal one. Discounting the cornice crowning over towards the lake, there was hardly more than comfortable room for our party. Unlike that of Lefroy, no rock pierced the virgin whiteness. To the north it fell away suddenly into a deep depression filled with gendarmes, separating it from a bastion, from which it seems hardly probable it will ever be approached. Immediately to the west a snow arête falls away less rapidly, rising again almost to our level in the most pointed snow peak I have ever seen. The sides meet in the perfect apex of an angle of less than 80 degrees. It seemed as if its point would prick the palm that should be laid upon it."

The descent was easy and rapid without any episode requiring record, and the chalet was regained at half-past five o'clock.

My own first introduction to Canadian alpine climbing was also on this mountain, a day in August, 1900, witnessing an interesting scramble to the summit of the northern peak. The Swiss guide stationed at the chalet, not knowing our qualifications as mountaineers, demanded a second guide to convoy our party of three (Mr. J.H. Scattergood, of Philadelphia, my brother and myself) up this simple peak; but the addition proved to be a great hindrance and a source of weakness, almost amounting to danger, to the party.

The chef got up to give us a recherché breakfast at the early hour of 3 A.M. We pulled across the lake under the starlit skies, the ghostly pallid summits beckoning us onward through the night. Soon we were far up on the stony flank of Mt. Whyte and entering upon the traverse of the upper glacier that streams from Mt. Victoria's long ridge. Turning north, we then climbed, ladder-like, a steep snow curtain, 700 to 800 feet in height, and landed on the razor edge that joins Pope's Peak to Mt. Victoria, a grand series of precipices marking the farther side. Along this ridge, heavily corniced upon the side of our approach, we now proceeded, a bitter wind blowing most violently, whilst the clouds scurried low along the faces of the mountains all around. Cautioning Zurfluh to be particularly mindful of the cornice, and give it a wide berth, for I have a special antipathy to these dread traps for the unwary climber, I followed in his and my brother's footsteps with a confidence which received a rude and sudden shock when, in an instant, I felt my previously solid resting-place quiver, totter, disappear, and I shot downward into space surrounded by a whirling mass of snow and ice.

For the benefit of the curious, who may wish, like sundry others, to know my first sensations, I can only tell the grim, prosaic fact that the sole thought that occupied my mind was that I should have to climb the whole of that long, weary staircase of 800 feet of snow all over again! I had forgotten all about the rope that bound us all together, but in a fraction of a second it brought its very real and tangible presence to my memory by a stupendous jerk as it tightened round my devoted waist, and there I hung, dancing on air, somewhat uncomfortable about the centre, but in perfect safety. The rope, which had been kept quite taut between us, cut into the soft snow and scarcely caused the slightest drag upon my two companions, and they held me without an effort. Calling to them to hold steady, with a few strokes of my ice axe I cut a step in the ice wall to stand upon, and two or three more quickly brought me to the top again.

The experience is one of real interest, though hardly sufficiently so to make one yearn for an encore, even under similar conditions of a safe issue, for which there was great cause for thankfulness; though it cannot be too strongly urged that, when the proper precautions are taken—being tied together, keeping right distance and a taut rope, with incessant watchfulness—there is little, if any, danger of a catastrophe, even should one of the party fall. In the case under notice, also, it should be added that there would have been no accident at all had the guide taken ordinary precautions to ascertain the width of the projecting cornice or to give it a reasonably wide berth.

It did not take us long thereafter to gain the snowy apex of the north peak, where, in a piercing wind, we obtained fleeting but glorious glimpses of as fine an alpine panorama as one could wish to see. The striking feature was the abruptness of the precipice of Mt. Victoria and. the marvellous ridge connecting our peak with the highest point, referred to by Professor Fay as "filled with gendarmes." It is as worthy of the term "knife-edge" as any in existence, but the knife has been sadly maltreated, like one used as a can opener or for some similar strenuous and unwonted purpose. It is serrated along its entire length by jagged pinnacles and towers, standing up in many instances for scores of feet from the narrow joining ridges, and in places overhanging one or other of the vast sheer walls that culminate in this appalling toothed arête.

Later I planned to try a climb along this route to the chief summit, which would in all likelihood provide as high a test of mountaineering skill as any in the world, but weather foiled the scheme and the ridge still awaits a conqueror.

The minor peaks around have all been scaled,—the principal, Mt. Aberdeen, by Messrs. Allen, Frissell and Wilcox in 1894, by an easy route; and the most difficult, without doubt, by Mr. Edward Whymper's quartet of famous guides in 1901. This is "The Mitre," a ragged rock pile on the ridge between Mt. Aberdeen and Mt. Lefroy, which proved a first-class little bit of rock work.

Mr. Whymper camped for several weeks that year at various

altitudes, doing very thorough work in his characteristically energetic and patient way, exploring in all directions and making valuable observations in almost every branch of scientific research.

The two famous peaks are, even with guides, beyond the powers or inclination of the multitude, yet many are attracted by the magnet of the glaciers, especially those to whom their power is new; and Lake Louise adds to its unique scenic charms the enjoyable feature of giving the opportunity for one of the most striking and picturesque lower alpine expeditions imaginable. This is the crossing of Abbot Pass to Lake O'Hara and the Cataract Valley, which is absolutely unapproached in interest, variety, and charm on the Continent of North America, and yet it is within the capacity of the ordinary walker.

Abbot Pass is a narrow V-shaped notch, cut deep between the lofty walls of Mt. Lefroy and Mt. Victoria, upon the Great Divide. It is a glacial pass, whose romantic and secluded summit, hemmed in between mighty precipices from which avalanches thunder with constantly reverberating roar, has an outlook to nought but naked peak and precipice, snowy steeps and cataracts of ice, wild pinnacles tossed to the sky from the dead world of rock and glacier, without a sign of life and scarcely even a stunted shrub or blade of scanty grass within the range of vision. It is a picture of weird wonder and desolate majesty, almost incomparable and boundlessly impressive in its might and its eternal suggestiveness.

This silent arctic passage links the bright environment of Lake Louise, on the Atlantic side, to the delicious valley where Cataract Creek, taking its rise in glacial heights, threads its torrential way down the steep, rugged slopes from frozen Lake Oësa, with brief resting-places as it merges with the still waters of sundry mountain tarns, to Lake O'Hara, fairest of mountain lakelet gems, and thence to join the Kicking Horse, or Wapta, River, forming the longest branch of that wild tributary of the great Columbia.

Abbot Pass takes its name from the distinguished climber Philip Stanley Abbot, a Boston man, the first and only victim of a mountaineering accident in Canada, who met his death upon the steeps of Mt. Lefroy in 1896, just above the little col. The pass was first reached by Mr. S.E.S. Allen, in 1894, from the O'Hara side, and subsequently, in 1896, from Lake Louise by the party which made the memorable first attempt on Mt. Lefroy, thus demonstrating its feasibility as a route across the watershed; but it remained uncrossed till Mr. R.F. Curtis and Professor Fay made the trip in 1898, and no one followed till, three years later, the latter repeated the expedition in company with Mr. J.H. Scattergood, Christian Häsler and myself, on July 23rd.

We were on our way to try the ascent of Mt. Biddle and chose this as the shortest, most scenic, and most sporting route. The trip was unique by reason of our being accompanied by a spaniel, belonging to the chef at Field, and "Nellie" proved herself a splendid alpinist, negotiating the difficulties of ice and snow, rock and scree, in first-rate style, and winning fame as the first of her sex and of her species to cross a glacier pass in Canada.

The customary, but ever fresh and delightful, passage of the lake in the early dawn led to the short tramp through dew-saturated grass and bushes to the Victoria Glacier. Scrambling over the rough moraine to the debris-covered ice, we made rapid progress along its dry surface towards the mighty walls of the encircling peaks which rose with snowy mantles and huge cornices in stupendous grandeur straight from the floor of ice. A striking specimen of a glacier table was met with, an enormous boulder, fully six feet high and about 30 in circumference, being balanced on a delicate ice-pedestal and surrounded by a circular basin hollowed in the glacier by the heat refracted from he sun-smitten rock. With some difficulty Häsler and I succeeded in clambering up the smooth, worn side, and, hoisting Nellie up, we posed for portraiture upon this singular monument.

Rounding the cliffs of Mt. Lefroy, the steep snow-covered way to Abbot Pass looms right ahead, the close-contracting walls of the two giant mountains climbing sheer above, overhung by the edges of the ever moving glacier masses that clothe their steep-pitched roofs clear to the narrow ridge that forms the roof-tree of the Continent. These glaciers are fully 200 feet in thickness at the point where they break off and avalanche from the summit of the vertical cliffs, and during the summer season many hundreds of tons of solid ice are daily hurled from their giddy eminence and shattered on the glacier below. The frequency of these falls and the extreme narrowness of the chasm caused its earliest visitors to shun the hemmed-in passageway, which they named suggestively "The Death-trap." Mr. Abbot, with greater perception and alpine experience, scouted the title and persuaded his companions to make the first passage, which has since been followed not infrequently: with reasonable care and common sense danger is wholly absent, and the early designation has happily become extinct.

Grand it is and wild and weird, as we thread our way amongst the numerous crevasses that cross our glistening white pathway, which lies deep-cut between the towering, close-pressing precipices. Onward and upward till in four easy hours from the chalet we gained the narrow summit of the notch, about 9,800 feet above the sea and 4,000 higher than our starting-point. Almost overwhelming in its sublimity and suddenness was, to quote Professor Fay,[14] "the wonderful prospect that opened so magically—the sudden plunge of the western gorge, snowless in its upper half, its sloping sides and narrow bottom lined with scree from the heights above; the sea-green lakelets at its foot, 3,000 feet below us; the pinnacle of Mt. Biddle leaping up like a petrified flame and pricking the clouds that levelled with the tops of Victoria and Lefroy themselves; the remoter array of peaks unfamiliar in this new aspect."

Surrounded by this galaxy of noble peaks,

> "Walls like the glittering domes on high
> Reared for the dwellers of the sky
> By heavenly architect,"

what food for solemn meditation is prepared; what memories, too, of human interest centre round these ice-bound crags!

In solemn awe we gaze on the glazed steeps of Mt. Lefroy, and our companion tells with bated breath of the long toil of the ascent, the alternate hope and fear as to the outcome, the satisfaction as at last success appeared within their grasp; and then the sudden ghastly moment of their leader's fall, the agonizing watching, of the inert body in its downward course, the helplessness to stay his sure destruction or to aid in any way; the slow descent with nerves racked and intense, the touching last farewell, the fearful night spent on the pass in drifting snow, the search for help, the long return, and final carrying of the corpse of the loved friend to Laggan. And then the eye lights up again as memory strides a year forward and on the anniversary the vanquished leader's plan is carried out triumphantly and the successful first ascent is recapitulated step by step. Next, turning round, the same intrepid pioneer tells us the tale of Mt. Victoria's conquest and of the first crossing of our pass.

Again, we look with mingled feelings to the triple mass of Mt. Goodsir, the mightiest monarch west of the Divide, which only a short week before had baffled us, when within a few short feet of its proud crest, by the extraordinarily corniced condition of the final ridge. Then to Mt. Biddle, with a confident hope that, barring accidents, we should be seated on its sharp pinnacle within two days, and we wonder as we study its sharp arêtes and bands of girdling precipice, which is the most vulnerable side and by what line of approach we are to make the first attack. And so, with all the fullness of interest of past and future, the present slips all too quickly by and Häsler summons us to hurry up.

Then down, down, down, glissading here and there on patches of old snow, striding with giant leaps through the loose slopes of debris till we halt briefly on the shore of little Lake Oësa, the "ice" lake, almost entirely frozen over even in mid-July, circled by precipices, fed by a glacier tongue. A tumbling streamlet issues westward, which we follow down through grassy, flowery meadows, past tiny lakelets, each with its own distinctive character and charm of form and colour and environment: soon the brook disappears only to burst forth from its subterranean channel some hundreds of feet below, and finally to leap in an exquisite cascade of interlacing silvery threads over a ruddy cliff in a frame of waving fir trees, plunge into the peaceful depths of Lake O'Hara and sink to rest on the broad bosom of that enchanting mirror-like expanse.

At the lower end of the lake we spy, not without mundane satisfaction, even amid these fairy-like surroundings, the white gleam of our tents, and soon we are reposing on the velvet turf, drinking in deep draughts of tea and scenery (an excellent mixture), and feasting upon Nature in its primitive simplicity and grandeur and upon her products as modified by the manufacturing and culinary arts of man.

The next morning, in contrast to the clear brilliancy of yesterday, dawned with weeping skies. Climbing was out of the question, but the day need not be wasted and, after vainly waiting awhile for a clearance, we tramped off to visit Lake McArthur and to prospect for the best route by which to tackle Mt. Biddle. Forest and swamp, equally wet, alternated until we rose towards McArthur Pass, and, rounding the rugged, stony shoulder of Mt. Schaefer, we soon arrived at the edge of the lonely lake. Lying between two lofty spurs that rise abruptly hundreds of feet above, it nestles close under the towering mass of the main peak, a fair-sized glacier thrusting its crevassed tongue far into the waters, which are frozen over almost all the year.

Our survey of the mountain resulted in the selection of a route that appeared feasible, and, having thus accomplished the immediate object of our jaunt, we faced towards Cathedral Mountain and started back for camp. The rain was heavier than ever, and hurry led to a near approach to a somewhat undignified race, when Professor Fay, in swinging off a ledge onto some loose stones slippery with the wet, unfortunately wrenched his knee severely and was put *hors de combat*. This misfortune was Christian's opportunity to display others of his sterling qualities, and he mounted the Professor on his sturdy shoulders and, with marvellous strength, agility and surefootedness, bore him on high over loose boulders and down narrow ledges to the flatter ground, whence he and Mr. Scattergood supported the limping invalid until I met them with a horse which I had raced to camp to bring to the Professor's aid.

The melancholy procession trailed into camp in due time, and on the following day proceeded in the still pouring rain down the rough banks of Cataract Creek, with sundry crossings and many a shaking up for the poor, suffering equestrian, till Hector station saw the termination of his woes and on a convenient freight train the remainder of the journey back to Field was comfortably made.

Mt. Biddle has since fallen to the prowess of that energetic climber Professor H.C. Parker, of Columbia University, and Dr. A. Eggers, who, under the invincible guidance of Christian and Hans Kaufmann, ascended by a long and circuitous route from a camp in Prospector's Valley. The approach was across several ridges to the south arête. "Here," Professor Parker writes,[15] "we enjoyed some most sensational rock work, for the arête narrowed to a very knife-edge and fairly overhung the vast depths of Prospector's Valley. The climbing was neither difficult nor dangerous, however. … After a time the arête ended abruptly in an almost vertical face of rock, but, as usual, Christian discovered a practicable route to surmount this obstacle, and, climbing through a most picturesque 'window' of rock, we came out just below the final summit cliffs. These cliffs, while not high, were unscalable from this side; so we made an easy traverse over a slope of rock and snow, and gained the northern side of the mountain just under the summit.

"The face of the peak, which here towers majestically over Lake McArthur, is extraordinarily steep for the last few hundred feet, but, had the snow slopes been in good condition, it would have presented little difficulty. In place of snow, however, we again encountered solid ice, and so were forced for a short distance to take to a slope of varied rock and ice, depending on the most uncertain of hand- and foot-holds.

"But soon we made our way upward by means of a short chimney, so narrow that I could not get through, but had to swing out over it. This passed, the summit lay but a few steps beyond, and the last peak … was conquered."

Cataract Valley I visited on two subsequent occasions: once, when traversing Cathedral Mountain after the first ascent of that peak; and again, when making the first demonstration of the possibility of reaching Lake O'Hara directly from Field, across the Dennis and Duchesnay Passes, an attractive but fatiguing expedition. The descent is by a beautiful, lake-strewn and finely timbered valley, which joins the main valley about midway between Lake O'Hara and the mouth of Cataract Creek. Making this trip entirely alone on a bracing October day, there was no check to the rapidity with which my lengthy legs bore me along, and the time taken so misled a party conducted by Professor Fay the following summer, in which some ladies were included, that I most unintentionally caused them to be overtaken by darkness long before the lower valley was attained, necessitating an impromptu bivouac with sundry attendant inconveniences.

Although fairly long, and somewhat wearisome as far as Dennis Pass, the route is grand and beautiful for almost its entire length, and for a good walker is undoubtedly the finest way from Field to the enchanting fairyland of Lake O'Hara and its neighbourhood.

Chapter v

THE TRAGEDY ON MOUNT LEFROY

The list of fatal accidents in the Canadian Rockies contains, happily, but a single name up to the present, though in perusing the records of the earlier climbers one is struck by the very special providence that has watched their initial efforts. Few of the pioneers had any real experience of the "science" of mountaineering: enthusiasm, natural athletic tendencies and some scrambles on comparatively easy and safe mountains constituted their chief stock, in trade, and only one or two had any practical acquaintance with the glacial world, or of crag work in its more difficult aspects. The rope and ice axe were also novelties to almost all.

These men climbed without guides, and ordinarily at least one complete novice was included in the party, sometimes more than one. To their intrepidity, sturdy resolution and natural ability their successors must offer a hearty tribute of admiration, mingled with congratulation at the good fortune that attended them. As one of the most prominent remarked to me: "Our ignorance enabled us somehow to achieve without accident what now our knowledge would cause us unhesitatingly to avoid." It is the old story of rushing in where angels fear to tread, and a special providence preserved them from dangers which often lurked unnoticed and unheeded, in numbers and of a character sufficient to appall the seasoned mountaineer.

Glaciers and their ways take a lifetime to understand fully. Snowcraft is an education which many guides, with the experience of years, are not yet masters of; and almost every season the treacherous snows will claim amongst their victims men who have spent years in studying their conditions. Many a vast abyss is hidden under an unbroken expanse of seemingly solid snow, where even the keenest and most practised eye cannot detect their presence; and frequently an intricate network of these huge crevasses may be gayly passed over by an unskilled party, perhaps unroped, where an experienced guide would have each individual on the *qui vive*, the rope held taut, the eye and hand watchfully ready, as he winds here and there, probing at every step and noting indications of the most subtle type.

My recollection takes me back to an amusing episode—amusing for all but one—some years ago which illustrates the dangers which even a good guide may fail to recognize. Four of us were traversing the wide sea of névé[16] at the upper end of the Durand Glacier, in Switzerland. The Col du Grand Cornier had just been crossed and the steep descent on the eastern side negotiated. Above us towered the grand precipices of the Dent Blanche and the Grand Cornier; before us stretched a gently sloping plain of purest snow, its surface scarcely marked by any fissure. Of course we were roped and ready for any emergency, although expecting none. Our guide was an experienced man, well versed in all the problems of the glaciers and was no stranger to the route. Not a depression of the tiniest description, no crack, no special softness of the snow, gave the least indication of the presence of a crevasse, although we knew that numerous huge caverns lurked beneath the heavy mantle of eternal snow.

The splendid summit of the Rothhorn rose in front, exquisitely lovely in the sunlight, and a halt was called to take a photograph. The photographer, who happened to be second on the string, set up his camera on the level surface and stepped back a pace to focus the picture, when, in an instant, he was not! Only a hole in the white crust was visible where but a second previously my friend had stood, and two narrow grooves cut by the straining ropes that bound the departed to his surprised companions. In a few minutes he was hauled out, none the worse, quite cool—he made some remarks about the temperature down below—and proceeded with his unfinished picture, after selecting another location, the stability of which he this time took the precaution of establishing beyond peradventure.

When I peered into the hole he had so ruthlessly made, I saw a chasm with glistening walls of ice, of every shade of blue most exquisitely graded to the deepest hues of night, where far below the darkness hid the bottom of the cavity from view. This specimen was probably at least 300 feet in depth, broad at the upper rims, yet so entirely masked that the guide and my friend passed over it unwittingly, and not one of us could tell where space ended and the solid ice occurred beneath the snowy covering.[17]

Still more appalling and even more difficult to recognize are the limitations of avalanching snow. The acuteness of the angle at which it lies, its consistency, the character of the substratum, are all-important factors in the questions of safety and speed upon a slope of snow; and considerable experience is necessary to know just where and how to traverse it.

A kindred topic is the glissade, one of the most delightful luxuries in a descent, but intensely fruitful in mishaps. There are so many possibilities of accident; from avalanching snow, from a patch of hard surface, where the glissader loses all control, from bergschrunds[18] or rocks at the bottom of an inviting slope. And the temptation is so great, the perils are so easily overlooked, that many a risk is run, sometimes with most disastrous consequences.

Then come the cornices, the bugbear of every climber, and they are far more frequently met with in Canada than in Switzerland. Almost every ridge possesses one at least, and I have on more than one occasion found on the same arête cornices overhanging each side in turn, and springing from the steepest curtains of soft snow and even from rock faces practically sheer. A foot too near the edge and the huge mass may break away and hurl the party to the depths of a fearsome precipice.

The difficulties of crag work are far less formidable or dangerous to the inexperienced. The average athlete, especially if he has scrambled amongst rocks and cliffs even on the lowest hills, requires a hundredfold less education to become safe or even expert on rocks than on snow and ice. He learns the limitations of his powers more rapidly. Dangers are more apparent and easily recognized. It is an open rather than a hidden and treacherous foe that he has to battle with; and certainly amongst amateurs for one thorough expert on snow and ice there will be found ten or a dozen in the foremost rank on rocks.

Yet there are many points to learn, apart from the mere physical ability to overcome obstacles. Many a novice has been trapped by making an ascent on a troublesome face of rock and finding himself utterly unable to descend, for almost invariably the former is considerably the simpler problem, as one's work is right in front and the centre of gravity tends inward. Often, too, it is necessary to note the landmarks very carefully; points look so very different when seen from the reverse direction, and often it is extremely difficult to recognize the gully or ledge by which alone a way back to the lower world is possible. Most precious hours of daylight may be lost in this way, necessitating a night out in the cold, foodless and weary, or perhaps an even worse disaster.

But the most dangerous of all the contingencies in crag work, one which is ever present and singularly aggravated in the Canadian Rockies, is the peril of loose stones and rocks. Sometimes they come in showers from above; sometimes the seemingly firmest of holds gives way most unexpectedly, and even masses of many cubic feet will break off as the climber rests his weight on them. Nothing must be taken for granted or given the benefit of the doubt. Each hold must be amply tested, and then be deemed more likely unreliable than not.

In addition to the actual features of the mountains and their surroundings, there is much to be learnt in the manipulation of the two invaluable accessories of modern mountain-climbing—the rope and ice axe. The ice axe is the first possession of the budding mountaineer, and what a thrill passes through the innermost being of the novice, who has caught the fever of the peaks, when first he grasps his own! The "ancients" used a long pole shod with iron, and when steps were needed dug out hollows laboriously with the point.

When more ambitious ascents commenced to be made and great stretches of ice walls and hanging glaciers demanded the hewing of a long staircase in the hardest ice, this early method was impossible and hatchets were carried for the purpose. Then the ice axe was evolved. The pole was shortened, and the top furnished with a steel head, fashioned with a pick at one end and a flattened scoop at the other. In hard snow the latter is sufficient to hollow out an adequate foothold, and the pick is employed to cut steps in the solid ice.

For anchorage purposes the axe is very useful, and comes in handy at times in pulling one's self up as well as in descending. Its uses are innumerable on and off the ice. In glissading it acts as a support and brake simultaneously; it clears away debris, probes for hidden crevasses, cuts steps, serves as a balancing pole when crossing streams on fallen logs, or as a balustrade for timid folks, chops wood for fires and boughs for beds, is a distinct success as a can-opener, and, on an emergency, comes in handy as a camera stand, two making a most effective substitute for the conventional tripod.

How to carry it to the climber's best advantage and the least danger to his comrades' eyes and limbs is not learnt in a day, and many a slip would be avoided and far more rapid progress made if its use were better understood.

As to the rope, its value can scarcely be overestimated. Although perhaps amongst experts it is rarely, if ever, in rock work called upon to help a climber physically, its moral support is quite incalculable. The difference in climbing up or down a really difficult cliff, with or without its presence, must be felt to be properly appreciated. The strain is minimized, the danger virtually nil, when the rope is there. And, as a precaution, no sensible man would be without it when there is any likelihood, or, in certain cases, any possibility, of a considerable fall.

Whilst of appreciable importance in rock-climbing, the use of the rope on glaciers and steep snow slopes is absolutely imperative. The masked crevasse, the slippery surface, the frail snow-bridge, the tendency to avalanche, demand every possible care to guard against an accident. And though on both rocks and snow instances may be cited when a rope has dragged one or more victims with the fallen climber to destruction, yet the cases where it has been the means of saving life and limb are vastly more numerous; and the frequency of wholly unnecessary disasters because of its neglect witnesses to the immense advantage of its use.

But *how* to use the rope properly is by no means so simple as at first sight appears. It is quite an art. To keep continually taut the 18- or 20-foot length between one's self and the next man in front is not at all easy when the varying conditions of the surface are taken into consideration. The "feel" of the rope behind as well as in front must be attended to, lest a sudden jerk catch the climber unawares, and instead of holding up he is pulled down himself. Watchfulness and readiness to aid on either side must be constant, and assistance, if required, given on the instant, or it may be too late. Beginners are apt to let the rope get slack or twisted, to catch on rocks, to sweep down stones and debris on the heads of those below, to jerk their neighbours unnecessarily, possibly in a ticklish place, and so on. Such constant care is most undoubtedly a nuisance and often causes a slower gait, but it may mean the difference between defeat and victory, between death and life.

Taking all these things into consideration, it is a marvel that there were not several fatal accidents in the Canadian Rockies in the early days. Fortunately the peaks immediately adjacent to the railway line present no serious difficulties for the most part, and the few really first-class climbs were wisely let alone. The stratification of the mountains of the watershed and their prevailing tilt cause many of the peaks to have one very easy line of access, and as the prime art of the first ascender is to find the simplest route, a long list of successes has been achieved with but one fatal incident.

My own experiences on Mt. Victoria, Cathedral Mountain, Mts. Habel, Collie, Vaux, Columbia, Lyell, and many others, together with observations of peaks that had been previously climbed, lead me emphatically to the conclusion that the average Rocky Mountain peak is extremely easy from the point of view of a fairly experienced mountaineer, and admirably adapted as a splendid field for the beginner in the study of the craft. Now that the Canadian Pacific Railway furnishes excellent guides, all danger is eliminated, and every possible facility is offered for the enjoyment of the exercise and scenery which are the glorious rewards of mountaineering and to be obtained through it alone.

By the strange fate that is so often noticeable, the victim of the tragedy on Mt. Lefroy was the most unlikely of all the climbers to meet with such an end. Philip Stanley Abbot was undoubtedly the most experienced amongst the pioneers who visited the Rockies. He was a Boston man, one of the most enthusiastic and probably the most expert of the members of the Appalachian Mountain Club, to whom all mountain-lovers owe so great a debt for opening up these fastnesses and calling attention to the preeminent position of this region as the American Switzerland.

He sought no bubble reputation, as, alas, is too often the case in these days of "records" and competition. He loved the mountains, studied them with all his energetic, thorough nature, appreciated their characteristics and their moods, enjoyed with all the born mountaineer's keen ardour the battle against the elements and all the varied forces of nature in its wildest, most titanic sphere. More than one season spent among the giants of the Alps had given him the opportunity of learning something of the craft of mountaineering. The opportunity, as was natural to a man of his rare calibre, was eagerly grasped, and characteristically made the most of. Then he joined the little band of pioneers in the Canadian Rockies, which he at once recognized as the natural home of alpine climbing in America, and brought his best powers of experience, energy and judgment to bear upon their problems in the field, and in the enlistment of the sympathies of kindred spirits and the rousing of the energies of eastern athletes to invade and conquer these new and matchless worlds, where sport in its highest, purest form can be enjoyed.

In 1895, Professor Fay, Mr. Abbot and Mr. C.S. Thompson were at Lake Louise, surrounded by the mountains, listening to the crash of the avalanche and the mysterious whisperings of the "Spirit of the Peaks," that lured them on to the enchanted land. The fires within, already kindled and brightly glowing, were fanned into a flame by the magnificent vision of Mt. Lefroy, as seen one afternoon from the shaley summit of Goat Mountain. The northern slopes in profile showed a most promising and really simple line of ascent, provided the top of the great cliffs, 700 to 800 feet in height, that girdle the lower portion of the mountain, could be reached. This vertical black wall was cleft at one point by a couloir, filled at its base with snow, and easy enough most of the distance up; but the details of the rocky fissure above could not be clearly seen and appeared extremely problematical. So a reconnaissance was made.

This couloir had previously attracted Messrs. Wilcox, Frissell and Henderson as perhaps a feasible approach to the enticing slopes above, and an attempt to climb it resulted in an accident that might easily have proved the first fatality in the region; strangely enough, upon the same mountain that afterwards gained such unenviable notoriety.

"On either side of us," writes Mr. Wilcox,[19] "there were overhanging walls, decayed limestone pillars, tottering masses of broken stone with daylight showing through the cracks, and a thousand rocks resting threateningly balanced and apparently ready to fall at a feather's touch. That we were not dismayed at this hopeless prospect proves that we were more audacious than prudent.

"At length when reaching upwards for a handhold, with a boost from below and my face against the limestone, I saw a large and dangerous-looking stone poised above us. 'Fellows, we must look out for that stone,' said I, 'and not let the rope touch it.' A moment after, Henderson and I were above this, climbing another rock ledge, when we heard the grinding sound of the large stone moving. We turned in time to see Frissell falling. The rope tightened and held him on a ledge ten feet below, but the tremendous stone, which must have weighed a ton, was rolling over and coming down upon him. For a brief but awful moment, helpless and immovable, as in a frightful dream, we saw the stone leap out into the air to descend upon our poor comrade, but he made a desperate movement, pressing hard against the cliff, and escaped the full force of the blow. Then the whole place resounded with the hollow rattle of falling stones as they danced in a shower of death below us.

"We found that Frissell could not stand, one leg being perfectly helpless, while he was so dazed by the shock that he fainted twice in our arms. ... Uncoiling the full length of the rope, one end was fastened round his waist, and the other round mine. With an ice axe buried to the head in the snow as an anchor, I paid out the rope and lowered our helpless friend fully 50 feet. Then Henderson went down and, anchoring himself in like manner, held him while I came down. This operation, repeated a number of times, brought us soon upon the comparatively level glacier."

Help was brought by Mr. Wilcox from the chalet, and the invalid carried thither on an improvised litter, where he was attended to by a doctor who arrived on a hand-car from Banff, 35 miles distant, and ere long he happily recovered.

The trio of 1895 met with no physical mishap, but, owing (apparently) to insufficient respect for the difficulties to be encountered, deferred their start until 3 P.M. and were most unfortunately overtaken by darkness at the critical point. Aided by a short and. narrow tongue of snow, just strong enough to cross, they reached the upper rocks and worked their way up a "chimney" for some distance till a *mauvais pas* was encountered, with the top still out of sight. Though impressed with the idea that a passage might be forced, there was no chance of effecting it before daylight disappeared, and, discretion being the wiser course, an immediate retreat was determined on.

Next morning they returned to the attack, but again the fates were contrary. A warm spell of weather and a drizzling rain had rendered the snow tongue unsafe, so a second chimney was attempted. This formed a most effective watercourse, with smooth sides glazed here and there with verglas, down which an icy shower was gayly plunging, soaking the climbers to the skin and overcoming the ardour of at least two of the party. Once more retreat was obligatory, and the problem of the couloir has, I believe, never yet been solved.

Since then a charming pathway has been found, clearly defined when snow is fairly fresh upon the peak, by means of an ample ledge running almost horizontally along the eastern face of the mountain, from the conspicuous mass of avalanche snow about its centre to the apex of the buttress at the northeast corner. Thus the summit of the cliff belt is easily attained, and the remainder of the ascent is of comparatively little moment, unless the mountain is in a glazed condition.

Meantime, however, this solution of the problem of Mt. Lefroy was not yet discovered, and a new line of ascent suggested itself to Mr. Abbot, in spite of the emphatic opinion of an earlier explorer, Mr. S.E.S. Allen, who alone had viewed the peak from the suggested point of attack. This was on the western side, directly from the pass now bearing the honoured name of him who conceived the bold scheme and in the execution of it lost his life. Mr. Allen had ascended the pass from the O'Hara Lake direction and examined the steep, white slope of Mt. Lefroy from close at hand. He judged that ordinarily so great a quantity of step-cutting would be involved as to render an ascent impracticable within the limits of a day, making a start from Lake Louise This verdict proved more of an incentive than a deterrent to Mr. Abbot, and the following summer found him, with his previous companions and the Rev. George Little, ready for another assault upon the fascinating peak.

On August 3rd, 1896, the chalet was left behind at 6:15—a somewhat noticeably late hour in view of the distance and the difficulties that lay before the party. In an hour and a quarter the glacier was reached, and 70 minutes later they roped up opposite the familiar couloir. Soon they turned the shoulder of Mt. Lefroy and entered on the new ground of the magnificent gorge dividing that mountain from Mt. Victoria.

The usual thunders of frequent avalanches greeted their ears, and the superb cascades of powdered ice and drifting snow were at their best. With but a single brief halt they pressed towards the narrow V-shaped nick at the head of the long snow slopes that rise steadily to the level of the cliff walls which form the confines of the glacier below.

Not till 11:50, however, did they gain the longed-for crest, and turned to scan the massive mountainside, whose ice-crowned pinnacle still towered 2,000 feet above the pass. Almost immediately the joyful exclamation came from Mr. Abbot's lips, "The peak is ours!" And (to quote from Professor Fay's intensely graphic account of the occurrence)[20] "surely his confidence seemed justified. From here an unobstructed way was seen leading up to the long summit arête, which still frowned nearly 2,000 feet above the pass. The vast mountainside rose in a sloping wall, ice-clad for the greater part, yet with here and there long upward leads of rock that probably could be scaled, as the dip was in the right direction. ... At 12:30 P.M. ...we again set forth to complete, as we fondly believed, the largest enterprise in the way of mountaineering that has ever [1896] been accomplished on Canadian peaks. Our record shows that in the first half-hour we made excellent progress, for at one o'clock our aneroid reading was 10,400,—300 feet above our lunching-place ... Of the next four hours and a half the writer of this narrative has a very vague recollection. ... These hours were spent either in cutting steps in our zigzag course up ice slopes, or in wary advance up the unreliable slopes of rock, the effect of a slip upon which would differ slightly in ultimate results from a slip on the ice itself. ... At 5:30 we drew up under an immense bastion possibly 75 feet in height, behind which lay the summit, of which as yet, owing to foreshortening, we had had no satisfactory view. This frowning face rose sheer from a narrow margin of tolerably stable scree that lay tilted between its base and the upper edge of the sloping ice that we had just left behind us. Looking past it on the right we saw, a few hundred feet beyond, the tawny southern arête, so shattered as to be utterly impassable. In one place a great aperture, perhaps 40 feet high and five or six in width, revealed the blue sky beyond. Evidently our course did not lie in that direction On the left the dusky northern arête rose with an easy gradient possibly an eighth of a mile away, but across an ice slope similar to that up which we had so long been toiling, and in truth a continuation of the same. To cross it was perfectly feasible, but it would take so long to cut the necessary steps that a descent of the peak before dark would have been out of the question.

"But now Mr. Abbot, who had moved forward along the rock-wall to the limit of the rope, cheerfully announced an alternative. His view beyond an angle in the bastion revealed a vertical cleft up which it was possible to climb by such holds as offered themselves. Bidding Thompson and me to unrope and keep under cover from failing stones, he clambered some 30 feet up the rift, secured a good anchorage, and called upon Professor Little to follow. This the latter proceeded to do, but while standing at the bottom of the cleft preparing to climb, he received a tingling blow from a small stone dislodged by the rope. A moment later a larger one falling on the rope half severed it, so as to require a knot. As danger from this source seemed likely to continue, our leader had Little also free himself from the rope and come up to where he stood. From here a shelf led around to the left, along which Abbot now proceeded a few yards and discovered a gully leading upward, unseen from the point first attained, and this also he began to ascend. To Mr. Little's question, whether it might not be better to try and turn the bastion on the shelf itself, he replied: 'I think not. I have a good lead here.'

"These were the last words he ever uttered. A moment later Little, whose attention was for the moment diverted to another portion of the crag, was conscious that something had fallen swiftly past him, and knew only too well what it must be. Thompson and I, standing at the base of the cliff, saw our dear friend falling backward and head-foremost, saw him strike the upper margin of the ice slope within 15 feet of us, turn completely over and instantly begin rolling down its steep incline. After him trailed our two lengths of English rope—all we had brought with us—which we had spliced together in our ascent over the last rock slope, in order to gain time by having less frequent anchorages than were necessitated by the short intervals of one 60-foot line. As the limp body rolled downward in a line curving slightly towards the left, the rope coiled upon it as on a spool,—happy circumstance amid so much of horror,—for not only did this increase of friction sensibly affect the velocity of the descent of 900 feet to the narrow plateau of scree above mentioned, but doubtless the rope by catching in the scree itself prevented the unconscious form from crossing the narrow level and falling over the low cliff beyond. Had it passed this, nothing, apparently, could have stopped it short of the bottom of the gorge leading up to the pass from the western side of the Divide, a far more fearful fall than that already made."

At 6:30 the slow and sad descent was commenced by the awed and heartbroken survivors. Without a rope the circumstances called for unremitting caution and great self command. Fortunately the steps on the ascent had been made exceptionally large, but for three long hours, while sunset radiance gave way to dusk, they worked their "slow way downward, and at length stood beside the motionless form that all this time had lain in full view. To our surprise life was not yet extinct. . . . A faint murmur, that my imagination interpreted as a recognition of our presence and an expression of gratitude that we at least had escaped from peril, alone broke the silence for a brief moment, and then we three bared our heads in the twilight, believing that his generous spirit was already passing."

He lived a short time longer, however, while with gentle hands they bore him to a better resting-place, and then he peacefully breathed his last. To bear the lifeless body farther without assistance and in the dark was utterly impossible, and, sorrowfully leaving the remains of their comrade on the snowy platform, the three survivors with difficulty retraced their footsteps of the bright, hopeful morning in the deep gloom of night and grief. The night was spent on the cold wind-swept pass, and, setting out at 5 o'clock next morning, they reached the chalet at 9:30 in the midst of a rainstorm.

Obtaining the willing aid of Messrs. T.E. Wilson and Astley, the party in half an hour were once more on the way. Reaching the pass at 2:30, mists and snow squalls enveloped them and made their task increasingly difficult. At four o'clock the work of lowering the body was begun, and even with the united efforts of the five it proved a long and perilous proceeding. Once the glacier was gained progress was more rapid, but darkness overtook them ere the lake was reached, and again the body had to be abandoned for the night The following day a party of bridge-builders, sent by the sympathizing officials of the Canadian Pacific Railway, carried the body to the station, and the long journey to the East concluded in the quiet service at Mt. Auburn on August 12th, when all that was mortal of noble Philip Abbot was laid to rest in hope and confidence of a future life.

The cause of the accident remains a mystery. Whether a slip occurred, or the climber trusted to a mass of rock which suddenly gave way, or was struck by a falling stone, cannot be determined. The intense rottenness of the Rocky Mountain quartzite lends strong probability to the view that a hold may have proved treacherous, and Professor Fay's "impression" gives additional weight to the idea. "I know not how to account for my immediate impression," he writes, "unless I actually saw something to create it during the momentary slackening of his swift rush past us, but it was an increase of horror lest a large stone, clasped in his arms, should crush him as he struck the slope."

Abbot's caution was proverbial amongst his comrades, though combined with an enthusiastic boldness, and a slip is the least likely of the three contingencies. The strange neglect to coil the rope is quite inexplicable to any experienced mountaineer, and the trail of its nearly 120 feet and liability to catch on the numerous projections and jerk the climber backward in a critical position, suggests another possible explanation of the fatal fall.

On the first anniversary of this terrible disaster a party of nine set out from Lake Louise to make a fresh attempt to conquer the mountain that had so fatally repelled the last assault. It was quite an international combination. America was represented by six members, Professor C.E. Fay and Mr. C.S. Thompson of the previous campaign, the Rev. C.L. Noyes, Professors A. Michael and H.C. Parker, and Mr. J.R. Vanderlip. They were joined by Professors Norman Collie and Dixon, of the Alpine Club, hailing from Scotland and England respectively, and Peter Sarbach, the first Swiss guide to visit the Helvetia of North America.

The route taken was practically identical with that made sadly memorable by the death of Mr. Abbot, and, although the abnormally large number of climbers, divided into three trios, was contrary to the accepted canons of mountaineering custom, a laborious but satisfactory climb resulted, and the proud peak was scaled successfully. Starting at 3 A.M. the pass was reached in five hours, and the summit at 11 o'clock. The snow was in fine condition and enabled them to ascend the steep slopes without the trouble of cutting more than a few steps here and there. The condition of this snow is the crux of the ascent. Even on that day of victory it was perilously near an avalanching state, for two days later when viewed from the crest of Mt. Victoria the snow had disappeared, leaving "an unbroken wall of gray ice. The entire layer from ten to 15 inches in depth, then welded to the ice beneath, had meantime evaporated under the intense rays of the August sun. Our attack was made in the nick of time. A day later would have made it perilous, and exceedingly toilsome, if not impossible."[21]

Since 1897 the peak has been ascended more than once, the regular route being the safer one by the ledge on the eastern face and up the northern slope. No longer formidable, the mountain still retains its interest. The shapely lines, stupendous cliffs and ice-capped crest still lay their fascinating spell upon the visitor, and this interest has gained an added power and intensity through the solemn and melancholy tragedy of that brilliant August afternoon in 1896.

The lesson taught at so terrible a cost has not been in vain. The enthusiastic love that Abbot had for Nature's noblest works has been transplanted by his death to other hearts The craft he so delighted in has gained adherents through his memory; whilst at the same time the awful shock of accident, occurring to a most skilful and habitually cautious mountaineer, has proved a valuable and perhaps much needed warning, lest undue familiarity, a moment's want of thought or care or adequate testing of conditions, should involve not one life only but very likely several.

Though the poor shattered body lies in the peaceful shelter of a New England tomb, the spirit of Philip Abbot lives again in many of those who knew him not, as well as those who had the privilege of intercourse and friendship with a rare personality; and his true monument is not within the lowland precincts of Mt. Auburn, but—standing majestically amongst the crags and glaciers he loved so well—the splendid peak of MOUNT LEFROY.

Chapter VI

THE VALLEY OF THE TEN PEAKS

Eastward from Mt. Lefroy, between the overshadowing heights of that peak and Mt. Aberdeen, projects a fantastic little pile of rugged rocks, appropriately named "The Mitre." On either side a narrow ridge connects the smaller point with its huge, massive brethren. From these sharp notches glaciers sweep down, uniting early in their course, and fill the valley east of Mt. Lefroy as they descend to meet the great Victoria Glacier.

A few days after Mr. Frissell's mishap in the couloir of Mt. Lefroy, the rest of his companions journeyed up this glacier on exploration bent. Their earliest adventure was the collapse of a frail bridge crossing a crevasse, which gave one member of the party a new and undesired experience, before he was pulled out of the icy chasm, and he reported that he could distinctly hear the gurgling of the water at the bottom of the depths over which he hung suspended by the precautionary rope.

Selecting the left-hand, or eastern, pass as having the easier appearance, Mr. Allen found strenuous employment in cutting steps up the steep slopes of hardened snow. "After three hours," Mr. Wilcox chronicles,[22] "of slow and tiring work we had climbed only 1,000 feet. It was a cloudy day with a damp and cheerless atmosphere, and at this altitude of 8,000 feet there were occasional showers of hail and snow. Chilled by the long exposure and the necessary slowness of our progress, every member of the party became silent and depressed. ... To judge by our surroundings alone, we might have been exploring some lonely polar land, for our entire view was limited by high mountains covered with glaciers and snow and altogether barren of vegetation. ...

"The last few steps to a mountain pass are attended by a pleasurable excitement equalled only by the conquest of a new mountain. The curtain is about to be raised, as it were, on a new scene and the reward of many hours of climbing comes at one magical revelation.

"Arrived on the summit of our pass, 8,500 feet above sea-level, we saw a new group of mountains in the distance, while a most beautiful valley, lay far below us. Throughout a broad expanse of meadows and open country many streams were to be seen winding through this valley, clearly traceable to their various sources in glaciers, springs, and melting snowdrifts. With all its diversity of features spread like a map before our eyes, this attractive place was seen to be closely invested on the south by a semicircle of high and rugged mountains, rising steeply from a crescent-shaped glacier at their united bases. ...

"At the time of our arrival on the summit, a sudden change took place in the weather. The wind came from another quarter, and the monotonous covering of grey clouds began to disclose blue sky in many places. The afternoon sun poured shafts of light through the moving clouds, and awakened bright colours over forests, meadows, and streams.

"This beautiful scene opened before us so suddenly that for a time the cliffs echoed to our exclamations of pleasure, while those who had recently been most depressed in spirit were now most vehement in expressions of delight."

The place was christened "Paradise Valley," and the climbers quickly descended the 1,500 feet between the pass and valley-bed, and traversed the green depths with many a hardship incidental to fallen timber, swampy ground and legions of mosquitoes, which must have interfered somewhat with their sense of the fitness of the just-given name, albeit to the eye this fairyland at every step revealed new wonders. Perhaps this disenchantment of the flesh may have had something to do with the transition to the name of "Sheol" given to the black bastion that projects into "Paradise" from the westward range. Eventually the inn at Lake Louise was reached in two detachments, one at 8 P.M., the other not until the following morning after a sleepless bivouac.

At the head of Paradise Valley another col, just opposite the Mitre Pass, opens to the south, between the spurs of Mt. Hungabee and Mt. Temple; and, a few days later, from its summit, the same party viewed for the first time the Valley of the Ten Peaks, then called by them, in contrast to the verdant vale of their approach, "Desolation Valley."

This mountain-circled valley, which is now becoming famous as one of the wildest and grandest corners of the mountain world, was thoroughly explored by Mr. Wilcox during the summer of 1899, and when I visited the place in 1902 a broad and easy pack-trail was almost completed to the borders of its central lake, preparatory to the establishment of a chalet where the modern traveller can enjoy in luxury the quondam almost inaccessible retreat.

Wandering eastward from the shores of Lake Louise, the wooded flanks of Fairview are first skirted, through alternating belts of timber, carpeted with bright green moss and brilliant flowers, and stretches of bare rocky ground, the track of old-time avalanches. And by the way, in their due season, a feast of berries often offers welcome refreshment in these woods and on these slopes. Soon, through the forest, looms the vast mass of Mt. Temple, the apex of whose gabled top rises some 6,000 feet above, ornamented by an exquisite hanging glacier.

The dark sheer walls, their horizontal strata frequently picked out with streaks of purest snow, stand almost perpendicular above the sunny depths of the sweet green vale that separates them from the scarcely less impressive cliffs of Mt. Aberdeen, terminating in the black precipice of "Sheol." This is the entrance to Paradise Valley. The sunlit Wastach[23] Creek, finding its main source in the Horseshoe Glacier, beneath the splendid summit of Mt. Hungabee, flows swiftly through the open meadows and dense forest growth to join the Bow, and, crossing its merry stream, we wend our way round the wide-swelling base of the great mountain.

But to see Mt. Temple in its noblest grandeur I would take you to the Saddleback. This is a broad green alp, nearly 2,000 feet above Lake Louise, a very favourite hour's ascent by trail, between Mt. Fairview and the projecting "horn" of the Saddle Peak. Crossing the plateau to the tree-fringed brink of the abyss beyond, our gaze is carried straight across the chasm, 1,500 feet in depth, to the huge peak, at whose far base nestles a small azure lakelet (Lake Annette), like a tiny bit of sky dropped from the heavens and almost lost in the depths of the sombre firs.

We can descend this abrupt mountainside and, joining the lower trail at the Wastach bridge, continue round the flank of Mt. Temple, till we reach the shores of Moraine Lake. This lake, which occupies the centre of the Valley of the Ten Peaks, is very similar in size to Lake Louise, and likewise hemmed in on three sides by the relentless mountains, but there the resemblance ceases. Our new location is wild and bleak and desolate. Mr. Wilcox, its real "discoverer," thus graphically describes the view from the lower extremity:[24] —

"Ascending a ridge about 50 feet high, there lay before me one of the most beautiful lakes that I have ever seen. This lake, which I called 'Moraine Lake,' from the ridge of glacial formation at its lower end, is about a mile and a half long. A green forest covers the north shore, while the opposite side is overhung by a high precipice. Two large piles of debris from the mountains dip into the lake and encroach upon its surface in semicircular lines. An imposing cliff, like a Tower of Babel, makes a grand terminus to the range of mountains on this side of the valley. Beyond the water is a succession of high peaks rising 5,000 or 6,000 feet above it, with a few short glaciers among them. The water is very clear and of the characteristic blue-green colour. A number of logs were floating on it in various places, while others crowded the shore and raised the water level by damming up the outlet stream. Part of the water escapes by subterranean channels among the quartzite and shale ledges of the moraine, and the rest flows out at the northwest end through an immense mass of logs. ...

"At the time of my arrival the lake was partly calm and reflected the rough escarpments and cliffs from its surface. No scene has ever given me an equal impression of inspiring solitude and rugged grandeur. I stood on a great stone of the moraine where, from a slight elevation, a magnificent view of the lake lay before me, and while studying the details of this unknown and unvisited spot, spent the happiest half-hour of my life."

North of the Tower of Babel opens out a little valley of singular beauty and restfulness, aptly designated "Consolation Valley," gemmed by pine-fringed lakelets and terminating in a snowy pass, above which rises to the right the icebound crags of Mt. Fay. From the latter stretch the Ten Peaks which give their name to the quondam "Desolation Valley." These summits were named by Mr. Allen from the numerals of the Stony Indian language: they lie upon the Continental watershed, commencing with Mt. Heejee (No. 1), swing round the curving head of the deep valley, which they wall in with a line of well-nigh vertical escarpments, and terminate in Mt. Wenkchemna (No. 10), which connects with Mt. Hungabee on the north, and with Mt. Temple on the east. The Wastach Pass, whence the first view of the valley was obtained, and a minor crest of rugged crags—Pinnacle Mountain—form the link with huge Mt. Temple, which fills the entire northwest side of the valley and dominates it in most strikingly majestic fashion.

Between peaks Nine and Ten lies the one easy pass the range affords, Wenkchemna Pass, leading over to Prospector's Valley, a tributary of the Vermilion River, which flows into the Simpson, itself a feeder of the Kootenay River, and this in turn joins the Columbia River beyond the Kootenay and Arrow Lakes.

So far as the writer has been able to ascertain, but two of the Ten Peaks have as yet been climbed. Neptuak (No. 9), lying immediately south of the Pass, was first ascended on the 2nd of September, 1902, by Messrs. Collie, Stutfield, Weed and Woolley, led by Hans Kaufmann. From the pass, to quote the narrative of "Climbs and Exploration in the Canadian Rockies" (p. 315), "turning to the left, we traversed a small but steep snow slope and got onto the arête. For some distance the going was easy enough, but presently we found our way barred by some formidable-looking walls and towers of rock. On our left we looked down the tremendous sheer precipice facing Desolation Valley: below on the right were shale slopes and couloirs, now sheeted with ice, down which stones and icicles were falling with unpleasant frequency. We therefore decided to stick to the arête; and the result was one of the best climbs of the trip. It was good hard scrambling nearly the whole way, the rocks being almost vertical in places and the handholds not overabundant; and, being a party of five on one rope, we made but slow progress.

"During the ascent we made a closer acquaintance with the variegated strata seen in the cliffs from below. First we encountered a layer of light-coloured limestone very much shattered; then came a bed of much firmer dark brown rock, then more pale loose limestone, and near the top almost black limestone with light veins. Towards the summit the inevitable cornice was encountered, and traversing some distance below it, we climbed a narrow ridge of rocks overhung with snow and found ourselves on the highest point at 3 P.M. Our height appeared to be 10,500 feet."

The chief amongst the Ten, however, is Mt. Deltaform, this title having been conferred by Mr. Wilcox, owing to the similarity of its form (as seen from Moraine Lake and the railroad) to the Greek letter Δ, and having unfortunately quite supplanted the Indian numeral "Saknowa," meaning No. 8. It has long appealed to climbers, but by reason of the practical impossibility of gaining the summit in one day from civilization, even as represented now by a camp at Moraine Lake, and the necessity of making one's base in distant Prospector's Valley, no attempt was made until on September 1st, 1903, Dr. A. Eggers and Professor H.C. Parker, guided by Christian and Hans Kaufmann, succeeded in making the ascent.

From Moraine Lake they climbed by couloir and arête to the crest of the ridge between peaks Four and Five, traversed behind peaks Five, Six and Seven, then, after a troublesome descent to the base of Mt. Deltaform, they rounded the shoulder of the latter into Prospector's Valley, and, in rain and darkness, reached a camp awaiting them beyond Wenkchemna Pass half an hour after midnight. Meanwhile, during their circuit of Mt. Deltaform, they had observed a very promising line of ascent, and next afternoon they moved their camp across the pass and located in a beautiful spot at the foot of Mt. Neptuak.

The account of the climb must be given in Professor Parker's words.[25] "On the morning of September 1, in fine, clear weather, we left camp about six o'clock and, skirting the base of Neptuak, made our way over the lower slopes of Deltaform to the foot of the couloir by means of which we had determined to commence the attack. Sometimes by means of couloir, but more often by means of treacherous rock slopes, we made our way steadily upward, and at last, emerging through a chimney, found ourselves on the crest of the southeast arête, and the summit apparently within our grasp but a few hundred feet above us. At this point we partook of a second breakfast, and then for a considerable distance made rapid progress until our way was barred by a great rocky buttress. Its walls were too vertical to climb, so we were compelled to make a traverse along its base trusting to insecure holds on the rock, and with a nearly sheer fall of thousands of feet below us.

"This difficulty passed, even worse conditions were encountered just beyond. The rock gave place to solid ice, so hard and flint-like that an ordinary blow from an ice axe seemed to make but slight impression upon it. But Christian, balancing in his steps, swung his axe with mighty strokes, and, sending the ice in showers of flying splinters down the slopes, hewed safe footholds. We kept close against the rocky wall and, turning a corner, made up a couloir to a rocky shelf above us. All this time, while Christian was cutting steps, we clung by most uncertain holds on rock or ice, chilled and numbed by a piercing wind. The shelf was covered by loose rock, and it required the utmost care not to send this flying down upon the companion directly beneath. From the shelf we crossed a couloir of solid ice, where Christian cut handholds as well as footholds,—for here our axes were of no avail as a means of securing a hold and a slip by any one of us might have carried the whole party from such precarious footing. Having crossed the couloir, we clambered through a narrow chimney and came out just below the summit cliffs. Here we met with a most trying slope of rock and ice, offering no holds that could be trusted.

"In one place, where Christian was only some four or five feet above me, he could not take another step either in advance or retreat, so great were the chances of a slip. Then Hans, with the utmost caution, slowly worked his way past me and with great care helped Christian down to a more secure position.

"Another attempt, and we scaled the icy slope, coming upon a splendid cornice leading directly to the sheer pinnacle of rock forming the summit. To me this final rocky spire looked inaccessible; but without a moment's hesitation Christian led us across the cornice and, saying our work was over, clambered up a narrow chimney I had failed to note, and presently we stood triumphant upon the utmost summit. ...

"The summit of Deltaform culminates in two great pinnacles of rock; the higher is the eastern one, on which we stood; the other terminates the western arête leading up from Neptuak. ... We had no sooner reached the summit than Christian said: 'We must not stay here; we must get down.' It had required ten hours to make the climb from our camp some 4,000 feet below, and it was now four o'clock in the afternoon. It must have taken nearly four hours to make the final climb from the foot of the buttress, possibly a vertical distance of 300 feet. ... At 4:25 we commenced the descent. If the climb had been difficult, the descent was decidedly worse; but somehow, after a space of what seemed like hours of almost imperceptible progress, we gained the foot of the buttress without a slip or mishap of any kind.

"The weather had been rapidly growing worse, and now on the arête we were enveloped in a driving snowstorm. We reached the halting place of the morning and commenced our descent through the chimney as the gloom of evening fell upon us. Then we plunged downward over treacherous rock slope, difficult cliff, and dubious couloir, in the semi-darkness. At times the moon appeared through the drifting clouds long enough to reveal the depths below, and then once more the veil would intervene.

"About two o'clock in the morning we rested on the rim of the last couloir, and as we waited heard the dull crash of a rock avalanche just beneath us. It was past three o'clock when we finally arrived in camp, after 21 hours of almost continuous work. The descent had taken 11 hours."

About six weeks previously Mt. Hungabee, at the head of Paradise Valley, had succumbed to Professor Parker and the same two splendid guides. It is one of the most striking peaks in the entire Rocky Mountain region, although, on account of its entourage of lofty summits, some surpassing it and others almost equalling it in altitude, and by reason of its rising from a very high connecting ridge on either side, it does not possess the grandeur and impressiveness of more isolated mountains. Its sheer sides, narrow arête and broken cliffs marked it as a problem of extreme interest to the mountaineer, but, as with Mt. Deltaform, the difficulties of approaching it prevented any attempt to climb its fascinating peak until, in 1901, Messrs. C.S. Thompson and G.M. Weed, with Hans Kaufmann, tried it from a bivouac high up in Prospector's Valley; but, after a fine climb, they were obliged to desist when not very far from the summit. Bad weather kept Professor Collie's party from the peak the following year, and the same cause frustrated my designs that summer. So it remained for the present party to achieve success.

Starting from Lake Louise, a pack horse carried their "impedimenta" to Moraine Lake, where they shouldered heavy packs and crossed to the head of Prospector's Valley by the Wenkchemna Pass. This pass was first traversed by Mr. Allen in 1894, during his exhaustive exploration of this range of mountains. On July 21st, 1903, at 3:50 A.M. they left their bivouac in the direction of Opabin Pass and had an easy climb for 2,000 feet by an arête. "At this point," writes Professor Parker,[26] "farther progress was barred by a wall of

86

vertical cliffs. Directly. in our path this rocky battlement was broken by a narrow icy couloir and a much narrower chimney filled with ice. After inspecting the couloir, Christian decided that the chimney would be the safer means of ascent, and so, after seeing that Hans and I were in as secure positions as the circumstances would admit, and with directions not to move from our places close against the rock, he disappeared around an angle and commenced the perilous climb.

"It was only by watching the rope that Hans and I could judge the progress Christian was making above us. For minutes at a time, it seemed, the rope would be motionless, then inch by inch it would slowly disappear up the chimney, and the crash of falling rocks and ice would warn us that we must cling even more closely and find what protection we could beneath the rocky wall.

"At last Christian gave the signal that I was to follow, first cautioning me most earnestly not to knock any rocks down on his brother Hans, for a slight mishap to any member of the party in a position like ours might mean a catastrophe for all. A short space of breathless effort, a strong pull on the rope from Christian, and I stood by his side at the top of the chimney. Then, slowly and carefully, Hans made his way up and joined us.

"Above us we could see a smooth steep slope leading to the final summit arête. This slope consisted of snow covering treacherous rock, but, thus early in the morning and while in shadow, it was in fine condition, and we made our way easily to the great shoulder of the mountain just under the final peak and almost overhanging Paradise Valley. On this shoulder a second breakfast was eaten, and we anxiously studied the route that we must follow. The summit was only a few hundred feet above us, but the arête, broken by vertical cliffs at this point, was impossible to scale. We had only one alternative left, to make an exciting traverse over a tremendously steep snowslope at the base of these cliffs and so reach the final cone.

"We did not discuss the possible dangers of such a course, but cautiously made our way beneath the cliffs, turned a most sensational corner almost in mid-air above Paradise Valley, and then scaled a nearly perpendicular cliff by means of a convenient crack. We were now on the arête and but a very short distance from the summit. Only one more difficulty confronted us: a narrow 'gabel,' or break in the arête, only a few feet in width, it is true, but with a nearly sheer descent of thousands of feet on either side. This gabel must be crossed to reach the summit. The arête was far too narrow to allow a jump being made with safety; so, slowly and carefully, while firmly grasping the rock on one side, Christian thrust his feet forward until they touched the other and his body bridged the chasm; then a strong forward swing and he stood safely beyond the gap. For me, aided by the rope, the matter was far less difficult, and soon we made our way over the intervening arête, gained the corniced summit, and Hungabee, the grim old 'Chieftain,' at last was conquered."

The ascent had occupied almost seven hours and the way down was fairly rapidly effected, with two unpleasant experiences. One, the snow-covered slope, where the hot sun was producing a disagreeable quantity and quality of slush, a portion of which, not many moments after they had crossed it, slid downward and avalanched over the cliffs below. The other was the passage of the chimney, which was now spouting water and demanded as quick a descent as possible; then, "somewhat wet but very happy," they proceeded onward to camp at 6 P.M.

While for the alpinist who yearns for a "first-class" climb with its attendant features to test his skill and pluck and energy, Mt. Hungabee and Mt. Deltaform are without a doubt the pick of the surrounding mountains, Mt. Temple still remains the monarch, alike in impressive majesty and isolation as it stands supreme in altitude. It rears its noble glacier-crowned crest 11,637 feet above the sea, and out-tops all the peaks of the Divide, as far as Mt. Assiniboine, 35 miles distant to the southeast, and Mt. Lyell, nearly twice that distance to the northwest. It is a strange fact that, in all that stretch of a full 100 miles (and half as far again at least if all the windings of the watershed are followed), the three most lofty and far the most prominent peaks are off the line of the Continental backbone; viz.

Mt. Temple and Mt. Forbes, projecting on the eastern side, and Mt. Goodsir, the king of the Ottertails, in a separate little group on the Pacific slope.

Mt. Temple, therefore, has its own particular attraction, and also merits distinction from the fact that it was one of the very earliest of the big peaks to lend itself to the explorer as a point of vantage from which the region could be surveyed in a bird's-eye view. The panorama is a truly glorious one, and, as the climb is by no means difficult, it affords one of the best opportunities for the ordinary mortal to indulge in the sublime experience of looking down upon a world where myriads of peaks, far-reaching valleys, countless glaciers, streams, and lakes, go to make up a vast, bewildering whole, that voices with its thousand tongues the praise of Him who made it all, and speaks to us in tones that surely must uplift our souls and bring them into closer touch with the Creator.

It was in August, 1894 (the 18th, to be exact), that Messrs. Allen, Frissell and Wilcox attained the summit of Mt. Temple. But this was not the first attempt. The previous year, the first and last named climbed nearly to 10,000 feet, where a steep precipice confronted them and the only visible means of getting higher was by a narrow gully, glazed with ice. There was a piercing wind, clouds drifted round the highest peaks, and then a snowstorm capped the climax and drove them back to camp.

The next attempt was undertaken under better auspices and with complete success. From a camp in Paradise Valley they ascended to the pass between the summit and its offshoot, Pinnacle Mountain. This is about 9,000 feet, and for 2,000 more the climb was "merely a careful selection of gullies and scree slopes, with occasional rock climbing.[27] . . . At a height of 11,000 feet we had a discussion as to the better route of two that appeared. One lay at our right and seemed easier, while the other probably lay to our left, and though it was concealed from view, the previous study of photographs convinced me that this would be the better route, and it took some time for them to agree on that point. A short scramble among flat shales and very rough cliffs led us suddenly to the great south slope of the mountain, and we knew our prize was all but taken. At noon we reached the summit and stood at the highest point then reached in Canada."

CHAPTER VII

FIELD AND MOUNT STEPHEN

MY HAPPIEST RECOLLECTIONS OF THE Rockies centre round Field. The pleasant sojourn of a week in 1900 led to its becoming my headquarters for the next two years. The little chalet of the former seasons and the larger Hotel that now exists were alike pervaded with a home-like atmosphere due to the personality of Miss Mollison, who "made" Field as an abiding-place.

Nestling close under the gigantic precipices of Mt. Stephen, beset on either side by rugged mountain crags, the little hamlet stands beside the eddying, glacial waters of the Kicking Horse River. Far up, the valley narrows to the Pass of the Divide; far down, the mighty pyramids of the Van Horne Range, their ruddy slopes streaked with snow and usually softened with deep purple shadows or wreathed in billowy clouds, complete the circle of majestic heights.

> "I lift my eyes, and ye are ever there,
> Wrapped in the folds of the imperial air,
> And crowned with the gold of morn or evening rare,
> O far blue hills."

The scenic way to come to Field is from the east; and by far the most satisfying method is on foot. My brother and I walked all the way from Lake Louise, some 19 miles, and the whole distance is well worth seeing thus if one is equal to the lengthy tramp, though most of the earlier stages can be almost as well appreciated from the train. But no one who can manage to walk six or seven miles downhill should miss the privilege of leisurely enjoying the succession of splendid pictures afforded on the way from Hector down to Field.

In journeying from Laggan, alternating with the retrospect of the ice-clad summits of Mts. Victoria, Lefroy and Temple, comes the glimpse up the broad valley of the Upper Bow, Mt. Hector prominent on the one side and the long escarpments of the Waputik mountains on the other. The wide fields of névé which clothe the massive shoulders of Mt. Balfour and Mt. Daly, breaking occasionally through the rampart walls, send forth many a glittering ice tongue into the dark forest world. Quite near the railroad track, one of the most important comes from the flanks of Mt. Daly, on our right as we traverse the gray wilderness of fire-swept forest that covers the entire region in the neighbourhood of the Great Divide.

The curse of fire, alas, has devastated thousands of acres of the grand primeval forests of the Rockies. In place of the dark sweep of feathery firs and pines that once lent stately grandeur to the rugged peaks, whose base they thickly clothed and towards whose lofty pinnacles they climbed with dauntless insistence, giving warmth and life and colour to the scene, now stands a countless host of bare, gaunt poles, mingled with blackened stumps and hollow, burnt-out shells of former giants, blending with the barren limestone crags and boulders in a wide gray expanse of desolate uniformity.

True, it has its picturesqueness, its weird beauty, its solemn majesty, but it is that of death, not life; of gloom, not joyousness; of human inroad on the domain of Nature's paradise. Civilization has its drawbacks as well as its advantages. The careless trapper or prospector, the construction gang of railroad enterprise, have all contributed to the great change from Nature's untouched glory to these too frequent scenes of desolation.

These fires are one of the saddest features of the mountain districts. The ravages of the past are visible in almost every valley; and every year fresh areas of living green are being swept by the pitiless flames and left a melancholy wilderness. The ease with which a forest fire is started is astounding and only rivalled by the rapidity of its progress when once it gains a hold upon the trees, and by the extent of the destruction ere the blaze is quenched. A single lighted match thrown carelessly upon the ground, a shower of sparks from a passing locomotive, a campfire insufficiently extinguished, may be the origin. And from this tiny cause, "how great a matter a little fire kindleth"

The masses of thick moss which carpet much of the forest land will hold the smouldering sparks concealed for days, and sometimes weeks; but gradually and silently they creep and spread, until a breeze fans them one day into a flame. The resinous needles of the pines and spruces are touched, and in an instant the sudden blaze leaps into the sky with a hiss and roar like a display of fireworks, and a tall tree becomes a giant torch of solid fire. Another and another follows till the hillside or valley bed is wrapped in flame. Vast columns of dense smoke arise, and, borne on the winds afar, obscure the light and obliterate the view for scores of miles around. The sun is hidden at midday and the giant peaks are blotted out.

For weeks this gloomy pall will sometimes float through the valleys and across the mountaintops, bearing the odour of the burning trees, and telling of the devastation of a wealth of scenery and many thousands of dollars' worth of valuable timber.

To the traveller, particularly the explorer, surveyor, and photographer, the existence of a large fire is terribly disheartening. Little or nothing can be seen, and the camera is practically useless. During the summer of 1901, the latter portion of our sojourn in the Yoho Valley was very largely spoilt. Mt. Stephen at a distance of five or six miles was quite invisible, and the haze at the best of times was far too dense to give clear views of objects even close at hand; yet the fire that caused the trouble was more than 80 miles distant in an air-line.

Each summer adds its quota to the sorry tale; some large, some small, but all bring melancholy ruin in their train, and spoil the holiday of many a nature lover in addition to the serious depletion of the forest area. More care, however, is now exercised by campers, and one may reasonably hope that every season will witness a diminution of the evil. The only consolation is that those who have seen the utter devastation and felt the thrill of disappointment and sharp pang of pain that fills the heart as one passes through these tracts of desolation and of death, must realize with a new intensity and added power the wondrous charm of the feathery forest growth, which, in the plan of the Creator, decked these rugged mountain valleys, softened the terrors of the frowning precipice, encircled peaceful lakes with a priceless setting, and outlined in bold relief the sparkling torrent and the gleaming glacier.

At the actual summit of the pass, 5,296 feet above the sea, a rustic arch has been erected, through which flow—when there is any water!—two tiny rivulets, the offspring of a single stream that takes its rise in the wild icy solitudes above. A few yards farther they diverge abruptly and, murmuring a soft farewell to one another, commence their infant pilgrimage towards the distant oceans where they finally will sink to rest.

> "From that cloud-curtained cradle, so cold and so lone,
> From the arms of that wintry-locked mother of stone,
> By hills hung with forests, through vales wide and free,
> Thy mountain-born brightness glanced down to the sea."

After 3,000 miles of rushing travel from the Atlantic seaboard, climbing steadily upward to the farthest source, we step across the little stream and face the sunset seas of the Pacific, with another trickling rivulet at our feet, commencing here its downward course, which we must follow through its troubled, wild career.

This is the Great Divide—the symbol of the turning point in man's career. A fraction of an inch to one side or the other at this "parting of the ways" determines the future course of many a little drop; thousands of miles sum up the distance of their goals. A moment in the balance, the slightest swerve, an influence almost imperceptible, and the decision is irrevocable; the Divide is crossed, the current, now fast, now slow, carries it onward, ever farther from the other stream, for good or ill, until the end is reached.

Just on the Pacific side a little reedy lake reflects the mountains for a fleeting moment; the downward grade begins, and in a couple of miles we arrive at Hector, named in recognition of the explorer who discovered this route across the watershed. A section house and water tank comprise the entire resources of the place. Wapta Lake, an almost circular sheet of the bluest water, usually a perfect mirror, lies to our right, a tumbling, turbulent cascade, the upper portion of the Kicking Horse, but here denominated Cataract Creek, flows in from the south, and points the way to beautiful O'Hara Lake, some eight miles distant by a good trail. This is the easiest way to reach that loveliest of lakes, but the approach, if possible, should be made by Abbot Pass, and this trail used as an exit only.

The white shoulder of Mt. Victoria's northern peak is grandly visible above the creek; right in front towers the northeastern spur of the Cathedral massif (whose topmost pinnacles were in full view on the Divide), and at the base of these splendid ramparts a deep, sombre chasm opens beyond the outlet of the lake. This is the famous Canyon of the Kicking Horse, and its passage on foot should be one of the most sacred duties of every visitor who enjoys majestic scenery. Ample time is thus given to appreciate the exquisite views that render every step of the way delightful, and, though the train goes very slowly, occupying 45 minutes for the seven miles, the artistic and nature-loving heart is always crying out for time to stop and revel in the grandeur of the succession of new and peerless visions. The engineering is of surpassing interest in itself. The gradient is one of, if not quite, the steepest on the Continent, averaging nearly 3 per cent, and reaching sometimes as much as 200 feet in the mile. In the ascent three or four locomotives are usually employed, one being necessary for every three cars on the train; and even then it is a strenuous climb, spasmodic puffs and the futile whirl of wheels that cannot grip being by no means an infrequent variation from the steady powerful pant and throb of the giant engines. In the slow descent the greatest care is always exercised and the train kept under complete control. Three safety switches are also in readiness, at judicious intervals, in case of any tendency to run too fast. They are kept always open, until a signal from the oncoming train that all is well permits them to be closed, so that a runaway, instead of rushing onward down the steep, sinuous track, would be diverted onto a straight stretch of rails and carried up a hill so sharply graded that the impetus would easily be checked and the flying train brought to a speedy standstill. It speaks well for the Company and the care exercised by the engineers that no passenger train has ever been obliged to have recourse to this extreme resort, or met with accident upon the "hill"; so that the most timid traveller may marvel at the thrilling triumphs of engineering skill and revel in the matchless scenery simultaneously without a qualm.

Many and many a time have I luxuriated in the delights of this section of the route, from dawn to sunset, and under the moonlight's spell. By train—inside the coaches, in observation cars, upon the top of a freight car, on a flat car, in a locomotive's cab, or on the cowcatcher; also several times on foot. The last is the best of all (particularly when the raspberries are ripe), but the cowcatcher or the top of a box car is the choicest of propelling methods, unless one can get a ride on a handcar or a speeder, with opportunity to slacken speed or stop whenever one desires.

Passing through a cutting, we leave the Wapta Lake behind (best seen at sunset with the glowing hues of evening lighting up the distant range of the Slate Mountains, reflected in the pearl-gray, placid waters in their darksome setting of the night), and plunge downward beside the tearing river, its waters clear as crystal and shining with that wonderful translucent tinge of green that marks the stream of glacial origin. Its bright cascades, hemmed in by rocky barriers, are fringed with spruce and graceful underbrush, and above them tower the cliffs of the Cathedral Mountain.

One afternoon, as we were slowly creeping upward past the almost continuous succession of foaming cataracts and eddying rushes, a fellow passenger inquired the name of this tumultuous and energetic river, and on being told "The Kicking Horse," chuckled with keen amusement and exclaimed, "Well, I guess that's about the fittest name a river ever got, for it's the darnedest style of bucking bronco that I ever ran across!" The history of the title is, however, rather different and bears no reference to the fascinating characteristics of these upper reaches. In 1858 Dr. Hector, probably the first white man who ever looked upon its waters, was journeying down the valley of the Beaverfoot, and arrived at its junction with an unknown river of considerable size, at a point close to the modern station of Leanchoil, some 14 miles below Field. When camping there, the Doctor's horse became restive and kicked him violently on the chest, delaying the expedition for a day or two in consequence; and in memory of the incident, the men bestowed the name "Kicking Horse" upon the newly discovered river.

Soon the sharp points of the Cathedral Spires appear, darting into the soft skies. What strangely weird little pinnacles they are! so tiny and attenuated that it seems impossible that any one could scale their smooth, steep sides and reach their sharp aerial summits; and yet we found quite a comfortable resting-place on the tip of one of them on a well-remembered September afternoon. Again the eventide is the finest time of day to see these gothic spires that nature has fashioned here on a colossal scale. Some fortunate circumstance enables the ruddy rays of the departing sun to break through the barrier of the western ranges and single out the towers and spires of this Cathedral of the Titans, amidst the general shades of night, for its superb illumination. Bathed in the glory of richest crimson colouring, each crag and pinnacle leaps like a fiery flame into the pale blue heavens.

Just below the highest safety switch a graceful steel bridge spans the ravine and affords a striking view of the deep wooded chasm below, where the surging waters flash in foaming cataracts amidst the sombre foliage. Round the base of the Cathedral we swing; Mt. Stephen's massive dome, adorned by a little hanging glacier, stands right ahead, and across the valley rise Mts. Field and Wapta, while to the right there gradually opens out the dark and wooded cleft of the Yoho Valley.

Away at its head gleam the eternal snows of the great Wapta icefield; the sharply pointed summit of Mt. Habel dominates the distant view, and a long tongue of glacier streams into the deep recesses of the verdant valley. This is the home of the far-famed Takakkaw Fall (the most imposing in the Rocky Mountains), the exquisite Twin Falls, and other beauties worth ten times the journey to behold.

An outlying buttress of Mt. Stephen projects across the track. Far up, the galleries of a silver mine are seen, clinging to the bare walls of nature's masonry; far below, the valley widens to a broad shingle flat, through which the river winds meanderingly in a maze of tortuous channels. A moment in the shadows of a tiny tunnel, and the lower reaches of the Kicking Horse lie spread before our gaze, the shapely pyramids of the Van Horne Range in the background, and Field immediately in front.

Tramping along one August afternoon, in the year 1900, hot and dusty after nearly 20 miles of walking, but well repaid by the feast of glorious scenery, the little chalet looked delightfully cozy and comfortable to my brother and me the day we first approached its hospitable portals. Miss Mollison's pleasant greeting made us feel at once "at home," as her tact and geniality invariably do, whoever the stranger may be. The domicile of "Scotland" in the Hotel register appealed to her national instincts, the offer of afternoon tea was gratefully accepted, and when real Scotch shortbread was produced for our especial delectation our hearts were won for good and all! Thenceforward Field became my Rocky Mountain home.

Field and Mt. Stephen are inseparable. That majestic summit. soaring 6,400 feet almost straight above the village is part and parcel of one's life at Field. The sojourner is never weary of gazing at its noble form, the same yet always different. Each month from sunny June to white December I have gazed at it. Always the same grand massive outline, yet each day, almost each hour of the day, brings out some new effect. Sunrise and sunset; brilliant noon and clear, calm night; sun, moon, and stars; the thunderstorm; soft, clinging cloudlets, or steely clearness, with all their variations, combinations, and contrasts, provide an ever changing series of wonderful, enchanting scenes.

To mountaineers, of course, its appeal is irresistible. It captured us at once, and the first evening of our stay we made arrangements to climb it on the following day.

Mt. Stephen is the most-climbed mountain in the Canadian Switzerland; with Mt. Sir Donald, in the adjacent Selkirk Range, an easy second. This is but natural, they being the most impressive and the most accessible of the larger peaks along the railroad, and admirably situated for panoramic views. Of the two, Mt. Sir Donald is the more difficult, and provides undoubtedly a finer and more interesting and varied climb; but both should be ascended and the intensely instructive contrasts of the rival peaks and ranges, in formation, climbing opportunities, and environment, will more than adequately recompense the climber for the double effort. The earliest record of an attempt to reach the proud summit of Mt. Stephen is inscribed upon a great cliff about 600 feet below the top, where in large black letters are painted the names of Hill, Whatman, and Ross, with the date, September 6, 1886. These men are said to have been connected with the railroad; but evidently the alpine character of the concluding portion of the peak proved too much for their powers, unprovided as they were with ice axes or even alpenstocks.

The first successful climb was made in the interests of science, by Mr. J.J. McArthur of the Dominion Land Survey, to whose enterprise and energy so much of our knowledge of the country is due. Impressed with the importance of the mountain as a topographical station, he determined to brave the difficulties and dangers of the ascent. Insufficiently equipped though he and his companions were with proper mountaineering implements, and unskilled in work amongst the realms of snow and ice, they persevered and overcame.

Mr. McArthur's accounts of his ascents in 1887 and 1892 are amongst the most thrilling ever published in a Government report; and though they sound exaggerated to a practised mountaineer, the experiences of the party must have been both exciting and hazardous, armed only with alpenstocks and apparently without a rope. Starting from Field at 4:30 A.M. on September 9th, 1887, they had to force their way through the bush and reached timberline at half-past eight. Finding considerable difficulty amongst the rocks and screes extending from treeline to the turreted walls of the final 600 feet and following a line which I find some difficulty in identifying but apparently a good deal more troublesome than by the regular slope that forms the skyline as the mountain is observed from Field, they eventually arrived at the lofty cliff, where they discovered the names of their predecessors.

Here the character of the climb changes entirely. From a scramble, fatiguing perhaps from the loose scree and rotten rock, but perfectly simple, one turns to formidable cliffs and icy gullies. The dangers are by no means few or far between for ropeless, axeless, inexperienced men. First came 100 feet of extremely steep ice, pouring down between precipitous rocky walls. "Foot by foot," writes Mr. McArthur,[28] "we worked our way, cutting steps with our alpenstocks, and in time reached the ledge of rock and looked back down the perilous slope. A slip on this glare surface meant death, and how we were to get down again caused us no little anxiety. Crawling along dangerous ledges and up steep narrow gorges we poked our way, expecting at every turn that one of the perpendicular walls would finally stop us with its impassable front. At last we reached the top of what we had judged from below to be the highest point of the mountain. We were not a little disheartened to see looming ahead of us another wall several hundred feet high. We moved along the broken ridge, and when almost at the foot of the wall we came to a deep chasm, which was the top of the ice-gorge up which we had already cut our way. The distance across was about three feet, and immediately opposite rose the perpendicular face from a narrow ledge. Leaving our alpenstocks behind, we stepped across and with face to the wall moved along the ledge to a slanting rift, up which we clambered, our entire weight sometimes dependent on the first joints of our fingers. After a perilous climb of about 100 feet, we reached a debris-covered slope leading to the top of the ridge. ... The top of this ridge was like a much-broken wall, in some places not more than three feet wide and descending in perpendicular sides, sometimes 40 feet, to the steep slopes of the ridge. It required all our nerve to crawl about one eighth of a mile along on the top of these half-balanced masses to the highest point on Mt. Stephen, 6,385 feet above the railway track."

Nine hours had elapsed during the ascent, and after an hour more on the summit the party commenced the return journey, and fortunately found the difficulties of the descent far less than had been anticipated. Timberline was gained by 6 P.M., and they were back in camp an hour and a half later, the entire climb having occupied 15 hours.

In 1892 Mr. McArthur desired again to occupy his station on Mt. Stephen, and on August 30th ascended to a camp near treeline, in order to give him a longer stay upon the summit. Next morning he and his assistant were off at seven o'clock, carrying a flag and a 15-foot pole to plant upon the summit. The route followed was practically the same as on the first occasion, but a surprise awaited Mr. McArthur on his arrival at the icy gorge, which was a source of so much difficulty then. Fully 200,000 cubic feet of rock, according to his estimate, had fallen into the amphitheatre below, and in consequence they were able to climb up easy rocks instead of an ice staircase. The ridge," by his account,[29] "must be at least 20 feet lower than at the time of my former visit, and where at that time we had but to step across a narrow chasm onto a ledge, we had now to reach the ledge up an almost perpendicular wall, and it seemed at one time that we were to be balked; but with the help of my assistant and the long flagpole I managed to surmount it, and then pulled my assistant up with the rope." This time five hours from timberline sufficed for the ascent, and the return was also far more rapid than in 1887.

In 1894 Mr. R.F. Curtis and Professor Fay made the first attempt from the mountaineering point of view, *pur et simple*. Time, aided by missing the path to the fossil beds, was principally responsible for the result of a compulsory return after the marked rock had been attained. But the following year, reinforced by other members of the Appalachian Mountain Club, a fresh assault was made. In spite of the previous repulse and the fact that two ladies were included in the party, a start was not made till half-past eight, and one is continually struck by the astonishingly late hours indulged in at these early times.

Thus it was 4:30 before the cliff was reached where the real climbing may be said to begin. It was soon judged quite impossible to get the whole party to the top before night. So Mr. Curtis and the ladies returned, while Messrs. Abbot, Fay, Field, and Thompson proceeded to the final task. This occupied two hours more, and nearly the same time was required for the descent, so that it was 10:30 when they reached the floor of the amphitheatre, and midnight had passed when their camp at treeline welcomed the belated mountaineers.

Though this attempt on the part of the fair sex to set their foot upon the summit was disappointed, the feat was successfully accomplished by Miss Vaux, of Philadelphia, in 1900, who thereby gained the distinction of being the first lady to ascend a mountain over 10,000 feet high in Canada.

Although already several times ascended, Mt. Stephen lacked nothing in interest to us, who were yearning for another panorama to fit onto those already seen from Cascade Mountain and Mt. Victoria.

In view of the past records, the great length of time occupied by every party, and the reputed difficulty of the last 600 feet, we resolved to get off as early as a September day would allow of. The "best on record" was seven hours from the Hotel; we wanted time to explore the fossil beds, plenty of leisure on the top, and the advantages of a morning view.

Modern conditions with a trail for more than 2,000 feet simplify the earlier stages immensely, and Christian Häsler, our guide, led us upward at a good, steady pace. In about an hour and a half we reached one of the most interesting-places in the Rockies. An extensive bed of fossil trilobites is here exposed on the flank of the mountain, nearly at timberline, and myriads of specimens strew the ground for a considerable area. One cannot avoid trampling on hundreds of them, and one can sit down and pick up dozens without changing his position. Many are visible at once, staring us in the face, whilst any of the countless slabs around can be easily split up and numbers of these wonderful relics of a prehistoric age displayed. Large and small, singly and clustered close together, perfect specimens are there in millions for the taking.

Thenceforward the march is more laborious, following the long, straight ridge that forms the skyline as we face Mt. Stephen from below. Ledges and rocky stairways, a short expanse of what Professor Fay graphically describes as a "stone lawn,"[30] and long, tiresome slopes of sliding debris are in turn surmounted, and just four hours have elapsed when the marked rock is reached, nearly 6,000 feet above the toy-like village and shining thread of railroad track.

Here Christian counsels a halt for a second breakfast before tackling the bit of climbing. I object. The weather, from a cloudless sunrise, is looking most uninviting. Mists are gathering on the mountainsides and so rapidly advancing that I want to hurry on and get the view before it is blotted out. "Surely 600 feet cannot take us long," I urge, "and we can breakfast on the top." "But it will take two hours," replies Christian. "Oh, nonsense, that is far too long for us," is my rejoinder. "I know that is the popular estimate, but we don't intend to take half that time." However, an hour and a half was the utmost limit that he would allow, and it was much better, he considered, to halt at once. Weakly I gave in and consented to remain. We wasted a precious 30 minutes at the base of the cliff (although we certainly were able to enjoy magnificently so much of the view as could be seen from this elevation, including almost as much to the west, south, and north as from the summit), and then we commenced the "terrors" of the "dangerous" part. The glare-ice slope does need step-cutting when it happens to be in bad condition, but it was preferable to the rocks just then; various ledges demanded care: one or two long strides and a rock scramble or two came in, and the limestone was, of course, extremely frail. But, including the steps, it only took 35 minutes, and we did not hurry at all!

Nevertheless, the halt had done the mischief. The driving mists enveloped us in an impenetrable cloud before the top was gained; and, though we obtained weird, shining glimpses of peak, and glacier, and valley, in a shifting frame of whirling cloud, as the strong wind opened a window here and there for us to get a tantalizing, momentary peep, the panorama was extinguished. After waiting more than a full chill hour on the narrow crest, covered with heavy snow, no better fate was granted, and we were forced to beat a sorrowful retreat.

Something, however, had been seen. The strikingly majestic pyramid of Mt. Assiniboine was visible in the far distance, and the Ottertails, particularly the magnificent three-headed mass of Mt. Goodsir, were extremely grand; and all the nearer mountains, wreathed with fleecy mists, and flecked with light and shade, displayed their rugged forms and richest colouring to the best advantage.

In the descent, instead of taking exactly the same route, we followed down the ice gorge, soon finding snow that we could traverse fairly fast and hurrying helter-skelter into the depths of the huge cirque of rocks to the southeast of the summit. The walls that stretch across the eastern side are very striking in their perpendicularity and form a noble rampart facing the less vertical, though steep and rocky, cliffs of the main peak, scored by ice-filled gullies and glistening with frozen snow.

No sooner had we got a few hundred feet below the top than we emerged from the obnoxious mists and enjoyed sunshine and warmth all the remainder of the day, though the great peaks were wrapped continuously in the gathering clouds. In the hollow we spent some time in an interesting search for crystals, which are to be found in great abundance, and some are really fine, though most are small and closely clustered. It is quite a neighbourhood for crystals. A cavern, just above the track, a mile or two from Field on the flank of Mt. Stephen, was a famous resort for some time, owing to the quantity and beauty of its crystals, until the place was blown up and completely ruined in an attempt to break away the sparkling masses. The greater number are yellow or clouded, but mauve and reddish ones are also to be found. I had the good fortune to obtain a specimen on the slopes of Cathedral Mountain which was said to be the finest seen there of late, and was honoured by permission to present it to H.R.H. the Princess of Wales, as a memento of her visit to the mountains.

A further prolonged stay at the fossil beds helped to make our rucksacks tremendously heavy for the rest of the downward journey, which was concluded at a tempestuous pace, and we were back in the hotel by 2 P.M., our actual time while on the move amounting to four and a half hours up and two hours down.

The result was terribly disappointing, both as regards the view, which, however, remains magnificent if only a fine day is secured, and, particularly, as to the climb. Previous narratives had led us to expect some stiff climbing, especially on the upper part, which we hoped would be really first-class, but the whole climb turned out to be absolutely simple for practised mountaineers, with or without a guide. The rock, of course, is rotten; the ice conditions may often be rather troublesome, and certain points undoubtedly are likely to be trying and even alarming for the inexperienced; but with a rope and axe and a guide or first-class amateur, there is no danger for even a beginner.

The ascent on a fine day will always be worthwhile, as the position of the mountain is admirable; the climb, though somewhat laborious and monotonous in parts, is short and easy; the start is made from a comfortable hotel; and varied geological interests are thrown in.

The weather during our first stay at Field was most unsettled. We snatched a charming day for a walk to the Yoho Valley, to see the splendid Fall. Of course we visited the Natural Bridge, which is less than three miles away, and which is a highly interesting phenomenon, besides being situated in most picturesque surroundings with Mt. Stephen as a superb background. The bridge is formed by the wearing of a narrow archway through a massive wall of rock, which stretches right across the riverbed, and the whole volume of the Kicking Horse foams through the contracted orifice in this mighty barrier with tremendous force and a fine display of lashing spray and turbulent disorder.

Barely two furlongs farther, the harassed river enters a narrow canyon, down which, with tortuous course and several thundering cascades, it tears its way between constraining cliffs, presenting a succession of effective "bits" to wanderers above on either bank.

The enchanting walk by the left bank of the river is, alas, largely spoiled by the new course of the railway. Although the farther wooded bank and the surrounding mountains abide unchanged and ever beautiful, the exquisite foreground has been torn and mutilated by pick and dynamite, trees have been overthrown by hundreds, and picturesque promontories defaced by cuttings; ballast and steel rails now take the place of a winding woodland path, and piles of debris that of shrubs and ferns and flowers. Thus has the picturesque to pay toll to the requirements of modern travel. I am glad I saw it and enjoyed it over and over again in the old days, for it was one of the loveliest walks in the whole mountain region.

But we had one other climbing ambition to fulfil during this first brief stay at Field, and that was to attack the delicately graceful spires of Cathedral Mountain and try to reach their topmost pinnacle. An attempt had been made earlier in the season by Professor Arthur Michael and Mr. J. Henry Scattergood, with Christian Häsler. After an arduous and lengthy climb in shocking weather, they were compelled to turn back, owing to the lateness of the hour, only a few score feet below the summit, having reached a position where they could see no feasible way of getting up the final cliff, which towered absolutely perpendicularly above.

We, too, were nearly frustrated in our desire, through an unfortunate misunderstanding. Our stipulated week was up, and the weather had prevented any climbing since our Mt. Stephen expedition; but a more promising appearance the last evening decided us to stay one further day if there was any chance of success. So we gave instructions that if the following morning were fine, we should be called at dawn and try the peak; but if it were wet, we would go on to Glacier. Between the two stools we fell. It was a glorious morning, but the message had got mixed and Häsler imagined that we were going away in any case; so when I woke about seven and found the sky cloudlessly brilliant, my disappointment may be imagined.

Coming down to breakfast, I discussed the matter with my brother and the guide, and wished to try the climb, however late. But Häsler stood firm, and in spite of our Mt. Stephen precedent demurred. The previous attempt had been frustrated largely by a late start (7:30); we could not possibly get off till nine, and to be beaten twice on the same mountain was not on Häsler's programme. Consequently my brother and I went in to breakfast and ordered lunches to be prepared, intending to go ahead without a guide. When this rumour filtered through the kitchen and reached Häsler's ears, he at once reconsidered his position and reported himself as ready to come along, despite the hopeless prospect.

So at last we got away. It was nine o'clock and a cruelly hot day for rapid going; but needs must and a good pace was set. Three and a half miles up the railroad track to a point some 500 feet above Field was the first instalment, and then came a rough scramble up the rocky sides of the mountain's base, through thickets of undergrowth, up stony gullies, clambering over boulders and charred fallen logs, till we reached a loose expanse of debris, the result of the constant erosion and disintegration of the limestone fabric that now towered like a titanic gothic façade high into the Italian azure of the sky. This was a weary bit of pilgrimage, but soon we got to the lower edge of a narrow glacier tongue, protruding at a tremendously steep angle from a snowfield above, between two close and lofty cliffs.

The Cathedral Mountain is a large triangular mass, filling the area between the valleys of Cataract Creek and the Kicking Horse. It has three main summits, besides numerous outlying spurs. The loftiest peak lies to the southeast and is invisible from the railroad after the watershed is crossed. The "Spires," so conspicuous as one descends the hill from Hector, form the northwestern corner of the massif, and a long buttress ridge projects from them towards the Great Divide. The Spires, our objective point, are undoubtedly the most fascinating of the three chief points, both from a structural and mountaineering point of view, hence their selection by the previous party and our own.

Our route lay up the small glacier that separates the Spires from the northern outpost. It led round to the northern face of the peak, by which side alone access to the top seems possible. The former climbers, having scaled a steep gully to the ridge east of the pinnacles, had to make their way to the northern side in order to attempt the final problem.

The ice was steep, slippery, and very hard, so Häsler had plenty of work for his ice axe, until we got well under the grand cliffs between which the ice tongue has forced its way. Bearing to the right, we kept close to the wall, occasionally making a detour on ledges or slopes of debris. We halted finally on one of these ledges for lunch, and then worked diagonally across a shoulder of the glacier, finding easier slopes beyond and being able to abandon step-cutting altogether.

Up the névé we circled round to the base of the final pinnacles, having a great advantage over our predecessors in facing the rocks we had to climb, and we were able to make a careful study of their difficulties. Two or three variations seemed fully practicable, and it was evident that the ascent was assured, and ample time remained. A few moments were permitted for breath, after a stiff snow pull to the foot of the rocks, and we then enjoyed an agreeable change from the somewhat monotonous ice and snow grind to the really interesting scramble up the rock face.

Although, of course, the limestone was extremely friable and called for constant caution, and some of the straight-up rocks, narrow ledge traverses, buttresses, and knife-edge ridges gave us an opportunity to exercise our muscles, skill, and experience, I was usually able to follow very closely in my brother's wake and to keep moving all the time.

The actual summit is more like a gigantic wall than anything else, sheer for about 80 feet on the west side, beyond which a twin wall rises at a few feet distance, equally sheer and almost of identical height The pinnacle, none too large or massive at the outset, seems to have been riven from end to end to form, this long, deep chasm. Our wall was often less than a yard wide near the top, constructed of nearly horizontal strata, the slabs of which were mostly loose. It was broken down in irregular steps at the eastern end, by which we approached, and provided a simple route, though balancing had to be resorted to occasionally.

Seated on our narrow perch, we could hang a leg over on either side and comfortably enjoy the extensive panorama. Being only 10,100 feet high, our view was partly cut off by Mt. Stephen and the main Cathedral peak, respectively 400 and 180 feet loftier, but the Ottertails and Lake Louise peaks were strikingly effective, and the vista up the Yoho Valley to the glaciers and mountains circling round its head, together with the tremendous drop from our aerial position into the depths of the canyon of the Kicking Horse between, was particularly beautiful and impressive.

Time would not wait to let us make the higher summit to the east, or even allow of more than an all too brief stay at our present resting-place. Soon we were off again on a very quick descent, taking only a few minutes to the rock base, and barely an hour to the end of the glacier. A perfectly exquisite sunset lit up with crimson flame the whole façade of the Cathedral from base to topmost pinnacle, illuminating each detail of its sculptured buttresses and towers and spires with richest splendour, and leaving a glorious picture indelibly impressed upon our memories as we hurried down the rocky and timbered slopes to the railroad track.

Darkness overtook us shortly before reaching Field, but we arrived at seven o'clock in splendid spirits, well pleased with our hurried but most successful dash.

A year later, after returning with Mr. Whymper from the Yoho Valley, I had the opportunity of finishing off my exploration of

Cathedral Mountain, by a traverse from Field to Hector by way of the highest peak. In company with two of Mr. Whymper's guides, Klucker and Bossoney, I left Field at 5:25 on the 26th of August, 1901. We followed up the railroad track for over an hour, going considerably too far, owing to some advice by Mr. Whymper, given by mistake, and had to work back as well as upward until we struck the arête descending to the west, at an altitude of 7,000 feet, the time then being eight o'clock. Looking up at the great southern precipices, I was much struck by the varied and brilliant colouring of much of the rock. Yellow prevailed, but it was banded by reddish, olive-green, and dark slate strata, and some of the cliffs were absolutely black. Disintegration is proceeding at a rapid rate, falls of rock, tons at a time, occurring at intervals during our climb. These masses appear usually to break away from the sheer faces in relays, commencing at the base, so that enormous canopies of rock overhang, one above another, and the actual summit projected several feet beyond the foot of the southern wall. The weather causes also a good deal of erosion, resulting in numerous sharp ridges and gendarmes, giving an appearance similar to the Dolomites.

The quantity of debris accumulated on the lower slopes, which we now had to traverse, was enormous and extremely loose: rolling stones and boulders, sliding scree and shifting shale, made progress slow, erratic, and intensely wearisome, as well as cruel for our boots. In time, however, it was accomplished, and, having passed the couloir by which Professor Michael's party had ascended towards the Spires, we turned up the last gully before the sheer cliffs of the main summit. This was filled with snow and ice and debris, not to speak of a cascade at one point, which we had to avoid by a small traverse and scramble on the rocks at its side. Steps were necessary at times, but on the whole we made good progress and scrambled to the top of the couloir by half-past ten. We found ourselves on the ridge connecting the chief peak with the Spires, which looked extremely well from here, although only rising 700 or 800 feet above the broad glacier which sweeps from the long arête towards the west (the tongue of our previous ascent) and the northeast.

Swinging round to the right, we mounted by narrow snow arêtes to the highest point (10,284 feet) in 35 minutes more. The summit is a small one, covered with fragments of broken rock, with its southwestern rim overhanging, and a short, gentle slope on the other side, falling away sharply a short distance down. One strange feature of this shaley surface was the forming of two or three circular basins and channels, the former four to five feet in diameter and sinking symmetrically to a depth of two feet or more. One was only six feet from the overhanging edge They appeared to be caused by the splitting of the rock beneath, forming a cavity down which the debris was working its way as in a funnel. It made one meditate on the transient nature of the actual summit, and, taken in conjunction with the repeated rock falls, renders it highly probable that the form and height of the mountain may be altered considerably every year, and that a tremendous smash may one day change its character at one fell swoop.

The view was of great interest, especially (to me) in the bird's-eye panorama of the valleys to the south; both were studded with bright lakelets, O'Hara Lake seeming to be the largest, but in the nearer valley, between Mt. Odaray and us, I counted eight beautiful little sheets of water, mostly set in trees and verdure, making the valley a most attractive spot.

We remained two hours on the top, and at 1:10 retraced our steps as far as the large eastern glacier. This we descended in the direction of Hector station, leaving the ice (2,000 feet below the summit), in 40 minutes, and, after a quick trot through the timber, we struck the Cataract Creek trail at 2:40, and were at Hector 35 minutes later.

Having plenty of time, I took the opportunity of going down the hill on foot: it cannot be too often done All the way down it was exquisite, the colouring magnificent and the views superb. We travelled at our leisure and spent a good 20 minutes indulging in a bountiful feast of raspberries, which live and appear to flourish amongst the cinders and coal dust that smother the track and its vicinity. They are, at any rate, famous for their size, abundance and superior flavour, and they were most acceptable to us after our long and rapid climb. Eventually we arrived back at our quarters at the Mt. Stephen House at 5:45.

Minor climbs and expeditions, some new, some old, but all enjoyable, and many repeated with small variations over and over again, abound in the neighbourhood of Field and have given me exercise and interest during sundry weeks at various seasons that I have spent at my beloved headquarters, alternating with the development of photographs. None of these merit a prolonged description, but one or two notes about some of them may be of passing interest.

One of the first was a "training walk" with Professor Fay and Häsler, preparatory to our Ottertail expedition. We climbed to Burgess Pass, the most enchanting of the smaller trips, scrambled up the shaley flank of Mt. Field, and, crossing the ridge, descended directly into the Yoho Valley. It had been our intention to try Mt. Wapta, but the weather emphatically forbade such a proceeding, and heavy rain caught us on the crest and followed us most of the way back. The descent was abrupt, enlivened by some glissades, in the course of one of which the feet of a distinguished member of the party sank in too deeply, halted that end of his anatomy with startling suddenness, whilst gravitation caused the upper being to continue the descent, with the result of a plunge headforemost in the snow and a complete somersault of transcendent grace, which would have done credit to a professional performer.

Farther down, we encountered thick woods and a dense undergrowth (which is often designated by the expressive term "shin tangle"), and, as every leaf was dripping with the heavy rain, we soon were saturated from head to foot and had a rough, wet march down the valley, which is blocked with huge masses of rock as well as fallen trees, both covered largely with moss, apt to scale off and cause a sudden fall. The uncovered boulders and rocks were slippery with rain, and progress was pretty hard work. Keeping well to the right, where the Yoho stream makes a wide detour we rounded the long, rocky spur of Mt. Field and reached the Kicking Horse a little way above "Silver City."

This imposing name was given to the two or three shacks which formed the habitat of the miners when the silver mines of Mt. Stephen were being worked, but at present both mines and city are left desolate. We crossed the river by a dilapidated and insecure log bridge, struck the railroad just above the tunnel, and returned home by the track. But the walk or ride on the opposite bank of the river is one of the most charming round Field. In the older, wilder days it was fairly rough, trackless in places, and frequently under water in sections, hence our preferring the other route; but now a carriage road has been constructed all the way, entirely on the level, and the views of Mt. Stephen and the Cathedral are extremely fine, by far the grandest obtainable with out considerable climbing.

A fortnight after this futile attempt to reach Mt. Wapta, Mr. Scattergood, Christian Bohren and I set off one glorious morning to have a good long day in the vicinity of Emerald Lake, incidentally including the aforesaid peak. We got it all: Mt. Wapta, and the day, very good and very long. We were lazy in the start and only got off at 9 A.M., but climbed apace, arrived at Burgess Pass at 11:05 and luxuriated in the inspiring view of Emerald Lake in its mountain and forest setting. Being in a comprehensive frame of mind, I suggested that we might have lunch on the top of Mt. Field and add its quota of scenery to the day's *menu*. The steep, shaley slopes are most fatiguing, the screes slip and slide beneath one's feet, and it took 40 minutes of really hard work to reach the more solid rocks near the top, where we arrived at one o'clock. The view of the peaks across the Kicking Horse is intensely imposing from this point. The summit is almost sheer above the riverbed, about 5,000 feet below, and the great walls and precipices of Mt. Stephen face us across this giant chasm and tower another 1,500 feet above our elevation.

After lunch and an hour's halt, we made our way along the ridge towards Mt. Wapta, looking for a feasible line of ascent in the precipitous cliffs of the latter. The walls facing us offered no inducement, so we skirted their base on the southern side until we came to a couloir, which might possibly provide a way to the top. We started up a slope of old snow, which gradually became steeper and icier, so we roped up and, by rocks and ice, with some step-cutting, worked up 200 feet or so, when the direct route became impracticable, sheer walls lining the gully beyond. Seeking a way of escape, we turned along a ledge to our right and tried a chimney. This would have been all right if a young waterfall had not been making use of the same passage that afternoon. I urged going on, in spite of the cascade, being out of the reach of the water at the time, but the other two, finding it cold and damp, besought an investigation first, in case a better way existed. Bearing still farther to the right, we worried round an awkward buttress and were fortunate in finding a broad and dry couloir running directly to the summit of the cliff belt, with no real obstacles en route.

Gaining the slope of loose talus that crowns the wall, we pushed rapidly upward to the second belt of cliffs, below the actual apex. Two or three ways up this are possible, for we examined its entire length, that from the near corner being most direct, but under certain conditions none too easy. So we preferred, as time was getting on, to traverse along about half the length of the wall, then, taking to a narrow ledge, with one or two objectionable corners to wriggle round, we gained. the eastern extremity of the final ridge and travelled up the jagged crest to the tiny rocky apex. Time, 4:55, an hour and 40 minutes from the bottom of the couloir.

Here, what a view was ours! The mountain, though little over 9,000 feet, is admirably placed and commands a superb panorama; the Emerald Lake and, above all, the Yoho Valley affording an admirable contrast of colouring and life to the wide chaos of peaks and glaciers that surround us on every side. For a bird's-eye view of the Yoho Valley, Wapta Peak is probably unsurpassed, though striking views are within my own experience to be obtained from several points, notably Cathedral Spires and Angle Peak. Certainly the picture of the green alps and sombre forests, the stream and waterfalls, little lakes and glaciers, and the entourage of mighty cliffs, is most entrancing.

The limitations of time demanded only a short stay, and by 5:20 we were off, descending quickly to the talus and romping down the snow slopes, scree, and grass of a large amphitheatre which opens towards the President Group. Striking across country, through bushes and forest,—a laborious undertaking,—we struck the Yoho trail at 6:45, and in an hour arrived at the shacks at the lower end of Emerald Lake. The sunset visions as we strolled along the water's edge, with all the glories of a sky lit up by the most vivid gold and crimson hues, the framework of dark precipice and forest slopes, and the unrippled mirror of the glowing lake, were like a peep into fairyland.

Arriving at the shacks, some friends, who were staying the night en route for the Yoho Valley, refreshed us with bread and jam and tea, and we wound up with a charming walk in the gloaming and the moonlight through the solemn aisles and avenues of pines and balsams, reaching Field at 10 P.M.

Two months later, on September 24th, I again ascended Wapta Peak, with Mr. Whymper, Häsler and Bohren, mercurial, cameras and theodolite. This time we started from the shacks, reversing our previous route and going up by the amphitheatre. We descended this way, too, and went to Field by Burgess Pass. On this occasion the beauty of the scene was greatly enhanced by freshly fallen snow, which mantled the upper world, and by a magnificent show of clouds just clearing the peaks and piled in all directions like gigantic, snowy billows.

Mt. Burgess and Mt. Dennis were among the smaller climbs, both easy but possessing delightful views, especially as one gets to know better and better each detail of the region and so many of the peaks both far and near. On the former I was on one occasion compelled, much against my will, to take a rough and highly objectionable route on my way down. When on the summit, I accidentally dislodged my camera case from its resting-place, and it started on an impetuous descent by increasing leaps and bounds of the most violent description. Selecting a steep gully in the direction of Mt.

Stephen, it disappeared from my view, and, though I had intended crossing the mountain to Emerald Lake, I was perforce obliged to go to its rescue. It was discovered more than 1,000 feet down, none the worse for its adventure, except for a few small scratches; but I was too lazy to climb up again and, in my attempts to get to the base of the precipitous cliffs in the line indicated by the truant case, a particularly interesting scramble resulted, with several considerable problems, but, eventually, sundry cracks and ledges, gullies and chimneys, were discovered in various directions, and by twisting here and making a detour there, the Burgess Pass trail was reached and Field regained in safety.

The route up Mt. Dennis from the railroad about two miles from Field is simple; but I had quite a climb one bright but cold October day trying it from Dennis Pass, between that mountain and Mt. Stephen. Earlier in the season traverses of ledges would in all probability enable one to make the ascent without difficulty, but when I was there ice and snow were prevalent. The ledges, sloping and treacherous with snow-covered debris, were far too dangerous for a lone man, and my progress, an exhilarating one by the skyline, was checked by an overhanging cliff, which could be turned only on the face, where these hazardous ledges formed the only way.

The same day, however, I reconnoitred a second pass, named after the late Mr. E.J. Duchesnay, which gave me a delightful trip a few days later. Dennis Pass, by itself, is of no real value, as it only leads into the narrow valley of Boulder Creek, and brings one down to the railroad track about four miles beyond the starting point, but in combination with the farther col it makes an interesting and direct mountain approach to Lake O'Hara from Field.

I cannot let the name of Mr. Duchesnay pass without my mite of tribute to his memory. Field and he are inseparably connected in the minds of all who have witnessed or enjoyed the development of the beauties of the vicinity, and especially of those who had the immense privilege of meeting him there in 1900–1901. No book on the Rockies could be complete without a reference to him.

To him are chiefly due not merely the facilities for reaching the places of interest, but also the inestimable advantages that result from the fact that an artist's eye as well as a master's hand was at work in laying out the trails and selecting points of view and sites for chalets. His love of nature and genius for grasping in an instant the picturesque and practical advantages together, were only equalled by the enthusiasm which inspired him and with which he infected all with whom he came in contact, be he visitor or labourer; and his kindly geniality and courtly gentleness and readiness to help, advise, or serve, were particularly attractive traits in his simple, noble character.

Apart from his high merits as a civil engineer, apart from the heritage he left in the opportunities to enjoy the beauties of the neighbourhood, as a worker, keen, conscientious, full of energy, one could not but admire him; but, better still, as a man, a Christian, gentleman, and friend, he inspired a deep and lasting affection. His tragic death, occurring characteristically in the course of helping another, through a fall of rock in a burning tunnel, evoked a sympathy and caused a blank in the lives of hundreds such as few are able to induce.

The news of the fatality, greeting me on my return in triumph from the sensational traverse of Mt. Assiniboine, took all the gilt off the climax of a successful season: he was the last to wish me success, none would have rejoiced more heartily in the achievement; but his warm, enthusiastic heart was stilled, one of the best of friends gone on to join the ranks of those who have passed within the veil.

The double pass to Lake O'Hara was suggested to me by Mr. Duchesnay himself, who was very anxious for me to investigate it and report on its suitability for a trail for horses, similar to that made by him across the Burgess Pass. This unfortunately I found to be impracticable, but for pedestrians it affords a charming trip, although perhaps a trifle long for all but first-rate walkers.

Following the path to the fossil bed, I struck off to the right towards Dennis Pass, close to the junction of the streams from the pass and the Mt. Stephen amphitheatre. This 1,400 feet of ascent occupied 40 minutes, but the rough going and deepening snow (it was in October) caused me to take just over an hour for the next 1,800 feet, and I arrived at the col (c. 7,300 feet) at half-past nine, having started at 7:45. Profiting by my previous experience, I made straight for the base of Duchesnay Pass, which connects the outlying ridges of Mt. Stephen with Mt. Duchesnay on the south. Keeping along the grassy sidehill, with a slight downward trend, a rough piece intervened before a steep pull up the rugged wall that marks the head of Boulder Creek. A large quantity of snow made the going heavy, and I frequently plunged in at least knee-deep. (There was sufficient to give me a delightful ride on an impromptu avalanche the first time I descended on that side.) Nearly an hour was required for this part before I landed on the broad summit of the pass, about 8,500 feet above the sea.

Lest any should be disappointed, in future expeditions by this interesting route, it may be well to state that, though the snow was a considerable hindrance, and would be absent entirely in summer, I went enormously faster than the average gait, being in good condition, alone, and impressed by the distance and novelty of the way, as well as the shortness of a mid-October day. My two and three-quarter hours might easily be almost doubled by an average pedestrian.

The long tributary of Cataract Valley which opens on the farther side is specially remarkable for the number of its lakelets, some of them extremely pretty, embosomed in trees and bordered by a fringe of shrubs and grasses. Swinging well round towards Mt. Odaray (on the right), I received much assistance from the snow in the descent, several glissades being available. Then came a long tramp from timberline, through forests, green and fire-swept, thickets and underbrush, over logs and boulders, till I struck the (then) poor trail from O'Hara Lake just at the end of the eastern spur of Cathedral Mountain. Being now in no hurry, I took my ease over the remainder of the journey, and arrived at Hector station soon after three o'clock, four and a half hours from Duchesnay Pass (including lunch), and seven and a quarter from Field. I was fortunate in finding a convenient locomotive just about to start, and finished my tour successfully in its warm and comfortable cab.

One more incident must be alluded to ere I depart from Field, and that is the visit of their Royal Highnesses the Duke and Duchess of Cornwall and York, who passed through Field twice in their journeys across Canada. As Field was the first place reached in British Columbia, a special welcome to the Province was displayed on the triumphal arch erected in front of the Hotel, which was simply but tastefully decorated in honour of the future King and Queen.

Happily the weather on both occasions, and throughout the royal stay on the Pacific slope, was all that could be desired, and both the Prince and Princess expressed themselves as filled with admiration and astonishment at the grandeur of the mountain scenery, and were most kindly interested in the accounts of mountain feats already accomplished and still awaiting the mountaineer, asking a number of questions about the scenery, the opportunities for sport and the details of climbing methods and adventures.

As the royal train started eastward, with five huge engines panting and puffing as they bore their precious freight up the steep incline, one felt that the mountains had gained new and lasting friends, and that their charms and grandeur had, as always, by their marvellous spell, enriched their lives with a precious gift of priceless, lifelong memories.

CHAPTER VIII

THE YOHO VALLEY

WITHOUT A DOUBT THE CHIEF attraction of Field, beyond the ever present glory of its mountain, is its proximity to the justly famous Yoho Valley and the Emerald Lake. The approaches to both are very different now to what they were in the days when I first was introduced to their beauties so recently as 1900, and they are accessible with ease and comfort for almost everyone.

In the year 1897 Mr. Jean Habel, of Berlin, an enthusiast in all that concerned the Rocky Mountains,—as indeed everyone must be who has once tasted the sweets of mountain exploration in that fascinating region,—and a charming man, whose sudden death in 1902 was a sad blow to all his many friends, spent 17 days exploring this valley, and was the first to call attention to the magnificent waterfall which is its chiefest pride. Entering the valley by way of Emerald Lake and the pass now known as Yoho Pass, he travelled right to its head and some miles up the long glacier beyond to the great Wapta snowfield. On his return he kept along the valley bed and emerged at its junction with the valley of the Kicking Horse, about four miles above Field.

The account he brought back of the beauty of the region, its grand icefields, and, above all, its splendid waterfalls, was the main factor of its exploitation by the Canadian Pacific Railway Company, and in 1900 a trail was roughly made to a lookout point opposite the Takakkaw Fall.

Desiring to see this fall, the fame of which was magnified at first by vast exaggerations as to its height, my brother and I determined to spend one day of our sojourn in making the pilgrimage to the Yoho

Valley. In order to have ample time, we were to spend the night in one of the log huts erected on the shore of Emerald Lake, and make an early start from thence.

The journey to the lake is one of my treasured memories. It was on a Friday, early in September; rain had been falling in torrents all the day and previous night. Towards evening it began to clear, and indications of better weather became so promising by six o'clock that we made up our minds in a great hurry to take advantage of the opportunity of a fine day on the morrow, in case Monday should be wet again.

Miss Mollison's ever ready help was secured; provisions were prepared and packed in our knapsacks, a railway lantern was procured from some kind official at the station; and off we marched in the gathering gloom. Crossing the river, we had an easy mile along the flat to the beginning of the woods, into which we turned in absolute darkness, save for the glimmer of our lantern.

The narrow trail was deep in mud, slippery and sticky by turns; the waving bushes and occasional fir bough swept across our faces and bodies in the darkness, streaming with the moisture of a 24 hours' rain. The tall, black spruces towered aloft on either side, sometimes meeting like the arch of a tunnel above our heads, at others disclosing a long, narrow strip of star-sown sky between their feathery tops. So, up and down, in the soundless solitude of this wild forest, black and weird; almost uncanny, yet infinitely majestic and impressive, we followed the little trail, plunging through the darkness and the mud, until a gleam of water shot through the densely growing trees, and in a few moments we stood beside the lake.

A brief spell of silent contemplation of the entrancing star-lit scene, and we passed into the welcome shack, lit a big fire, made some good hot tea, dried our saturated garments, and then tested the merits of the camp beds under a mighty pile of thick, warm blankets. We needed them all, too, for the night was cold and frosty; but we slept well, got astir fairly early, made an excellent picnic breakfast and were off by seven o'clock.

Nowadays, a luxurious wagon road leads to the lake; and a most charming chalet, well appointed and supplied with every comfort, takes the place of our old-time shack. But the lovely lake, the noble forests and the castellated mountains are the same. The drive is a lovely one, particularly where the "long-drawn aisles" of stately firs open out a vista piercing the tall, tapering trees, that form a grand enshadowed avenue nearly a mile in length, beyond which the white sunlit crest of glacier-crowned Mt. Vaux leaps high into the heavens.

The lake does not belie its name: it is a gem of perfect beauty, whose colouring is marvellously rich and vivid, constantly changing under the shifting lights and shades, and the varied effects of morning, noon and eventide. The chalet is situated on the edge of a small, wooded promontory, lapped by the peaceful waters, with pleasant paths meandering through the forest growth along the shore, and cozy corners everywhere for rest and scenery to be enjoyed. It stands beset by alpine slopes and rocky pinnacles, Mt. Wapta's castled ramparts and the splendid precipices of Mt. Burgess; and in front, the sheer face of President Mountain, with its snowy curtain and encircling glaciers, far above: the whole rich setting reappearing in sharp detailed duplicate upon the mirror surface of the tree-girt lake.

On the occasion of our first visit there was but one trail, along the western shore. Then, quitting the lake, a stretch of gravel flat was crossed, and a steep path wound past some pretty falls and ere long buried itself in the thick woods, through which we steadily ascended until the summit of the Yoho Pass was gained, at an elevation of just 6,000 feet, between Mt. Wapta and the eastern spur of President Range. Here, nowadays, a trail converges from the right, a beautiful alternative by which to come direct from Field or to return.

It is a way replete with lovely pictures. The pines and firs and lowlier growth upon the slopes and ridges of Burgess Pass form a succession of admirable frames and foregrounds for many a striking view, so that the 3,000 feet of ascent, by a good pony trail, seems scarcely half the altitude, so constantly enjoyable has been the scenery—down the valley where Mt. Vaux's elegantly moulded glacial apex shines against the blue; up the narrow, wooded canyon to the Great Divide; or straight across to Mt. Stephen's splendid mass (seen here perhaps to better advantage than from any other point) and the Cathedral's ruined spires and towers.

As the narrow ridge of Burgess Pass is crossed, the President Group bursts on the sight, with the bright lakelet in its leafy setting 3,000 feet below, more exquisitely emerald in colour from this vantage point than from a lower altitude, whilst the tremendous wall of Mt. Burgess towers above our heads.

The trail now skirts the bases of Mts. Field and Wapta, trending downward at an easy angle, to join the lower one on Yoho Pass. A few score paces on the farther side a restful little lake comes into view, enshrined in forest, with a fairy peep of whitened summits far beyond, and a sharp rock peak its dominating feature in a backward look. This has been dubbed the "Parsons' Peak" locally, in commemoration of our ascent of it on the afternoon of our first visit to the Yoho Valley; but some other title is more likely to be officially adopted for the small but striking pinnacle.

We passed round the lower end of Yoho Lake, crossed the little stream debouching from it, and resumed our pathway through the forest. Ere long a booming as of distant thunder reverberated with ever growing volume and intensity, and in half an hour we emerged from the trees in full view of the grand Takakkaw Fall,[31] on the far side of the valley and about a mile across in an air-line.

The great névé between Mt. Balfour and Mt. Niles gleams white above; a crevassed glacier tongue streams down a narrowing gully, worn in long ages in the face of a tremendous wall of rock, nearly 2,500 feet in height; the torrent, issuing from an icy cavern, rushes tempestuously down a deep, winding chasm till it gains the verge of the unbroken cliff, leaps forth in sudden wildness for a 150 feet, and then in a stupendous column of pure white sparkling water, broken by giant jets descending rocket-like and wreathed in volumed spray, dashes upon the rocks almost 1,000 feet below, and, breaking into a milky series of cascading rushes for 500 feet more, swirls into the swift current of the Yoho River.

Down the far-stretching steeps, clothed with a wealth of living green, or rugged in their barrenness, dash other silvery cascades; the river gleams below; majestic lines of cliff and jagged pinnacles cleave the clear sky, and glaciers and snowfields lie along their base.

Such a scene as this compelled a lengthy stay at the Lookout point, but at last we resumed activity, and, to vary the route and try to get a yet more extensive panorama of the neighbouring mountains, we struck straight up the slopes, along the track of an ancient avalanche, that had cut a broad swath through the timber, leaving a steep, open pathway, now green with tiny trees and bushes. Keeping to the left of the fringe of glacier which stretches along the base of the President cliffs, we soon reached the divide, 1,000 feet or so above the Yoho Pass.

As we were bearing round the rocky shoulder of the "Parsons' Peak," I suddenly came face to face with a magnificent specimen of a mountain goat. He was advancing gayly round a buttress on a somewhat narrow ledge as I was soberly progressing in the opposite direction. He was so surprised that he stood still for several seconds in sheer amazement, and I was very nearly able to pull his venerable beard ere he recovered from the shock and saved himself from such a gross familiarity by a most unceremonious departure in a whirl of dust.

Making the ascent entirely on rocks, we succeeded in obtaining quite an interesting scramble to the sharp peak we were aiming at, and quickly reached the little pinnacle, about 8,500 feet above the sea and 2,500 feet above the pass. It proved to be the terminal point of the long eastern ridge of the President Group, but little elevated above the arête connecting it with the next in the series of minor peaks, yet presenting quite an imposing appearance from below. We crossed the peak, descended on the farther side, and made a rough and enterprising way down the cliffs to the head of the cascade above the Emerald Lake flats. Then swinging along beside the water's edge, we picked up the remnants of our possessions at the shacks and completed the impressive forest journey down to Field by dinner time.

Many a time since then have I visited the lake, and had the great privilege of spending more than a fortnight in 1901 in the upper portions of the Yoho Valley as Mr. Edward Whymper's guest, having the pleasant opportunity of doing the first mountain-climbing from that attractive centre.

On August 6th, 1901, Mr. Whymper and I, with Christian Klucker (one of Mr. Whymper's four Swiss guides), Christian Häsler and Tom Martin, spent a day in following up the North Branch of the Kicking Horse (now the Amiskwi River) to the mouth of its chief tributary, Kiwetinok Creek. This stream rises near Kiwetinok Pass, which separates its headwaters from those of the Upper Yoho Valley, where Mr. Whymper's camp was situated, and our object was to reconnoitre this side in order to find out whether a satisfactory route could be made from the camp to Field by way of the intervening pass.

Next day we started for the camp by way of the Emerald Lake trail, driving to the lake and tramping across the Yoho Pass. Mr. T.E. Wilson and Klucker completed the party. Leaving Yoho Lake upon our right, we struck off along a trail made only the previous week by Mr. Whymper's men. Ascending a few hundred feet through the woods, timberline was soon passed, and we skirted the end of a series of glaciers that cling to the rugged base of the President's eastern spur.

A magnificent view of the Takakkaw Fall here challenges attention: our elevation is almost exactly that of the top of the upper fall, and the glacier tongue, the rushing torrent from its icy cavern and the gigantic fall of seething water form a complete picture of remarkable interest and effectiveness.

Part of our way lay over alps, clothed, as usual, with luxuriant flowers, the yellow mountain lily very prominent, and flaming painter's brush, purple asters, white dryas, and anemones also abundant. A rough traverse of an ancient moraine and the crossing of a mountain torrent lent variety, and as we rounded the shoulder of the northwest buttress of the President Group, a splendid view of the entire valley was vouchsafed, with the Upper Yoho tributary descending from the south.

An amusing roundup of an antique porcupine, to enable me to take a portrait of his excellency, was somewhat unsuccessful in its main result, as it was too dark for instantaneous work and the subject was too flustered to look pleasant or remain quiescent. About dark we struck the camp, situated at the edge of a flat meadow, fringed with fir trees and overlooked by jagged and snow-clad peaks. Here we were heartily welcomed by Mr. Whymper's three other guides, Joseph Bossoney, Christian Kaufmann and Joseph Pollinger, Bill Peyto, the outfitter of the camp equipment, and Jack Sinclair, his aide; and we spent a cheerful evening round the roaring fire.

One of the chief delights of camp life is the fire. Its cheerful blaze and lusty crackling logs lure everyone to its vicinity and invite the greatest sociability. It is a democratic institution of the most powerful and valuable type. All are equals under its potent influence, and conversation flows apace. The yarns attributable to its influence are endless and of infinite variety, though sometimes perhaps there is a lack of absolutely historical accuracy, which does not necessarily detract from their interest or their value. Tales of the mountains of this and other lands, of hunting experiences and cowboy episodes; tales of the goldfields mingle with the stirring themes of war, and adventures, grim and gay, by land and sea, in almost every clime, contribute to the nightly entertainment and while away the passing hour. The Yoho camp was one of the most interesting possible, for Mr. Whymper and Pollinger had been in South America, among the Andes; Peyto was one of the Canadian contingent in South Africa, and had an ample share of work in the fighting line; Sinclair had hunted gold in Australia and the Pacific islands; and I had wandered in most of the countries of Europe as well as Palestine and Egypt.

Plans and preparations for the succeeding day took up some time, and finally we turned in and buried ourselves cozily in the depths of blanket sleeping bags, upon a springy couch of scented boughs, beneath the white canopy of our comfortable tents.

Next morning (August 8th) we were early astir with a double programme in view. Mr. Whymper, with Wilson and Klucker, intended to cross Kiwetinok Pass, at the head of our valley, enter the Kiwetinok Valley, (the tributary of the Amiskwi up which we had prospected two days before), swing round the shoulder of the President massif and so reach Field, making an entire tour of the group. This they accomplished successfully after a long and fatiguing tramp of some 17 hours, being much impeded by heavy timber work on the slopes of Mt. McMullen.

Pollinger and Kaufmann were told off as my companions for a reconnaissance to the northwest. Both parties started together and leisurely mounted the easy slopes which lead to the pass. The President Range stood on our left, with considerable glaciers sweeping down into the valley: rocky spurs rose to the right, outliers of the main ridge running southeast from the peak known as Signal 18, one of the Dominion Land Survey stations. Just below the col, a picturesque tarn lies at an altitude of about 8,000 feet, nestling beneath the sheltering cliffs of a minor peak, which terminates the above-mentioned ridge, and forms one of the guardians of the narrow pass. The lake was still almost wholly frozen over, and a small glacier appeared to run right into the upper end, where deep snows were massed upon the frozen surface and the shore.

In two easy hours from camp we arrived on the summit of the pass, a desolate plateau of brown shale and debris, patched with snow and strewn with angular blocks of limestone. Before us opened out the bright, green expanse of the Kiwetinok Valley, trending sharply downward between steep grassy banks and as a thickly wooded canyon disappearing from view round the final buttress of Mt. McMullen. Away in the distance rose the Selkirks, gleaming white with their splendid mantle of perpetual snow, beyond the ruddy pyramids of the Van Horne Range.

A photographic halt ensued, and we bade farewell to the Field contingent, turning our footsteps upward towards the peak above the lake. Good snow led to a steepish climb, a scramble over an awkward schrund, and a breaking through a little cornice, but we soon reached the long arête and, continuing by its edge, in an hour gained the rocky summit (9,600 feet).

We were now perched on a pinnacle overlooking the two streams that unite to form the Amiskwi River, with a splendid array of peaks around us. The President Range, close at hand, was naturally most conspicuous, with the fine pyramid of Mt. McMullen particularly striking. But to me by far the most interesting outlook was to the distant mountains of the north, and I obtained my first glimpse of the region I had read and dreamed about, the region of the Freshfields and Mt. Forbes, Mt. Bryce and Mt. Columbia. Our view only took in the southwest corner of this vast mountain region, but Mt. Mummery and the Freshfield Group, with their grand glaciers, gave a first impression, deepened and extended by subsequent views, which eventually led to the most fascinating summer holiday that I have ever known.

Of course photography and sundry observations were indulged in,—ça va sans dire in this vast land where such huge areas are unknown and unmapped,—then, christening the peak "Kiwetinok," the Indian name already given to the stream and valley which it overhangs, we retraced our steps to the point where we had gained the ridge. Pollinger returned to the pass to carry back some instruments of Mr. Whymper's, and Kaufmann and I continued along the arête towards Signal 18. Passing over two subsidiary points, each with a spur extending to the Upper Yoho Valley and giving the appearance of a peak from the depths of our camping ground, an hour sufficed to bring us to the snowy summit.

We found the survey cairn set up, and spent some time enjoying the fresh beauties of the scene unfolded here. The distant view was very similar to that of the earlier peak, but the magnificent sweep of snowfield now lying at our feet was worthy of any alpine region. An upland glacier stretched from the crest of our mountain on either side of a strangely shaped rocky island—named Isolated Peak—to the Upper Yoho Valley and the far larger Habel Glacier, a huge expanse filling the semicircular basin above which Mt. Habel rears its sharp, white apex. Beyond this, without a break in the snow-covered surface, the névé of Mt. Collie leads to the yet vaster Wapta icefields (from which the Yoho tongue flows into the valley of that name), and they, in turn, curve round the valley head and, behind Mt. Gordon, unite with another dozen miles or so of glacier that forms the snowfield of the Waputik.

This succession of glaciers, some 30 miles in length, sends down long tongues on both sides of the watershed between each pair of peaks that form the retaining walls of its enormous arctic mass.

At 11:30 we left the top to return to camp by way of Isolated Peak and the eastern glacier. As we skirted the ice cliffs above the Habel Glacier, we espied upon the snow, close to the edge of a wide-yawning crevasse, a dark, round object, which at first we could not recognize. Changing our course to get a nearer view, we saw it was a monster porcupine. But whether he was dead, asleep, or wrapped in meditation, it was impossible to tell. Venturing as far as was prudent to the upper lip of the crevasse which separated us, I photographed this candidate for alpine honours, and then, to find out his condition, ignobly snowballed him. This took immediate effect. At the indignity, he hastily uncurled himself and waddled off along the rim of the deep fissure. Again I took his portrait, just before he disappeared behind an icy projection. A moment later we saw him try to turn, but, alas, he slipped and fell, and the last seen of the unhappy mountaineer was a faint wave of his black tail as he crawled slowly over a snowy mass wedged far down in the recesses of the frozen chasm, apparently unhurt but hopelessly unable ever to return. And there we had to leave him, another victim to the dangerous habit of climbing alone and of venturing upon a glacier without a rope!

What he was doing or seeking at an altitude of nearly 9,000 feet, 1,500 above timberline, I cannot say, but it was certainly a surprise to meet with him upon the chill expanse of a large icefield, with a long and difficult, as well as foodless, journey evidently accomplished to reach his record situation.

Our scheme for August 9th was the ascent of the highest point of the President Range. It is formed by two ridges, containing a number of more or less prominent peaks, converging to a sharp angle, thrust like a wedge between the Upper Yoho and the Yoho Valleys: within the angle lies the Emerald Lake. The highest peak, "The President," stands almost in the centre of the principal ridge, running nearly north and south. It rises about 6,000 feet above the lake, but not much more than 3,300 from our camp, so that for shortness and also ease the Yoho Valley starting point is much the more advantageous.

Off at 6:50 with Pollinger and Kaufmann, 50 minutes were spent on stones and dry glacier before we roped up, when we made rapid progress over the névé towards a narrow dip east of the chief peak. Numerous bad crevasses were encountered, but in two hours from camp we reached the white pass, at a height of about 9,800 feet. The travelling speed of our trio was in all our expeditions well above the average, and any who may follow in our footsteps should make due allowance for three special elements: splendid mountaineering craft (whichever guide was leading), the ideal number on the rope, and a constitutional tendency towards rapid going in all three of us.

Mr. Whymper and C. Klucker were the first and up to date, the only ones to cross this col, the Emerald Pass. They traversed it early in August, en route for Field. Its glacial conditions demand experience, but otherwise there are no special difficulties and by far the most disagreeable and fatiguing part was the descent through trackless thickets to the flat above Emerald Lake.

On the morning of our climb the weather was singularly unpropitious: after a clear dawn, clouds gathered thickly, threatening snow, and, what was far worse to me, a loss of view. So we made but the briefest halt on the col, and turned to the steep snow slope of our mountain, which forms one of the abrupt walls hemming in the pass Kicking or cutting steps in frozen snow or ice, we zigzagged upward till an easier gradient and better footing on rock or solid snow furnished a simple approach to the summit. A splendid cornice overhung the eastern face, whose curtain of purest snow was scored by the tracks of falling masses of ice from the wide arctic eaves above.

We found the altitude to be about 10,200 feet, very slightly higher than Mt. McMullen, the pyramid that terminates the massif to the south, and than the peak immediately to the north of us, which in form strongly resembles that on which we stood and bears the name of "The Vice-President." The view was interesting in the extreme. Far below, some 6,000 feet, lay the brilliantly emerald waters of the lake; the imposing precipices of Mt. Burgess and Mt. Wapta rose beyond, and my old friends, the mountains in the neighbourhood of Field and Laggan, stretched grandly across the distance. Again the far northwestern peaks were visible, and the great sweep of the icefields, surmounted by prominent summits, was seen to good effect.

One of my principal objects in making the ascent was to determine which of the many points in the group was the one climbed in 1900 by Professor Michael and Christian Häsler. The designation of that point by the title "Emerald Peak" had naturally given the impression that it was the chief summit of the group of that name (the names "President Range" and "The President" having only recently been substituted for the earlier designations of "The Emerald Group" and "Emerald Peak"); but the details of the ascent by way of the glacier under "Parsons' Peak" led me to conclude that they had only reached a minor elevation on that ridge.

On arriving at our peak, evidently the highest of the range, my surmise was confirmed by the absence of any cairn such as was stated to have been erected to commemorate their climb. I was anxious to ascertain beyond a doubt which was their peak, and we should have traversed the entire ridge had not the weather taken a share in the argument and falling snow decided us to seek the shelter of the camp, as no satisfactory results could be obtained in the circumstances. The col was reached in 20 minutes, half an hour later we unroped, and finally arrived in camp after just an hour and a quarter's going from the top.

Four days later the investigation was resumed, and we ascended the Vice-President, lying next to the main peak on the north. A glacier and col,—President Pass,—somewhat similar to those on the opposite side of the highest peak, divide the two summits. Our way lay up the centre and right bank of the glacier to a rocky spur protruding westward from our objective peak, and along this we next proceeded, sometimes on rocks, more often on the snow, and finally by zigzags on frozen snow to the white top. This occupied three hours, including one or two brief halts, and the elevation is approximately 10,000 feet.

Finding no traces here of Professor Michael, we followed along the crest of the arête to a sharp point where the ridge turns abruptly at less than a right angle towards the east. This snowy little pinnacle, which I called Angle Peak, is a magnificent coign of vantage from which to obtain a survey of the Yoho Valley. It projects into the angle between the Upper Yoho and the Yoho Valleys, rising as a glittering cone above the dark forest slopes and deep canyons 4,000 to 5,000 feet below.

Still keeping to the arête, in a short time we came to a little elevation, slightly lower than the Angle Peak, where we discovered the "remains" we sought,—a tiny cairn, a good-sized bottle, and a record, bearing date "Sept. —, 1900." Their climb had been a very long and most laborious one from the shacks at the lake shore, and the length of time taken, together with the shortness of a September day, prevented their going farther; otherwise, no doubt, they would have made for the second peak and perhaps the highest, though the eastern side of the latter is anything but a pleasant problem to undertake.

We lunched on the spot, took several photographs, especially admiring the grandeur of the chief peak from this point of view, and then made tracks directly for the col above our camp (35 minutes), and had our customary quick descent over the glacier in 40 minutes more.

Mr. Whymper had meanwhile returned, and on the 14th we made a triumphant expedition in force to the top of Isolated Peak. All the four guides, Mr. Whymper and I were of the party, as a large theodolite, with a huge, cumbersome tripod, a Fortin mercurial barometer, large camera, and sundry smaller articles had to be transported to our destination. The height of the little peak is not of imposing dimensions, being barely 9,300 feet, but its position is extremely valuable for a survey of the glaciers surrounding the head of the Yoho, and of the various tributary valleys.

It was a strictly business enterprise, though the grandeur and wild beauty of the whole environment is thoroughly enjoyable. As regards the climb, it is scarcely worthy of the name. A pleasant pull up through the trees and over flowery meadows was succeeded by a bit of steep, dry glacier, till snow and schrunds rendered a rope advisable for a short distance, and finally an easy tramp up a gentle slope of debris landed us on the small, rocky apex.

A tiny col, to the north, unites this little helmet-shaped peak to a long whale-back ridge separating the Upper Yoho Valley from that of the Twin Falls, and connects our icebound peninsula with the world of life.[32] Everywhere else its base is swept by the moving masses of snow-covered glacier, which stream down from the wide slopes of Signal 18, and, surging against the promontory of our Isolated Peak, flow down on either side into the tributary valleys of the Yoho River.

Two specially interesting routes were carefully observed with reference to future expeditions: one, to the summit of Mt. Habel, and the other, across a glacier pass to the north of Mt. Balfour, leading to the upper valley of the Bow. Some hours were also spent by Mr. Whymper in making an exhaustive series of transit readings and a complete photographic panorama of the scene.

The following day, August 15th, we made our highest and far most interesting ascent in the region—to the summit of Mt. Habel (10,600 feet). The mountain is a conspicuous one, and is well seen from the railroad about halfway down the "hill" above Field, strikingly sharp and white above the wide stretch of glacier that circles round the head of the Yoho Valley: and it obviously held an unequalled position for a survey of the scarcely known mountain world of the northwest, reports of which had established it as the grandest section of the Canadian chain.

The great distance demanded an early start, but it was 4:45 before we got off and commenced the slow ascent towards Isolated Peak. Bearing to the right, we scrambled to the rocky little col to the northeast of the peak, 2,000 feet above the camp, in somewhat less than two hours, and had to descend sharply for 300 feet on the farther side to the main level of the Habel Glacier. Thence ensued a monotonous tramp across its several miles of almost level surface for about two hours more. The snow was in fair condition, uneven but not soft, yet the pace was slow and wearisome, and a little island of rocks just at the foot of the southern arête of our peak was hailed with joy, and 20 minutes' rest gave us a pleasant relaxation. The day was exquisite: an Italian sky set off the purity of our environment of dazzling white snow, but the hot sun and glare were almost too severe to conduce to the perfect comfort of the *corpus vile*.

The peak loomed close above us now, with a circular basin of steep névé embosomed between two long arêtes. This was full of crevasses, some of them very large, but the advantages of the route over the alternative of the rocky ridge were overwhelming, and by nine o'clock we were once more on the upward grade. The snow was softer than before, but our pace improved a little and we steadily mounted to the centre of the ice basin; then, bearing to the left, we made directly for the arête.

This was guarded by an enormous bergschrund, but a sufficiently stable bridge was found leading to the steep snow curtain that rose beyond the broad crevasse. It was laborious work clambering up this almost upright wall of softest snow, in which we sank occasionally up to the hips, but eventually we struggled to the crest and halted in a little circular recess hollowed in the snow, with a small pool of water in the middle, and a magnificent outlook from the edge of the mountain's western wall.

Sundry refreshments were most acceptable, especially Mr. Whymper's particular mountain luxury, fizzy lemonade, and in half an hour (10:50) we resumed our climb. We were already 1,500 feet above the isle of rocks, and only about 500 feet remained. But all the toil was over: only an easy slope of shale and scree, with patches of snow and a few stones and boulders, intervened; the rope was not needed and half an hour was ample for a leisurely completion of our task.

By 11:15 we stood upon the summit, which was crowned by a really splendid cornice overhanging the tremendous northern precipice, and took our fill of the glorious fresh air and the enchanting scenery. For two and a half hours we basked in the warm sunshine, turning again and again from point to point of the enormous sea of peaks till the entire panorama was fixed upon my memory.

And how superb it was! First and foremost, of course, was that new region to the far northwest, dominated by the dark pyramid of Mt. Forbes, behind whose shoulder distant summits of surpassing whiteness stood out clear against the sky. One of these,

"Whose sun-bright summit mingles with the sky,"

is Mt. Columbia, 60 miles away, more than 12,500 feet above the sea, sovereign supreme of all this realm of mighty peaks. Nearer, the Freshfield Group and dark Mt. Mummery are prominent, the southern outposts of that vast alpine territory.

The better-known mountains of the Waputik Range, with Mt. Hector rising beyond them, lead the eye onward to the striking summits on the farther side of the railroad, Mts. Temple and Hungabee, Victoria and Lefroy, Stephen and Cathedral, and the Ottertails, whilst the ethereal-looking snowy ranges of the Selkirks stretch right across the horizon in the west.

Far below us, in the narrow gap between the sheer walls of Mt. Habel and Mt. Collie, a glacier pass leads to the upper waters of the Blaeberry, and in the opposite direction we looked down almost as steep a descent to the broad, green expanse of Baker Pass, bearing a shining lakelet on its ample bosom, whilst the sombre depths of the North Saskatchewan cleave the mountains to the north.

On the southern side of Baker Pass the Amiskwi River takes its rise and joins the Kicking Horse about three miles below Field. The pass is a bleak upland, sloping gently towards the south, but pitching very abruptly to the valley of the Blaeberry. It was first crossed (since Indian times) by Mr. G.P. Baker and Professor J.N. Collie, in September, 1897, led by Bill Peyto. The ascent on the Blaeberry side is a terrific one and most probably horses had never been taken over it before, but, being lightly loaded and in good condition, the cayuses were brought across successfully. Peyto repeated the trip with Mr. Wilcox in the midst of the October snows, but it has not found favour as a regular way, and if it be used as a means of communication between the Kicking Horse and upper waters of the Blaeberry or North Saskatchewan (now that fallen timber has rendered the lower Blaeberry Valley impassable), it should be on the southward journey alone, the danger of descending with horses on the farther side being considerable.

At 1:30 we turned our faces homeward, and had an easy descent to the rocky islet in 80 minutes. A three-quarter-hour halt ensued, during which we amused ourselves by stalking some stray ptarmigan in an endeavour to catch them, first by camera and then by hand. The former was the more successful, though the tameness of the birds permitted us to get within a few inches of them time after time. Both the ptarmigan and tree grouse, or foolhens, are remarkable for their freedom from fear; they can be readily approached, and we have on several occasions knocked them down with sticks or stones when the larder has been low.

On the long snow stretch, conditions were still admirable, and we arrived at the rocky col at ten minutes after five. Thenceforward there was plenty of leisure and lemonade, and we reached our tents at 7 P.M.

Next day we struck camp, leaving the pleasant upland meadow where it had been located for more than a fortnight. Peyto, Sinclair, the guides and I, at various times and in various combinations, had been investigating most thoroughly the lower reaches of the valley in an endeavour to find some route to the main Yoho Valley suitable for horses, but without success. One by the left bank was located, curving round a shoulder of the Whaleback ridge, and it has since been cut out by the Canadian Pacific Railway Company, but it involved far too much timber-cutting for our purposes. The lower portion of the upper valley is draped heavily with trees of varied foliage, screening an exquisite little lake which we discovered on the shoulder of the hill during our explorations, and the torrent's course, rugged always and broken by repeated cataracts and miniature canyons, grows deeper and more abrupt as it plunges downward to a final headlong leap over a splendid belt of cliffs to join the foaming Yoho River.

This long cliff belt and the thick and fallen timber obliged us to send the outfit all the way back to Yoho Lake and round by the regular trail, which zigzags to the bottom of the valley close to the foot of the Takakkaw Fall. Here we pitched our tents for the night, with the thunder of the giant fall reverberating between the lofty walls on either side.

The following morning we moved on to the head of the main valley and found a charming little camping ground amongst the trees about two-thirds of a mile from the end of the Yoho Glacier. Numberless attractions arrest one's attention in this ideal valley. First I went off alone to see the big fall at close quarters, and incidentally passed through a wood where huge, fallen trees were lying in such continuous profusion that I was able to travel for more than 400 yards without once putting my foot upon the ground, and frequently my log pathway was many feet above the soil.

Soon I was standing by the river brink, face to face with the great cataract, whose glistening mass of foaming water seemed to pour straight from the blue firmament that crowns the frowning walls, and crashed with a ceaseless thunder on the boulders at their base.

Traversing shingle flats, green, sunny meadows, and shady forest groves, we passed a shallow lake, named after Mr. Duchesnay, to whose initiative, enthusiasm and energy the opening up of this exquisite corner of Nature's rich domain is chiefly due. The waters are wonderfully warm and full of marvellous living, creatures; and the shores are thickly strewn with tiny shells. Fine cliffs guard it on the farther side, and Yoho Peak, so often visible as we ascend the valley, rears its pure snowdome above the firs, and forms, with the white, gleaming glacier, the central feature of the background.

Hard by, the river passes through a narrow, crooked flume, worn deeply in the solid rock, a turbulent and seething flood; and a short distance higher up, two considerable tributaries enter from the west. First the Upper Yoho stream, leaping from out the dark green woods that cling to the steep cliffsides, makes its lofty plunge close to the trail, forming the Laughing Fall. Two hundred paces farther, the torrent draining Habel Glacier comes impetuously down, and our way now lay along its course. A good trail, with some ascent, was followed, and soon, athwart the fir trees to our left, a glimpse was gained of what by many is considered to be the chief glory of the neighbourhood—the Twin Falls—not equalling in grandeur the Takakkaw's single leap, yet still more picturesque.

A few minutes later we were at our new abode, where we were destined to sojourn for another week.

The next day was Sunday, August. 18th, and a general day of rest, so I went off on a solitary, meditative ramble. The direction of the Twin Falls was naturally taken, the trail of the previous day being retraced to its junction with the path to the falls' base The ascent is fairly steep and amounts to some 300 feet, but delightful peeps of the tumultuous stream are continually obtained as one wanders through the shady woods, and a superb gorge is passed, with vertical precipices over 100 feet in height, whose crests are almost touching as they overhang the boiling torrent.

Forty minutes from the camp brought me to the foot of the falls, and from a wide, sloping terrace, covered with undergrowth and shrubs, I paused to gaze at the noble cliff, which rises abruptly 400 or 500 feet and stretches right across the valley. From two deep grooves worn in the centre of its upper rim, the parted river pours its glittering twin streams in ceaseless cataracts, which rush united downward in a succession of turbulent cascades and sweep below me wildly in their headlong haste.

I found quite a company gathered at the attractive spot; for Miss Vaux and Mr. George Vaux, of Philadelphia, had come up from their camp near the Yoho gorge, accompanied by Mr. Duchesnay, C. Häsler and Tom Martin, with Hansen, the foreman of the trail-making gang. Mr. Vaux was much elated at being five minutes ahead of me and the first to take a near photograph of the Twins. Mr. Wilcox had been there earlier, but one of the streams was indisposed, suffering from a landslide in its upper channel, and refused to work. So Mr. Duchesnay, with his usual readiness and thoughtfulness, had despatched the workmen to remove the obstruction, and this was the first appearance of the invalid since his illness. He still showed some traces of his recent ailment, but the effect was nevertheless quite superb, and a long time was spent enjoying the beauties of this charming spot.

Then I wandered downstream with Mr. Duchesnay and Hansen. Frequent cascades and foaming rushes, miniature canyons and meandering curves, form many a lovely picture, set off by the varied greenery of bush and plant, and framed by massive trunks and over-arching boughs. Crossing the stream, another characteristic Yoho Valley lake came suddenly into view amidst the trees, and from its lower end, above the heavy fringe of firs, we catch a distant glimpse of the Twin Falls, and see them again reflected in the clearness of the water, whilst the murmur of their far-off thunder fills the ear.

Returning to the foot of the falls, I left my friends at half-past 11, and scaled the cliffs which form a barrier across the valley. I now found myself in a charming open valley, green and fresh, a perfect garden of autumn flowers, walled in by the ridges of our old friend the Whaleback and the Yoho Peak, and sloping gently upward to the three-tongued Habel Glacier. Turning to the right, I struck the southeast arête of Yoho Peak, and following its crest, reached the first of its three points in a little over an hour from the falls. The ridge is extremely narrow, but the going was particularly easy; one could almost run along, either on the rough crest or on a convenient little ledge from one to three feet lower, so that for scarcely a foot of the way was my head below the skyline.

The next point, slightly higher, also a rocky pinnacle, was gained in 20 minutes more, a second cairn erected, and then a steep descent made over rocks to a nick between the ragged ridge thus far traversed and the snowy dome of the highest peak. Half an hour was occupied in the transit, and I found a "stone man" to greet me, built two or three days previously by Messrs. Campbell, Dubois and Palmer, who were the first to climb the little mountain, which they did by way of the Yoho Glacier, an easy but not so interesting route as the one by the ridge.

The summit is not more than 9,200 feet, rising out of the great Wapta snowfield, and (except that it has a striking appearance during the ascent of the Yoho Valley) of no significance save as a viewpoint; but in that character it would be hard to beat for a glacial panorama. A wide expanse of snowfield, edged by noble peaks, almost surrounds it; the one exception is to the southeast, where the fine vista of the green Yoho Valley breaks the uniformity of white, and carries the gaze down its deep wooded cleft to the long, indented range of splendid mountains beyond the railroad track. One of the most notable features of the view is the appearance of Mt. Forbes, exactly in the centre of the icy gap between Mt. Habel and Mt. Collie; and the interesting medial moraine crossing Balfour Pass is well seen from this vantage ground just opposite.

My return was a helter-skelter of glissades and scurries over grass and debris to the rim of the enormous wall that turns the Yoho glacier tongue sharply eastward near its extremity, and from its sheer elevation of about 1,000 feet a striking survey of the glacier is obtained.

On the 19th Mt. Collie was our objective point; and, anticipating a long day similar to the Habel expedition, chiefly on snow, we were on the move at 4:45. A quarter of an hour from our camp brought us on a sudden face to face with the vast tongue of glacier that pushes its relentless way, between huge barren cliffs, from the great life-bereft snow regions far above into the verdant heart of the warm lower realms of life and vegetation. A fine ice cave usually marks the source of the Yoho River, just 6,000 feet above sea level, but it had recently fallen in and blocks of ice lay strewn around the now low and insignificant exit. Crossing a rough slope of loose stones and detritus, we soon set foot on the ice and had to cut a considerable staircase up the snout. Three guides (Klucker, Pollinger and Kaufmann), besides Mr. Whymper and myself, composed the party, which was the same as on the Habel climb.

After an hour on the ice we came to a delightful stretch of heathery turf, gay with flowers and broken by clumps of trees, bushes and rocky outcrops. Several little streams cascade across it, coming down from the imposing walls of Yoho Peak above. It would be an absolutely ideal place for a climber's hut, giving about two hours' advantage over a starting place in the valley, which on the vast snows of the Wapta névé would be invaluable under soft conditions. The glacier is considerably broken opposite this alp, but above it the névé commences, and ere long (7:30) we took to the ice, keeping away to the left on the upper glacier connected with Yoho Peak and, in its farther reaches, Mt. Collie, and leaving the main Wapta icefield below us on the right. The configuration of the various snowfields here is interesting; the Habel and Wapta névés are separated by an upland plateau running from the main ridge of Mt. Collie to Yoho Peak; cliffs occur along almost the entire length on either side, but occasional gaps permit the overflow from this upper glacier to connect with one or other of the larger fields.

Our way lay nearly up the centre of the raised glacier, but crevasses drove us frequently towards the Habel side, and some fine views of that mountain were obtained. As we proceeded, the great stretch of the Wapta icefield was more and more disclosed up to the Continental watershed, with Mt. Baker prominent above it in the distance. The snow was wonderfully satisfactory, and we plodded steadily along across a considerable elevation running at right angles to the direction of our march, and dipped into a lower basin, where the snows embosomed between the two great arms of Mt. Collie sweep into the upper portion of the Wapta névé through a fine portal at the farther end of the line of cliffs retaining the higher glacier.

Then we made for the main southeastern arête of the mountain, crossed a large bergschrund, clambered up a steep and soft snow slope and struck the ridge at about 10,100 feet at 20 minutes to 11. At this point, though only 400 feet below the summit, I struck for something to eat: we were six hours out from camp, and breakfast had been a light one; the weather was perfect, and the top might still require some little time. The motion prevailing, we had a satisfactory rest and some refreshment before tackling the arête. This, though very narrow, proved of no difficulty, firm snow leading with scarcely a break right to the top, and 35 minutes sufficed for the ascent.

The summit is formed by the converging of three sharp and long ridges, and is about 10,500 feet above the sea—a full 100 feet lower than Mt. Habel. The view is, naturally, very similar to that from the latter mountain, though more extended to the east; but, unfortunately (especially as Mr. Whymper's large camera had been brought along), a tremendous forest fire was raging somewhere near the headwaters of the Columbia River; and, although we were more than 80 miles distant in an air-line, the smoke was sufficient to obscure almost the whole view towards the railroad and rendered even that to the north extremely indistinct. Mt. Habel was wonderfully impressive as we looked at it across a narrow glacial pass from the edge of the absolutely perpendicular southwest face of our peak. In the opposite direction, the chief interest lay in ascertaining the practicability of glacier passes from the Yoho Valley in various directions, particularly to Bow Lake and Peyto Lake, at the headwaters respectively of the Bow River and the South Fork of the North Saskatchewan.

Mt. Collie had been attempted once before, on the 6th of August, 1898, by the Revs. H.P. Nichols and C.L. Noyes and Messrs. C.S. Thompson and G.M. Weed. Ascending from Bow Lake by way of the Bow Glacier, at 9 A.M. they reached an outcrop of rocks on the snowfield which marks the Divide. An hour later they commenced a toilsome trudge across the fast-softening snow towards the peak, suffering greatly from the intense heat. By noon they entered the trough of glacier above-mentioned as flowing from the summit to the Wapta névé and worked their way up the snow slopes of the southern face for some distance, finally turning directly to the edge of the eastern arête.

"This way," writes Mr. Noyes,[33] "simple as it looked, developed difficulties which checked progress all the way and grew quite tantalizing. The snow was very soft, and seemed unstable to indefinite depths. Soon we found ourselves in to the thighs and going deeper at every step. This was not only disagreeable, but seemed dangerous, and proved so; for our footing was shelving down to the brink of a crevasse, into which the thrust of the axe at last broke so suddenly that the leader was glad of the steadying check of the rope from behind. This brusque stop was the more baffling because there was no surface sign of crevasse; and as there turned out to be quite a series of them, running irregularly, with connecting bridges thoroughly hidden by soft snow lying deep above, we could not see, but had literally to feel our way with scrupulous caution. A way there was, and at last, after much greater waste of time and patience than we could have forecast, we reached the gray ice above.… The edge soon rose into a parapet, along which we had to slab our way on crumbling screes of icy footing above the jaws of ragged schrunds. But the snow arête was close at hand, and we promised ourselves a cleaner if still stiff piece of climbing there. But it proved the turning point of our ascent and day's progress. Before we had made a rod along its edge, we found it undermined by a cavernous schrund; beyond, it presented a nice dilemma between its crest dangerously corniced and a traverse over ice very steep and lubricated by melting snow; and so on to the top the whole way bristled with obstructions, each of which, manœuvred past, would only lead to the next, as difficult or dangerous."

It being then 4 P.M., they turned back, reaching their camp at ten o'clock. The conditions were against them, and, being without a professional guide and not experienced in such objectionable features as the névé and slopes of Mt. Collie certainly present, their failure is the less surprising. So it was left for us to be the first to attain the summit, without any difficulties, though the skill of Klucker on the glacier had much to do with the ease and comfort of our climb; and I imagine that our ridge is possibly the simpler of the two.

We stayed two and a half hours on the top, but photography was at a discount and bearings were unsatisfactory. Leaving, as usual, a stone man to guard the summit, at 2:30 we commenced the descent, which was devoid of incident, except for a detour or two I made for photographs and special observations of the Wapta névé. In two hours we were on the flowery alp, and two more, in spite of several stops, saw us again in camp at half-past six.

On the 21st we had a little climb to a ruined tower on a serrated spur of Mt. Balfour, which had been called by Mr. Habel "Trolltinder," or the Witch's Peaks, after a famous and much pinnacled ridge above the Romsdal in Norway, the legend saying that the points represent a wedding party turned to stone by an evil genius.

It was an absurdly simple climb, though somewhat laborious, except for the last 50 feet, which gave us a really good gymnastic scramble.

Leaving camp at 7:25, we crossed the glacier snout, descended the left bank of the river to its junction with a mall cataract from one of the Balfour glaciers, and proceeded up the steep right bank of this tributary. The rocks exposed here are of peculiarly brilliant red and yellow striation in assorted widths, giving a striking effect in contrast with the dark trees, green undergrowth and sparkling water. It is a not uncommon formation in the region and was met with again on Mt. Assiniboine. I also found on the Yoho Glacier some remarkable pebbles, which we called glacier eggs. They were lying in small hollows in the ice, just like nests, six or eight pebbles in a nest, about the size of pigeons' eggs, worn perfectly smooth, white and almost circular. Doubtless it is a variation of *moulin* on a miniature scale.

Going steadily, at 8:50 we were at the top of the steep ravine, and, crossing the stream, we worked diagonally to the south end of the main ridge. Thence it was a wearisome pull up sliding shale and scree to the base of the shattered tower, which is perched in isolation on the apex of the narrow ridge. I arrived, *solus*, at 10:50, but not quite liking the look of the last bit without a rope, waited for Mr. Whymper and the guides to arrive.

Three sides of the massive block are absolutely sheer, two above precipices several hundred feet deep, and the third above the end of as jagged and sharp a set of rock needles as ever graced a narrow ridge. On the fourth side fortunately the rock had broken off in huge slabs, leaving a few ledges, extremely slippery and occasionally sloping disagreeably outward, with bare vertical faces, four to six or seven feet in height. We were obliged to pull ourselves up from one to the other, or swing one leg to the level of the shoulder and thus get a purchase which enabled us to raise ourselves to the next storey.

From the tiny top of this quaint watchtower, 9,600 feet in altitude, a fine view should be had on a clear day, but the smoke was still triumphant on the occasion of our visit. The larger peaks loomed through the haze like phantoms, and even the tributary valleys opposite (the Upper Yoho and Twin Falls) were hopeless for detail and photography: a great disappointment, as that was one of the chief objects of the ascent. Mt. Collie was singularly featureless from our position and elevation; its broad, white face and steady upward gradient were so foreshortened as to appear almost flat, and, as Kaufmann remarked, "No one would say it was a mountain at all!" Nevertheless, from some other points of view it is a really striking peak. Mt. Balfour was a splendidly imposing sight, an absolutely sheer precipice many hundred feet high and of considerable length rising close in front of us. Then, lower down, across a ravine to the southeast, where a green lake lay peacefully radiant in the sunshine, were two extraordinary ice cataracts, perfectly vertical, like titanic columns of sculptured ice, hundreds of feet high, connecting the glaciers above and below the mighty cliff down which these frozen cascades had been precipitated.

We made a lengthy sojourn on the summit and a leisurely descent in two hours and a half, with no occurrences of note en route.

Next morning, Kaufmann, Pollinger and I bade farewell to our companions and the Yoho Valley, to seek an exit by a more novel and exciting route than the prosaic trail. Starting at six o'clock, we crossed the snout of the glacier and advanced up the moraine and debris on its left side, rounding the shoulder of a huge outlying spur of Mt. Balfour, until we reached a lateral valley between that mountain and Mt. Gordon.

On the way we came across a bountiful supply of large ripe strawberries, growing abundantly on the bare, stony slopes at an altitude of more than 6,000 feet, but time did not permit of more than a hurried sampling of them as we passed. The lateral valley, into which we turned at 7:15, is distinguished by a series of four flat, circular or oval basins, occupying the entire width of the valley, and separated by ramparts varying from 50 to 200 feet in height. The lowest and largest has a most picturesque cascade, foaming through a rocky trough-like channel from the top of the grassy wall at the upper end. Climbing this steep barrier, which looks like a large dam, built right across the valley, we found a stone-strewn flat above; the next basin higher was carpeted with bright green turf, whilst the topmost one was, in turn, stony, with a large glacier descending into it.

The glacier tongue has retreated and left a succession of outworks, formed of moraine deposit, some fully 15 feet in height, barring the way to its icy territory. It is a desolate spot. Lofty cliffs, hung with ice, hem us in on either side; behind, is a scene of barren rock and glacier; and in front, another glacier (an outflow from the Waputik snowfield, with two giant arms, separated by a great wall of rock, over whose crest the central portion sweeps in constant avalanche) leads to the wide unbroken fields of névé and the dark precipices of Mt. Balfour.

The snout is wide and spreading, so easy in gradient that no steps were necessary. Crossing one tongue, we approached another on the Mt. Gordon side, equally easy and buried in moraine. Following this up, most of the debris was soon left behind, but a remarkable medial moraine remained, acting as an indicator of the direction we ought to take. Sometimes on this, sometimes on the snow at the side, we tramped gayly along and reached the broad plateau of the pass (named Balfour Pass) at about half-past eight. It is difficult to say where the centre of the pass occurs, so broad and level is the summit of the Divide, but the altitude is approximately 8,400 feet. The medial moraine continues without a break right across the Divide, stretching like a rough road the whole way from the Yoho end to the icefall of the Balfour Glacier.

Here Mt. Hector came in sight, and shortly afterwards we could see Hector Lake, very gloomy in its dark setting at the base of the frowning cliffs that confine its sombre waters. The day was cloudy, some drops of rain falling about noon, and the smoky atmosphere helped to deepen the tone of murkiness.

The lie of the land being quite unknown to us,—none of us had ever been in the Upper Bow Valley before,—we got into difficulties by taking too direct a line towards the lake, and before long we were pulled up on the verge of a huge vertical cliff and could see no feasible way of getting to its base, so we prospected on the side of the glacier tongue, as likely to be the more direct and practicable route. This led to an extremely interesting descent from our lofty situation to its broken surface, which we crossed just above a splendid icefall. The glacier was much crevassed, both longitudinally and latitudinally, but Pollinger displayed great skill in finding a way, with scarcely a moment's hesitation, amongst the intricacies of the maze of fissures; and we went frequently at a run down the steep slopes and slender ridges between the big crevasses!

Whilst crossing the tongue we perceived that the better route would be to follow the medial moraine clear down to the icefall, which appeared not only practicable but quite simple. The lower icefall is absolutely impassable, so we took to the rocks on the southern side, skirting the base of the cliffs at a hand gallop, for showers of stones and ice were almost continuous. A short distance farther we were able to get onto a large tributary glacier from the south, which has a fine, regular tongue down which we had no difficulties to negotiate. An effective view of the Balfour icefall and the great cliff opposite, which had impeded our advance, was obtained from the glacier, and a graceful cascade streaming down the lofty face of rock added considerably to its charm.

The junction of the two glaciers was soon passed and we were off the ice by ten o'clock, only four hours from camp in spite of the detours! At the point of the tongue was a magnificent cavern of enormous size, from which a considerable stream debouched, flowing through stony flats for about a mile before it merged with the green waters of the lake.

We had a very bad time of it when we struck the north shore of the lake. Afterwards we were told the south side was much better, but the problem of crossing the Bow River below the lake would have been a most serious one, and for a horseless party probably our rugged route was really best. All traces of a trail had disappeared, so we had to fight our way through a trackless tangle of trees and shrubs, frequently being driven to the water's edge, where, partly in the lake and partly on the banks or sundry stones, we worried along as best we could.

It was a toilsome and disagreeable process. At noon we halted for lunch and three-quarters of an hour's rest. After that the way improved somewhat; the woods thinned, but numerous muskegs took their place. At half-past one we reached the Bow River, just above its entrance to the lake, and crossed it by a convenient fallen tree. Twenty minutes later, after some circuitous wandering, we struck the trail down the Bow Valley, and thenceforth had a beaten track to follow.

Going pretty hard,—for we were unaware how long it would take to get to civilization,—with one or two brief halts, we arrived at Laggan at 6 P.M., and were not sorry to rest in the comfort of the Lake Louise Chalet at the close of our long and arduous journey, which, though accomplished in 12 hours, is really a tremendous day's expedition.

CHAPTER IX

THE OTTERTAIL GROUP

THIS PICTURESQUE GROUP OF FINE peaks, surrounded and intersected by beautiful valleys, and containing several striking glaciers, was practically unknown up to the summer of 1901, yet it is without doubt one of the most interesting corners of the Rocky Mountains, and possesses attractions far beyond the ordinary for the artist, scientist, and mountaineer.

The noble snow-crowned summit of Mt. Vaux is a conspicuous and magnificent object from the Emerald Lake region and the heights round Field, and it is also visible from the railroad track west of that station. Seen from Emerald Lake on a summer evening, softly glowing with the delicate rosy lustre or flashing brilliantly beneath the red-gold glory of the sinking sun, framed by the dark rocks and sombre pines of the southern portals of the intervening valley, its graceful form and wondrous hues reflected in the peaceful, paling waters, Mt. Vaux presents a picture to live forever in the inmost shrine of one's most cherished memories.

The Chancellor, again, that mighty pyramid whose frowning precipices, black and forbidding, loom aloft nigh upon 7,000 feet above the Kicking Horse River, cannot fail to impress the traveller with a sense of awe and grandeur, as he approaches eastward from the grim gateway of the Lower Canyon or passes along its base at Leanchoil.

Mt. Goodsir, however, the third great peak of the group, greatest and grandest though it be, is scarcely known to any but the few who have been privileged to scale one of the loftier heights along the line; although the western tower, remarkable, even in the diminution of distance, from its massive character and strikingly overhanging attitude, and the main peak behind it, can be seen from the windows of the railroad car at the far end of the vista of dark cliffs and rugged points that overtop the wooded southern slopes of the Ottertail Valley. From almost every mountain top and some honoured few of the lesser and more accessible altitudes within an immense area of the Rocky Mountain and Selkirk Ranges, the triple mass of Mt. Goodsir is a marked feature of the landscape, towering aloft 1,000 feet above the tallest of its immediate neighbours, striking in form and most impressive in its stately grandeur.

The area covered by this splendid trio of mountains and their lowlier attendants is roughly rhomboidal in form, with sides ten to 12 miles in length, bounded on the east by Goodsir Creek and the headwaters of the Beaverfoot River, which turns at an acute angle round the southern extremity and continues as a boundary on the southwest; westward by the Kicking Horse, and on the north by the Ottertail Creek. In the centre, the mountain mass is cleft by a narrow V-shaped valley, down which a rushing, swirling torrent pursues its headlong course; a beautiful spot, cradled between the double ranks of rugged, snow-hung crags that form the ridges trending southward, peak on peak, from Mt. Goodsir's and the Chancellor's proud eminence.

Far up, the valley head is closed abruptly by a wall of cliffs, down which the gleaming, broken waters of several picturesque cascades leap from ledge to ledge, like threads and bands of silver, from the upper slopes of snow and glistening parapet of ice that crowns the whole and acts as sponsor to the river and its valley bed.

Another interest of this small but fascinating gem of Nature's handiwork is found in its peculiar formation from a geologic point of view. Almost alone and to by far the greatest extent, so far as is at present known, amongst the hosts of ranges in the Canadian Rocky Mountain chain, the Ottertail Group provides exception to the prevailing Middle Cambrian to Lower Carboniferous strata, and here a belt of syenite runs right athwart the centre of the limestone mass from east to west, severed itself by the sudden cleavage of the Ice River Valley.

Considerable mineral wealth is likely to be stored within the rocky treasure house of these everlasting hills; zinc, mica, sodalite and the richer ores have already yielded their quota to the miner. It is also a good region for the sportsman; the woods that clothe the lower slopes, the bleaker ridges, and the broken crags, harbour the bear and deer and offer advantageous haunts for mountain goats, whilst silvery trout gleam in the streams below.

Albeit thus prominently situated in full view of railroad engineers, surveyors, and the countless throng of tourists journeying along this favourite line, since the days when Dr. Hector, as far back as 1858, skirted the mountains' base as he proceeded down the Beaverfoot and up the Kicking Horse Rivers, pausing at the mouth of the Ice River; past the far later date of 1885, when Dr. Dawson visited the region in his geological survey; but for an Indian hunter now and then, or a stray prospector passing through in search of richer prey, the beauties and the grandeur of these vales and peaks have lain unnoticed, unappreciated all these years.

Such is the district whose rumoured treasures filled the hearts and minds of at least three poor mortals with eager desire to explore; treasures of scenery, healthful vigour, and of boundless opportunity. The peaks looked difficult enough to tempt the most blasé of mountaineers. The charm of the unknown added its potent influence. The tales of prospectors assured us of an interesting expedition. So Professor Fay, Mr. J.H. Scattergood and I arranged to make this our first objective point in the campaign of 1901.

Mr. Scattergood had already established a prescriptive right to be the first climber to attempt the three great peaks. The previous summer, lured by the possibilities of mountaineering and topography, he had endeavoured to ascend Mt. Vaux and throw some light on the vexed question of the nomenclature of the district. Misled by the vagueness of the information he was able to obtain, he and his guides, Jacob Müller and Christian Häsler, climbed the peak which terminates the ridge on the east side of the valley, under the impression that it was Mt. Vaux. He subsequently discovered that this was a mistake, and gave the name of Mollison to the mountain, in honour of the hospitable manager at Field Hotel.

The route taken involved a wide detour, as they went by train to Palliser and had a long tramp thence up the valley of the Beaverfoot. Four hours on the afternoon of August 18th, and more than 12 of journeying the following day, brought them to the mountain's base, where they bivouacked at an altitude of 4,300 feet. On the morning of the 20th they were off at 3:45, in perfect weather, and, after an easy climb of five hours and a half, including halts, they reached the summit, 9,350 feet above the sea. The return march, like the journey in, proved most laborious, timber and rivers combining to delay and to discomfort them. Another night was spent among the trees, after a 20-hour day, and four and a half hours more were necessary to bring them back to Palliser.

Professor Fay had long had designs upon this particular region, so we three, with Christian Häsler, started from Field on July 15th, with a laborious programme in prospect, but in the highest spirits and full of confidence. Miss Mollison, Mr. Duchesnay and Mr. Carey, of the Canadian Pacific Railway, with kindly interest afforded us all possible advantages, and helped our expedition in many ways; so, on a brilliant morning, seated on the cowcatcher of a locomotive, surrounded by impedimenta of knapsacks, ropes, and ice axes, we were speeding down the grade en route for Ottertail bridge, from which point we were to leave civilization, as represented by the railroad and a miner's shack, and plunge into the solitude of the mountain fastnesses.

Mr. Lindsay, the owner of a silver-lead mine close to the bridge, gave us a hospitable welcome and a hearty send-off, entertaining us to dinner and supplying us with some information about the valley. Then, shouldering our packs, at one o'clock we started off with his good wishes ringing in our ears.

A recently constructed trail leads for some miles up the valley, which heads in towards the southeast, but it was overgrown in places and occasionally blocked by fallen timber, over or under which we were obliged to climb or creep. A hot sun and the weight of our baggage made us glad that we had but a short programme for the day and plenty of time. We followed the trail for about three miles, most of the way high above the rushing stream, and later converging towards it, till we crossed the torrent by a rustic bridge, close to its junction with a tributary from the south, and meandered up the banks of this smaller branch, named Haskin Creek. An ancient trail assisted us for some little distance, but soon we were obliged to turn in to the trackless forest that clothes the eastern slopes.

The chief disadvantage of pioneer mountaineering is the laborious nature of travel below the timberline. Trails are few and far between, often ancient, overgrown and covered with fallen tree trunks. Sometimes they are practically only blazed, and usually are absent altogether. Every year, however, sees a marvellous difference in the facilities for reaching both near and distant points of beauty and of interest, through the energetic development of the district by the Canadian Pacific Railway Company and the Government, so that the approaches nowadays are easy to all but the most out-of-the-way peaks.

This afternoon we were very fortunate: the grade was steep, but the woods were comparatively open. Still, the weighty packs upon our unaccustomed shoulders, all out of condition as we were, gave us work enough.

An open-air bivouac and the uncertainties of mountain exploration necessitate considerable impedimenta. Between us we bowed beneath the accumulation of two full days' provisions, changes of garments, blankets for the night, mackintoshes, aneroids, compasses, levels, cameras and other minor paraphernalia, including a large axe. Our leisurely ascent continued till half-past six, when we reached the timber limit and sought a snug location for the night.

Unfortunately our desire to be as high as possible, in view of the next day's prospects, outweighed our discretion, and, while wood was plentiful and shelter abundant, the third desideratum of a camp could not be found in combination at that altitude, and the nearest water was 15 minutes' scramble from our halting place. Rather than descend, we made a pilgrimage to the cascade, and had our supper at its side, returning to the shelter of the trees, where we built a huge fire, cut down pine branches for our beds, rolled ourselves in blankets, put our boots beneath our heads, and wooed sweet slumber with more or less success.

Morning began to dawn with fair promise; we broke camp at 3:50 and halted a quarter of an hour later by the stream for breakfast,—a somewhat chilly repast, owing to the early hour, the frost of the previous night, our exposed situation and the ice-cold beverage which had to take the place of tea. At 4:40 we were again on the march, striking upward towards a noticeable dip between Mt. Hurd, the northern outpost of the massif, and Mt. Vaux.

An hour's steady going over firm snow and easy rocks brought us to the base of a steep snow curtain, up which we zigzagged and soon stood upon the broad expanse of Hurd Pass, face to face with a resplendent vision of snowy ranges, glistening in the morning rays, as peak after peak of the mighty Selkirks pierced the sky. Several of these, Sir Donald, Dawson, Eagle Peak, and others, were recognized as old friends, but even more interesting at the moment were the steep sides of Mt. Vaux, now first revealed to us at close range. We were relieved to note that the one hitherto unseen portion of our projected route appeared quite feasible; for we had no previous knowledge of the character of one intervening section between Hurd Pass and the upper elevation of Mt. Vaux, which might have presented difficulties insurmountable and rendered futile all our plans.

After a halt to photograph and enjoy the landscape, we turned southward and entered on a rocky scramble along a broken, jagged arête for nigh upon an hour, stopping at 7:30 for a brief repast on a narrow col at the base of a lofty, very steep snowdome that barred our progress towards the highest peak and had to be surmounted. Great ice cliffs fell sheer to the Ottertail slopes upon our left, whilst it was equally impossible to work a way round to the right, so over the top we had to go. This proved the most fatiguing portion of the climb; the acclivity was at a very sharp angle and rose fully 800 feet above our resting-place; and, laden as we were, on this our first ascent of the season, breath soon became a scant commodity. Twice we stayed for a brief respite ere we gained the summit at an altitude of about 9,950 feet.

From this coign of vantage we had an unobstructed view of Mt. Vaux's topmost glacial peak immediately in front, offering an easy access to its hitherto untrodden pinnacle. A glorious view of our three objective mountains was disclosed; Mt. Vaux, in spotless purity, with giant cliffs abruptly falling to the Kicking Horse on the right, and the stately flow of its magnificent glacier trending majestically to the left, walled in by the low parapet that, on its farther side, drops almost sheer into the valley of the Ottertail.

Above it rose the black, forbidding precipice of Chancellor, fringed to the east by hanging glaciers; and farther yet, the awesome western tower of Mt. Goodsir, with its castellated buttresses and almost overhanging northern face.

Only one drawback threatened, in the mass of ominous clouds that were now sweeping towards us from the western ranges and across the Beaverfoots; so we descended hurriedly to the dip that separated us from the highest peak, and, leaving our packs upon the snowy col, climbed the slope of névé that sweeps away below us to the southeast, bearing well to the left to avoid the great crevasses that barred a direct approach and circling towards its narrowing final ridge.

Long ere we gained it, we were wrapped in clouds; hail fell with tingling force, swept by the rising wind; flashes of vivid lightning cleft the murky curtain of advancing storm, and thunder crashed above us and reechoed far and near from crag to crag. Thus we struggled upward to our goal, at length arriving on the snow-clad apex, where, in front, the precipices yawned in awe-inspiring suggestion of immensity below, as, through the wreathing billowy clouds, we looked down into space apparently unlimited.

For half an hour we huddled on this narrow ridge of snow, some 10,750 feet above sea level, with the thermometer below the freezing point, whitened with falling flakes and hail. Occasionally fleeting but precious glimpses of the world around were gained; no simultaneous panorama, but spectacular effects of peak and vale, gleaming in sunlight often, beyond the pathway of the transient storm. With chilly fingers aneroids, level and compass were manipulated at lucid intervals, but at 11:15 we deemed it best to beat an ignominious retreat, and ran down rapidly to where our rucksacks lay almost engulfed in snow. Thence we followed the glacier, glancing up at the Chancellor again and again to see if any route suggested itself up the rugged northern side, but in vain.

The weather rapidly improved, the sun shone out again, and the views extended, though the loftier peaks were mostly veiled in mist. By good going over easy snow we soon arrived at the rim of the great cirque of ice-hung cliff and craggy steep, which closes in the head of the Ice River Valley. It lay below us in its beauty, the brightness of its verdure, far beneath us, threaded by the clear, winding river, sparkling in its tumultuous course; the sombre pine-clad slopes merge into snow-tipped pinnacles, bare, rugged cliffs and beetling, broken crags; and, away beyond its bounds, in striking contrast, a line of bright ethereal mountains closes in the view.

It was with feelings of satisfaction that we descried, far down the riverbank, a small white tent, sheltered by trees, with curling smoke hard by, and horses tethered in a rich tract of pasturage beside the water's edge. This was to be our home for the next few days. Our packer, Ross Peecock, had come up by the Beaver-foot trail, and now awaited our arrival by the untried route over the mountain wall.

Snow slopes led steeply downward, affording some glissades, until the cliffs arrested progress and demanded careful searching by ledge and cleft to find a passage to their base, and caution during the abrupt descent. Eventually, after an awkward crossing of the foaming glacial torrent and a swift glissade over the hard snow at the foot of the cliffs, we reached the valley and made our way along the riverbank, plunging through thickets of alder and willow, crossing and recrossing the ever-growing stream, till finally the welcome camp appeared, and Peecock greeted us with voice and teapot.

A bath in the swift-flowing, ice-fed creek was the first delight, and then we looked around our new quarters to make arrangements for the night.

At the first blush things did not seem too grand; for a misunderstanding as to the supplies had most unfortunately arisen. The tent was only large enough for three instead of five, and kitchen and dining room utensils were provided for but a solitary man. However, there was food enough to last the week out, and to a cheerful party like ours the situation was not bad enough to spoil our appetites or joviality. Forks, spoons and ladles soon were fashioned out of wood, smooth slabs of stone did duty for the plates, condensed-milk cans, retired from public life, made serviceable cups, whilst, for the night, a bower, formed of poles and boughs, provided a superior sleeping apartment (except during thundershowers), and Mr. Scattergood and I took up our quarters there.

An excellent hot supper and a lovely night succeeded in due course, with well-earned rest till far into the morning, which was spent in laziness and minor occupations. Hässler displayed great ingenuity and skill in fixing up an ice axe, the shaft of which had broken off close to the point, and which was now repointed as a baby axe some 30 inches long. Peecock was busy baking a supply of bannocks for our next expedition, and some of us after our conflict with the brush had tailoring to do.

In the afternoon we started off to bivouac high up, preparatory to an assault on Mt. Goodsir on the morrow. From our headquarters, at an altitude of about 5,000 feet, we walked some little distance down the valley, then turned to the left, up the steep, sparsely timbered slope to round the rugged shoulder of Mt. Goodsir's southwest buttress. Here several tracks of bear were seen, but we had not the good fortune of our packer, who, the previous afternoon, close by the camp, had watched for a full hour a large-sized grizzly disporting himself on these very slopes.

A stiff and steady pull took us to timberline, and as we turned in to a lofty torrent valley that drains the southern side of Mt. Goodsir, that splendid mountain burst upon our gaze.

Across a rough expanse of debris rose the titanic mass, crowned by a long, serrated skyline with three huge peaks, from which its mighty ribs and snowy couloirs descend to meet us, overhung by rugged cliffs and broken pinnacles; westward the formidable, bare, black tower that had been visible along the line of our approach from Field; eastward, the thin-ridged triangle of the highest point, set obliquely on a high-pitched gable; and between the two a smaller peak rises upon the sharp connecting ridge.

On the green tongue that forms the base of the great central buttress, under twin trees that made a spreading canopy above our heads, we bivouacked some 6,800 feet above the sea, beside a tiny brook. The fire lighted, fuel gathered in, branches cut down and strewn to form our beds, all things made snug, we supped in luxury and laid ourselves down to rest, conscious that next day would bring us genuine work to do, a giant to be wrestled with, one of the noblest in the land.

With brilliant radiance, Jupiter, the evening star, rose over the ridge of Mt. Goodsir, and soon the cloudless heavens were studded close with gleaming stars, which kept watch over us, whilst the murmur of the failing water crooned a lullaby.

An early rousing was in store for us. Breakfast was quickly over, our blankets and superfluous baggage hung in the trees to keep them from the inquisitive and voracious attentions of the marmots, and at 3:45 we were on the march.

Crossing a long tongue of snow to the east of our camp, we commenced the ascent by the long ridge leading to the prominent eastern shoulder of the chief summit The gradient at first was easy and the going fairly good, so rapid progress was made. High up we passed one of the location posts of an adventurous prospector's claim, and, after ascending 2,000 feet in an hour and a half, reached the first snow upon the ridge. Amongst other geological "finds," we came across several specimens of a brilliant blue stone, like lapis lazuli, called sodalite, which is to be found in immense quantities in the Ice River district, but has not been met with elsewhere in the Rocky Mountains.

Slopes of talus and broken rocks marked the way for another 700 feet, and then, at about 9,500 feet, we roped at six o'clock. The character of the climb soon changed. The arête grew steeper, narrower, more broken. The rocks, like those of almost every mountain in the Rockies yet explored, were friable and often broke away at the slightest touch; sometimes, large pieces of an apparently solid mass would split off or tear away when least expected. This in itself necessitates incessant care, not only on one's own account, but also for the sake of those below. Snow, too, lay fairly deep and covered treacherous holds, and here and there the rocks were glazed with a thin coating of fresh ice, which added largely to the difficulty of the way.

Our progress consequently became extremely tedious, yet it was progress. Now we were balancing upon the attenuated crest of a steep ridge; now traversing beneath a spire we could not overtop, edging along the slippery ledges above deep ravines, down which loose stones were bounding in a suggestive fashion to join the mass of debris far below.

Two hours and a half spent in covering 1,300 feet was certainly not a certificate of speed for our party, but it was full of interest almost all the way, and we imagined that there was no tremendous cause for hurry. It was now 8:30, and a halt for rest and breakfast was in order, as we felt that both had been fairly earned. Certainly both were thoroughly enjoyed.

Here in our lofty eyrie, 10,800 feet above sea level,—already more than 100 feet above Mt. Vaux,—we drank in the pure air and rejoiced in the scenery around us. To the north and northwest our mountain was all our view; but beyond the jagged arête of our ascent, with glistening cornices overhanging its upper rim, rose in the foreground the boundary range between the Ice River and Beaverfoot headwaters; across the former valley the Chancellor and his long line of attendant peaks; above, beyond them all, stretching to either side as far as eye could reach, white crests, sharp pinnacles, and glacier fields—the Selkirks, monarchs of the western realms. Yet farther to the left, the mountains bounding the Vermilion Valley are the first to catch the glance, then distant Mt. Assiniboine, a head and shoulders taller than his fellows, Mt. Ball and countless lesser eminences.

But there is plenty to be done before the day is ended. A few minutes bring us to the angle of the eastern shoulder, and an extremely narrow, nearly horizontal ridge intervenes between us and a ruddy cliff that forms the base of the great final peak. It is a picturesque, yet somewhat fearsome, ridge. A spotless curtain of pure snow hangs draped by Nature's supreme hand on either side, as steep as snow will cling, corniced along almost its entire length of some 400 feet with delicate, clean-cut crests, some large, some small, and two reversed. We balance sometimes actually on the narrow edge; anon we traverse gingerly along the slopes of snow, a soft, insidious hiss of wonderful suggestiveness greeting each step, as the top snow slides downward at the touch, and, gathering speed and volume, races to the bottom in a miniature avalanche.

Thus, forward to the cliff, a straight-up, almost smooth wall, 100 feet or more in height. At first, gymnastic exercises, with scarcely a crevice for hand or foot to rest upon, are needful; then, bearing round above the glorious depths of the precipitous northern face, we find a cleft, up which we clamber without difficulty but extremely carefully, for loose stones abound and cannonade the men below. One larger mass almost capsized Mr. Scattergood, breaking off in his hands, and it was with great difficulty that he prevented it descending on my devoted head.

As I, who am the last upon the rope, appear above the edge of the buttress, I see by my companions' faces that something out of the common lies ahead, and that it bodes ill for the completion of the climb. The prospect of defeat is staring us full in the face.

A marvellous ridge it is upon whose lower extremity we stand, worth coming all this way to see, even if it does spell defeat. Far longer than the last, far narrower. A snowy curtain still depends upon our right, stretching into depths 5,000 or 6,000 feet below, and much too steep to dream of setting foot upon. Upon the left, the snow has yielded place to rook too sheer for snow to rest on, and without a ledge, apparently, by which a traverse could be made. Then, in the centre, first a single heavy cornice, before the rock becomes too steep for snow, and, farther on, a spectacle that I had never seen or read of previously, and which is unequalled in the experience of several experts I have since consulted,—a triple cornice, with the central flange reversed, two springing from the rock face upon a base but a few inches wide.

Two alternatives alone suggest themselves to overcome this formidable barrier. The one, to beat down all the cornices with the ice axes,—a tremendous job; the other, to tread down a narrow pathway, exactly above the razor-edged ridge which forms the base of each, and, balancing without a touch to right or left along this aerial kind of tightrope, with a fall of several thousand feet upon each side and the possibility of the entire cornice breaking off as we pass, to gain the farther side.

The consultation was not a lengthy one, for our party was not expert enough for such a feat. Moreover, it would have occupied considerable time, and one member of the party was already thinking with much anxiety of the glissading snow slopes of the lower ridge. So, with a swift survey of the extensive panorama, now including all the northern mountains near the railway along the Continental backbone, and many farther still, and a final lingering look on Mt. Goodsir's yet unconquered summit (scarcely a 150 feet above and not 200 yards away), we clambered down our awkward rocky wall, crept softly along the treacherous arête, and sorrowfully retraced our steps, by cliff and ice slope, scree and snow, down to our bivouac at 4 P.M.

The turn was made at half-past ten, when our elevation was estimated (the mean of three aneroids) at about 11,300 feet.[34]

From bivouac to lower camp took but little more than an hour, rain falling as we neared our goal, with promise of a heavy shower and more to follow. So it turned out, and our improvised shelter of branches proved most inadequate against the torrents of a succession of thunderstorms. A huge fire, replenished at intervals during the night, kept us warm, and we were none the worse, though neither Mr. Scattergood nor I obtained much sleep amidst the drip and splash of baby waterfalls.

Morning broke with clouds enveloping the mountaintops and a more than doubtful weather prospect. Long deliberation eventuated in a determination to try Mt. Chancellor next day, going to a high camp as usual in the afternoon, and sending off our horses and paraphernalia to Leanchoil.

The day improved as it wore on. Some pictures were obtained, and after dinner we mounted the thickly wooded slopes along the, course of a torrent that descends in bold cascades from a high side valley opening from the west just opposite our camp; our purpose being to try the ascent by the long spur which strikes the main arête about a mile from the highest peak.

At our usual altitude of about 6,800 feet, we found a spot in which to spend the night; and, as thunderclouds looked threatening, at once prepared an elaborate nest, hollowed amongst the roots of a large spruce fir, and filled in with small trees and branches. It looked a cozy retreat, and it was wonderfully waterproof; but; alas, when we turned in, we found it had one serious defect. The surface of our quadruple bed was not completely level, and, being by mischance at the lower end, I was soon conscious of a great oppression, as Professor Fay, crushed downward by the ponderous forms of our two heavyweights, forced me against the barrier of spiky trunks and boughs which closed us in. Hours of expostulation and hilarity, varied by experiments of a serious and jocular nature, which gravity defied and defied gravity, culminated in an uneasy slumber, from which we rose without much reluctance at an early hour.

The storm of the previous afternoon, a grand display of vivid lightning, and tremendous thunder which reverberated almost interminably among the mountains round, had cleared away at sunset and given us an immortal vision (like a peep into the glories of Paradise) of Mt. Goodsir, powdered with fresh, sparkling snow alight with crimson flames and circled by soft, clinging wreaths of tenuous cloud, most delicately tinged with tender roseate hues and palest gold.

Now, in the brilliance of a cloudless sky, the sun rose clear and augured well; 4:40 saw us on the move, beginning with a wearisome ascent up slopes of fine, sandy debris, which slipped beneath our feet at every step. At half-past five we struck the edge of the spur at 8,000 feet, and, during a brief halt to inspect our route, had a delightful view of ten or a dozen mountain goats, browsing and clambering about on another spur a long way down.

Then up to the main arête, to reach which required the cutting of a breach through the long cornice which extended right across the point of junction. This ridge stretches almost due south from the summit of Mt. Chancellor and contains ten minor peaks, ending rather abruptly in the angle between the Ice River and the Beaverfoot Valleys The point we now were on was the fourth and attained an altitude of about 9,000 feet. Three more remained to be traversed before we could reach the dip at the base of the chief peak, and the arête was long and often narrow, much broken by gendarmes, especially towards the farther end. It was evident that our course must lie practically along the crest of the ridge, and that none of the summits could be avoided, All went well for some time; the work was interesting, if slow, and we had struck an igneous outcrop, the syenite was firm and solid, and good grips and stable footholds were the rule. Nevertheless, with fresh snow covering much of the mountain, all traverses had to be extremely cautiously undertaken, and there were a considerable number of them, varied by grand gymnastics on the pinnacles.

The ridge proved infinitely more serrated than we imagined. The gendarmes multiplied into squads and companies. Spires and towers 50 and 60 feet high had to be scaled, their summits traversed and an abrupt descent immediately made. A few yards only would be gained in actual advance, and in a moment or two the process would have to be repeated.

Huge cornices frequently hung over on the eastern side, above great glaciers that yawned with gaping fissures, and sometimes there would be a spell of our old enemy, the limestone, so that an almost sheer finger of rock, protruding abruptly from a ridge 2,000 to 3,000 feet in height, would have to be negotiated with the warning from the ever watchful Häsler, "You must not touch the snow, and that rock" (pointing to the only one which could apparently be utilized at all) "is not safe!" On the tops of one or two pinnacles the edge was so intensely narrow that some members of the party sat astride and worked themselves along it in that posture, whilst I preferred to grasp the crest and worry across the less vertical side by the aid of friction. And all the while these acrobatic performances had to be perpetrated we were loaded with heavy packs.

At length, in front of an even more perpendicular tower than before, we faced the situation. Several more gendarmes intervened before the Chancellor Peak itself could be attained; a long and difficult scramble was assured upon its slopes, probably a four-hour job for our weak party; provisions remained for only two more light repasts; no knowledge was possessed as to the possibility of a descent upon the western side, by which it was practically imperative to make our way; and it was 12 o'clock. To go on seemed to render inevitable a night out on the mountain, perhaps at a great elevation, and we had no food for another day. One of our number, in addition to the other considerations, did not at all like the appearance of the gendarmes ahead, and reminded us that he had a wife and family at home; so discretion was deemed the better part, and sadly, for the second time in three days, we retraced our steps, repulsed.

Returning to the top of the last peak surmounted (that nearest to the main summit), we had some lunch and then descended the buttress towards Leanchoil. A long, steep slope of snow came next, down which we plunged, my lengthy strides and rapid gait obtaining for me (who led) emphatic and reiterated objurgations, but we arrived in fairly good condition at the bottom and turned into the wide, deep couloir directly south of Mt. Chancellor's black pyramid. We soon unroped and were able to make our own way and speed along its snowy course, till a sudden drop between two splendid precipices compelled us to make a detour across several ribs of rotten rock, supporting the mountain's base, down gullies full of shifting scree to timberline, and thence, through swamps and bushes and over countless fallen logs, to the broad flats opposite Leanchoil station at five o'clock.

Here, alas, the river barred our way and was impassable without a boat or horses. We had heard of a boat, but our search for it was vain. Peecock was waiting with the horses, but we struck the river too high, and, through a misunderstanding, failed to make connection. So we were compelled by force of circumstances to try the trail that, we had been informed, led by the east bank of the Kicking Horse to Ottertail, where the railroad crosses the river.

Five miles does not sound a lengthy journey, even to tired men, but distance is not always the only consideration. The trail proved to be of great antiquity; often it was quite obliterated; at best it was indistinct, difficult to trace and constantly blocked. Its devious nature, false turnings, scrambling over fallen tree trunks, fighting through dense undergrowth, pushing between the dry, sharp fir twigs, manœuvring round muskegs, jumping little streams, hauling logs to cross the larger creeks, clambering up cut banks, detours here and twistings there, made it the worst experience any of us had ever been through.

After two hours we had to stop for the night; on the edge of a swamp, serenaded by crickets and mosquitoes, short of food and thoroughly done up, we turned our toes up to the sky for the sixth successive night, and tried to sleep. Hopefully we started out next morning, although tea and a mouthful or two to eat was all our breakfast, but four more solid hours of hard and steady going took all the exuberance out of us before the bridge by which the Canadian Pacific Railway crosses to the right bank of the river appeared in sight, and as, half in exultation, half in weariness, the cry, "The Bridge!" rings out, we wonder if the famous "θαλασσα! θαλασσα!" of the classic story brought an equal sense of deep relief.

Eight more miles to tramp, and still no breakfast! But we were now upon the railroad track, a smooth and direct route, and spirits rose again. Welcome refreshment again at Mr. Lindsay's shack sent us on our last five miles to Field in first-rate trim, except for sundry damages to our sartorial effects, with six days of interest and enjoyment to look back upon in spite of disappointments and hardships one of the grandest and most pleasant trips in any of our memories.

Foiled once, we were enabled to conquer the Chancellor before our time expired, though Mt. Goodsir was too distant to attempt again.

A week later, Mr. Scattergood, Häsler and I, with Mr. George M. Weed, of Boston, were deposited at Leanchoil for another attack. Unfortunately the accident to Professor Fay's knee near Lake O'Hara prevented his having his revenge upon the mountain. This time we were to try it from the west, and, in order to avoid the awful trail experiences (which Mr. Weed, in company with Mr. C.S. Thompson, had twice undergone when attempting to reach the same peak during the previous week), we brought a sackful of spikes, rope, etc., to construct a raft, on whose frail structure we expected to have to entrust ourselves and all our goods.

None of us had ever made or navigated a raft, but that was a mere detail, although I, for one, had serious doubts whether we could manufacture one fit to hold together in the rapid, turbulent flood of the Kicking Horse, or steer it safely once we were embarked. But, happily, thanks to Mr. Duchesnay's kind assistance, we were spared the necessity of making the dubious experiment; a boat was discovered and a crossing made in two sections with a portage in the middle.

Thence we headed for the mountainside, traversing the swampy flats and the heavy, log-strewn underbrush of the Chancellor's lower slopes. Bearing to the right of the direct spur, we mounted to nearly

7,000 feet, but found an utter absence of water in the upper gullies, and were obliged to pass still farther round the shoulder and descend a few hundred feet before we came upon a suitable location. Our bivouac was made eventually on the steep side of a deep gully, with scanty pines scattered along its slopes, an enormous vertical wall behind, cleft by a narrow chasm, down which a torrent pitched in headlong rushes and picturesque cascades. Here we were most comfortable, under the benign influence of a lustrous full moon and clear-shining stars.

Determined to have plenty of time at any rate for this attempt, before three o'clock on July 30th we were stumbling upward over fields of sloping scree, in the uncertain, fitful moonlight. Day broke ere long, and, as the sun rose, radiant beams lit up successive peaks till finally the entire chain of snowy Selkirks was bathed in the golden glow.

Two obvious lines of ascent suggest themselves to the mountaineer approaching Mt. Chancellor from this direction: one, the more sporting, right up the steep and jagged ridge, which, broken by occasional vertical cliffs, ascends directly from the west; the other, a more certain route, by the deep snow couloir at the southern base of the above-mentioned ridge, leading up to a depression just below the towering summit, and thence by the skyline to the top. This couloir we had already traversed for most of its length in our previous descent.

We chose the former, however, as likely to afford the more exciting climb, leaving the other for the return, or as an alternative in case of need. The lower part was simple, although the rocks were absolutely rotten. Then a gully had to be climbed and some ledge work negotiated up to the base of the first sheer cliff, just beyond the junction of the two foundation spurs. This point is about 8,800 feet in altitude and we arrived at five o'clock.

Some prospecting was necessary here to turn the precipice, and an awkward but apparently feasible way was located on the right side. After a slippery traverse, the initial piece of straight-up climbing was effected by a gymnastic effort up an overhanging mass of rock, with scarcely a crack to get the slightest hold upon. Called to the front, by means of extra length of limb and a step made by Häsler's axe, I managed to hoist myself up to the top of this obstacle and gain, by somewhat easier clambering, a narrow rift, from which point of vantage I could with the rope facilitate the arrival of the rest.

Slow, cautious climbing ensued for some little distance: a rock tower called for a rough scramble, ledges and cracks on slippery slabs had to be traversed, but finally, from a point unseen by me, Häsler announced that we could go no farther by that route, and that we must return and try the lower way. This I reluctantly assented to, though I am still strongly of opinion that the ridge might have been gained by a divergent line; but time was slipping away so swiftly,— two hours had already been spent on this short bit,—difficulties as great or greater might be met with above, the party was not at all quick on rocks, so once again we had to persuade ourselves that discretion was the better part, and we slowly made our tedious way down the precipitous face, and hastened down easier rocks and couloirs, till we could find a means of access by the rocky wall to the snow gorge below. It was ten o'clock by the time the base was reached, at a point just about an hour and a quarter's distance from the bivouac, six precious hours having been spent in the futile though delightful rock scramble and its approaches.

After a meal, quick progress up the gully followed and zigzags up the rocks and snow of the ridge wall by any available ledges and miniature couloirs, till shortly after noon we stood on the crest of the arête dividing the Kicking Horse and Ice River Valleys, about 10,000 feet above the sea, and 200 or 300 yards beyond the point at which we had turned back at our previous attempt.

From the dip we looked up interestedly at the steeps of the final struggle. Under good snow conditions this would be a quick and easy matter, and the climb will probably be done some day in less than four hours from the timber limit; but on this occasion the snow lay thin over hard and slippery ice, ready to avalanche at any moment, and it was useless to think of trying it. So nothing but the rocks were left, and they were mainly huge slab sections, tilted sharply in the direction of ascent, too slippery as a rule to scramble up and, therefore, necessitating frequent turnings first on one side and then another, passing along cracks and ledges, one so closely overhung by a great rock that a serpentine wriggle alone could bring us through the gap. Clefts, sometimes lined with ice and graced with trickling waterfalls, had to be ascended vertically; huge buttresses were swarmed by dint of close embrace and friction, and quite an amusing series of interesting and effective situations was afforded by the varied niceties of climbing that were brought into the short ascent.

But it all took time, a great deal too much time, and only at three o'clock did we stand at last, at our third attempt, upon the summit, 10,780 feet in elevation. The peak is a double one, the western portion being crowned by a massive cornice. The day was exquisitely clear, but with a lovely sky massed with effective clouds. The view was consequently at its best, and it is most magnificent.

The noblest features, from which the eye can hardly wander, are the gleaming glacial heights of Mt. Vaux and the huge triple mass of Mt. Goodsir, one of those mountains which exert a fascination indescribable and inexplicable. But when we could look beyond, what a sea of alpine crests spread round us, reaching to the horizon in a stupendous circle! The Selkirks, always glorious in their whiteness and ethereally bright; the mighty monarchs of the north, untrodden, almost unexplored and practically still unknown. And the familiar forms of the great peaks of the Continental watershed, Stephen and the Cathedral, Hector and Balfour, Habel and Collie, Victoria and Lefroy, Hungabee and Deltaform, with the grand ice-clad helmet of Mt. Temple shining resplendently above the line of giants, behind which its massive form conspicuously towers.

Our observations and photography occupied us fully; but Häsler's urgent calls had to be heeded all too soon and at 4:15 we turned to ordinary earth once more.

Descending to the dip was nearly as slow a process as the ascent, and ere we reached the unbroken snows at its base, the setting sun had flooded all the pure slopes around us with its rich crimson, dying glow, which faded to the cold and weirdly bluish hue of snow that waits the fall of night.

Huge strides and numerous glissades were welcome after ropes and caution, but darkness gathered rapidly as we came down the last loose slopes of debris and tumbled into camp at 9 P.M., just 18 hours after leaving it.

A good night, a quick run down the canyon bed next morning, a more tedious tramp to the riverside, a tumultuous crossing in our borrowed boat, and we were at Leanchoil, from whence on "No. 2" we later arrived at Field, well satisfied that on the third appeal we had secured a judgment in our favour from the Chancellor.

Two years elapsed before Mt. Goodsir had another challenge, and a second time his topmost crest remained inviolate, a snowstorm driving back Professor Parker and his guides from an altitude of about 10,000 feet, early in July, 1903. A few days later, a third attempt was made, the party being composed of Professor Fay and Christian Häsler, representing the first invaders, and Professor Parker and Christian Kaufmann, of the second contingent. All four had, therefore, some old scores to settle with the peak.

On July 12th they left Leanchoil at 1 P.M., and five hours later were in camp in the Ice River Valley, about two miles below our former camp, thanks to a bridge and road constructed by the Government since our experiences by boat and trail in 1901. Next afternoon they ascended to a high camp in Zinc Gulch, not far from our old bivouac and about the same altitude. There they were detained by a snowstorm, and it was not until the 16th that they were able to attack the mountain. The dawning day was superb, and a start was made at 3:40. The rocks were free from ice, the snow in perfect condition, and a steady pace was maintained until eight o'clock, when a halt was made for a second breakfast at a height of nearly 10,000 feet.

"From here on," writes Professor Fay,[35] "even to the top of the seemingly vertical cliff at whose upper edge we had turned back in dismay, our ascent was little other than a repetition of that former one [in 1901]—save that the snow was in far better condition, remaining firm and crisp to the very summit. Arrived at our previous altitude, we found the situation on the summit arête entirely changed, the remarkable 'reversed cornice' having entirely disappeared. ... The distance from the top of the cliff to the summit is perhaps 500 feet, with an ascent of 150 feet at the most. So near had we once already been to victory! But it is indeed a most interesting bit. On the left (westward) for much of the distance it falls vertically, perhaps even slightly overhanging a tremendous descent, so that anything let drop might go 1,000 feet before striking, and then would ricochet 3,000 or 4,000 more before coming to a state of rest; on the right, a snow slope of at least 50 degrees descends for perhaps 2,000 feet, ending at a precipitous fall of doubtless three or four additional thousands. On the knife-edge in which these slopes met I saw one of the party astride at a certain point with one leg pretty nearly vertical and the other at no uncomfortable angle from its mate.

"At 11 o'clock we stood upon the summit. ... First, a broad expanse of snow slightly tipped westward and northward, and perhaps 15 feet in breadth—but of this a full third is cornice, overhanging towards the Ottertail Valley; this small plateau is prolonged in a narrower extension 100 feet or more, ending in a gable that we did not think it worthwhile to look over. It is corniced all the way. No later comer will find a 'stone man' on Goodsir's summit; there are no stones,— nothing but pure white snow. For the view, one word only must suffice—it is magnificent!"

The results of boiling-point observation gave an estimate for altitude of 11,925 feet.[36] An hour later they were en route for camp, reached at six o'clock, and Mt. Goodsir had joined the ever growing host of peaks included in the roll of "First Ascents."

Chapter x

THE VALLEY OF THE UPPER BOW

Ho! FOR THE FAR NORTH; for the untrodden summits of Mt. Columbia and its vast icefield, Mts. Forbes and Freshfield, Bryce and Lyell, and other such peaks, named or unnamed, as might lure the explorer with their subtle fascination, if time and weather be propitious. Ho! for the Great Divide, whose numerous eccentric crooks and windings, bastioned with sturdy outpost peaks, and riven with passes never visited by man, with their attendant spurs and valleys hitherto unknown, present so wondrously attractive a problem for the mountaineer to solve.

It seemed almost too good to be true, but we were really off at last! Despite many a difficulty and many a disappointment, my dream was in very deed beginning to be realized. Ever since the first fitful glimpses of the "beyond" from out the driving mists upon Mt. Stephen's top, I had longed for an opportunity to wander in the region of the Giants, where Mt. Forbes and Mt. Columbia held sway over a realm scarcely invaded by the foot of man. Again the next summer from a score of summits the far peaks called and called again, till finally upon Mt. Habel the summons came so imperatively that it would not be denied, and the first plans were laid, to bear fruit ten months later.

The officials of the Canadian Pacific Railway, from the highest down, showed the very greatest interest and kindness in furthering the project. In addition to numberless courtesies, they most generously placed at my disposal for the whole season the services of the ablest of their contingent of Swiss guides, Christian Kaufmann, who had been my companion on many interesting occasions when he was attached to Mr. Whymper's staff. But, unfortunately, my two expected comrades were at the last moment prevented from accompanying me, and I was left in the unpleasant predicament of having a most inadequate climbing party, which threatened ruin to the mountaineering portion of the trip; for two on a rope on the great icefields and unknown, but presumably difficult, big peaks to be explored, was anything but an ideal arrangement. Since the mountaineering element was the most important feature of the whole undertaking, as it was imperative to seek the summits to obtain most of the required data, it was that or nothing. With almost any other guide but Christian I should have shrunk from the attempt, but his skill both on rocks and on ice is so consummate, and his experience so considerable, that I was ready, if he were willing to trust himself with me alone. This, to my great relief, he volunteered to do, and our mutual confidence was amply vindicated by the achievement, without mishap or accident, of the first ascents of eight peaks over 10,000 feet in altitude (besides two others in conjunction with Professor Collie's party), and the exploration of several new passes and extensive glaciers and snowfields.

Of course Bill Peyto was my outfitter, but his growing business needed so much of his attention that he could not spare the time to spend eight or nine weeks away from his headquarters, and he could only accompany us as far as the Saskatchewan, leaving the camp in charge of Jim Simpson and Fred Ballard, both experienced hunters and trailmen, and both excellent cooks, particularly Fred. This latter is by no means the least qualification, and the ability of the chef especially on a long trip, is a most important factor of the comfort, health and "condition" of the explorer. I have seen bannocks, tough and solid beyond all idea of eating, which have stood the ravages of wind and weather without a trace of wear, let alone dissolution, for four long years! *Verb. sap. sat est.*[37]

Laggan is the starting point for the far North, as the extraordinary valleys, characteristic of the Canadian Rockies, running parallel to the main line of the Divide, permit of a route in almost a perfectly straight line alongside the watershed and seldom more than half a dozen to a dozen miles away. The start had been delayed a week by heavy rains which made the swampy valley of the Bow well-nigh impassable, but, on July 8th, 1902, Christian and I spent our last night for many a week surrounded by the comforts of a civilized abode at Lake Louise, equipped and eager for our lengthy wanderings.

Next morning Peyto, Jim and Fred appeared from Banff with 14 horses, not to mention an irresponsible and irrepressible two-year-old colt, and a full stock of provisions. Almost every previous party that had explored the headwaters of the Saskatchewan and beyond had suffered regularly from the running short of their supplies, necessitating a hurried return and the abandonment of sundry plans, accompanied by privations more or less severe. Such a contingency Peyto and I were mutually determined should not occur on this occasion, his first as an outfitter for the long trip, and mine as an independent traveller. As a result we had an abundance throughout our two months' trip and some to spare.

These stores, together with my impedimenta and Christian's modest kit, loaded our ten pack horses heavily, the others being used for saddle purposes. Some description of the contents of the packs may be of use if not particularly interesting. The provisions, to commence with the most important items, consisted of a mainstay of flour and bacon; canned goods of various descriptions, including milk, corn, tongues, boneless turkey and other birds, beef, and jam, sugar, salt and other seasonings (Fred made the best mustard I have ever tasted anywhere); baking powder, dried fruits,—apples, pears, prunes, apricots and raisins; rice and oatmeal, cheese and chocolate, tea, coffee, cocoa and a varied assortment of soups about complete the tale, and we fared sumptuously every day. Two small tents accommodated the four of us, bestowed in pairs; blankets and sleeping bags, according to individual taste, completed the night equipment; kitchen and table utensils, strictly limited to bare necessities, made up the balance of camp furniture. Our personal baggage varied from the little more than change of raiment of my three companions to my own dittos, stuffed into a common sack, together with my solitary luxury and sundry instruments required for semi-scientific purposes; and four ice axes formed a most harassing climax to the number of the packs.

The instruments consisted of two cameras, 5 × 7 and 3¼ × 4¼, with some 40 dozen plates and cut films, and the etceteras necessary for changing plates and other incidentals; a mountain transit, with tripod, most kindly supplied by Mr. E. Deville, Surveyor-General of Canada, along with a Watkin mountain aneroid and one of ordinary make: these were supplemented by my own pocket instrument, and the three served as valuable checks to one another, besides enabling me to leave one down in camp to be observed regularly by an assistant whilst the other two were being operated at various altitudes; a fairly accurate correction for weather variations was thus obtained. A sextant, clinometer and small plane table, fitting onto the tripod of my camera, three thermometers and a pair of field glasses, besides an assortment of maps, notebooks, accounts of previous explorations in the vicinity, and a few minor addenda, made up a fairly bulky but very valuable load, which caused me many an anxious moment, in spite of strong wooden cases, for the contrariety of the cayuse is proverbial, and amid the close tree trunks of a dense forest or on the occasions of the swims across the broad Saskatchewan the delicate instruments and cameras were fortunate in coming through unscathed.

I have referred to my one luxury, which brought me some chaff and scarcely veiled contempt at the outset from my comrades, but ere long it was conceded to have some merits, and before the confines of civilization were again attained they wanted to know where one like it could be got. Each evening on our arrival at a new camp, after tents were pitched, boughs gathered and spread within and all made snug, I appeared from the recesses of my tent with a flat package, 15 inches long, eight wide, and one and a half thick, and a machine like a small accordion; unfolding the former, an air mattress of waterproof cloth was displayed, which the "accordion" soon filled to a convenient size, and lo, an ample bed, seven feet long and two and a half feet wide, with a bulging pillow at one end, lay ready for a comfortable night.

Old bones get painful after eight weeks night by night on Mother Earth's hard lap, even with spruce boughs plentifully spread; and many a disturbed night of tossing in search of softer spots was saved, besides racked bones and possibilities of rheumatism obviated by the use of my beloved mattress. The memory is fragrant yet,—with a fragrance born of India rubber that was its only failing, particularly in its earlier days,—and we shall be inseparables on any future camping trip of any length.

The first night, camp was pitched only three or four miles from Laggan, Kaufmann and I walking over from Lake Louise in the evening. Reveille was sounded early. Jim and Peyto hunt up the horses and bring them in; Fred looks after breakfast; Christian and I strike tents, fold blankets, pack the baggage and help with the saddling. Then breakfast is in order, the dishes are washed, saddles cinched up, packs loaded and fastened with the mysterious but invaluable "diamond" or "three-quarter-diamond" hitch, the fire is carefully extinguished, we mount our steeds, and off we go along the trail.

It is just 7:20, but each day sees the routine of packing more nearly perfected and the time occupied in getting under way grows less and less. Peyto leads on his well-tried black mare, followed by the string of pack horses, which make occasional dashes for the leadership, shaking up their packs and bumping into one another or any trees that they can hit. The packing and the "hitch" are early and most fully tested. In the middle of the bunch comes Fred, and Jim brings up the rear; both have considerable "driving" to do, as the commencement of a march invariably calls for some discipline and training: some of the cayuses were new to pack train work, and all were on their first trip of the season and apt to be a little slow and contrary, until they got into good condition and their regular routine of place and method was established.

Kaufmann and I were unattached, and the pursuit of photographs took me sometimes ahead or left me far in the rear. The latter proceeding did not agree with the gregarious tastes of my first steed, which objected strongly to being tied up when the other horses disappeared along the trail: on one occasion he broke his tie rope and left me in the lurch, and on another he uprooted bodily a sturdy 12-foot spruce and cantered off in glee with the tree swinging at the end of the stout cord. So Christian good-naturedly shadowed me in future and took charge of the delinquent.

Fred Stephens, another admirable "outfitter," was on his way with 15 horses and two foals to the mouth of Bear Creek, packing in supplies to cache in advance of Professor Collie's party, which was to follow thither in two or three weeks' time: so the combined strings formed a striking cavalcade.

The weather was perfect as we slowly wound our way along the old trail, probably largely the same as that taken by Dr. Hector in 1858, when the first white man sought the sources of the Bow. Behind us rose the well-known peaks beyond Laggan, Mts. Victoria, Lefroy and Temple grandly prominent. To the right, a fire-swept desolate expanse extends to the southeastern spur of Mt. Hector and gradually leads the eye to the sharp, fortress-like apex of that peak, the dominating mountain of the Upper Bow. On the left, wooded slopes merge in the rugged escarpments of Mt. Daly and its neighbours, till, in the distance, the palisades are broken by a sudden gorge, where the vast icefields of the Waputik sweep down to Hector Lake, and on the farther side a wooded spur juts far into the valley, culminating in Bow Peak and folding the shining waters in its close embrace.

The late spring and recent heavy snows, which had delayed our start, rendered the trail—troublesome at best—well-nigh impassable. The sloughs were full of water, the trails thick with soft and sticky mire. The poor horses, with their extra-heavy packs, sank deeply in, and only with constant effort and many a resounding squelch were their captive limbs withdrawn. More than one fell and had to be rescued; they would persist in wandering from the pathway, in search of better footing, and driving meant some exercise for hand and voice Once "Kootenay" stuck fast, his pack between two little spruces and his hind quarters sunk in a deep mudhole, utterly helpless and incapable of movement; and it took the combined efforts of the five of us, after a prolonged struggle, by dint of pull and push, easing and straining, to hoist the poor beast at last to terra firma. Though trembling in every limb and slightly wrenched and strained, he fortunately was not seriously the worse of a mishap such as has frequently cost a pack animal its life.

Thus, leaping fallen logs, crossing wayside creeks, ploughing through swamps, the march proceeds beside the rushing waters of Bow River, till shortly after noon we find a pleasant camping ground close to the eddying current and about a mile from the lower end of Hector Lake. An ample supper of splendid rainbow trout witnessed to a part of the afternoon's occupation, and a stroll to the borders of the lake gave me an opportunity of learning a little more of the topography. The ground was more or less familiar, as I had already had a journey along the tangled shore after crossing Balfour Pass nearly a year before. This is the first respectable adit to the Waputik icefield and its peaks from the Bow Valley, and it is by this approach that the earliest explorations have been made.

On the other side of the valley towers Mt. Hector, a lofty peak, 11,205 feet, but with a very easy way of access to its final turret from the northern end; its aspect from the south and west, however, is imposing and precipitous. It was first assailed in 1895 by the late Mr. Philip Abbot, Professor Fay and Mr. C.S. Thompson, and though there is nothing of thrilling alpine adventure in the narrative contributed to *Appalachia* by Mr. Abbot, the humorous and racy style of his account makes it one of the most delightful articles in that delightful periodical.[38]

He sums up the features of the expedition in his opening paragraph: "Our party that climbed Mt. Hector cannot, I am afraid, lay claim to much glory therefrom. We had no hair-breadth escapes; we did not even encounter great hardships, except such as are familiar to every bricklayer's apprentice. We did not need to exercise great generalship: the mountain was in plain sight, we walked to its base,—some distance, I admit, and not exactly over a paved road,— and then walked on till we reached the summit."

But the view from the lofty and isolated peak was of unusual grandeur. "In the single element of savage desolation—unrelieved, monotonous, boundless, and complete—I have never seen anything which equalled the view from the summit of Mt. Hector, and I do not expect to see anything which will excel it. But impressiveness and picturesqueness of detail, beauty of color, and, of course, human interest—except the imaginative interest which came from the mere immensity of the solitude—were, on the whole, lacking.

"These are large deductions; but on the other side there are to be said two things. So far as the Club is concerned, Mt. Hector is the first alpine peak (and it can fairly be called alpine) which has been conquered for the first time by an Appalachian party, as such, climbing without guides We do not claim to have achieved greatness, but we do expect to have greatness thrust upon us, as being the first parents of a very long and illustrious line to come. Secondly, the expedition was an interesting one to ourselves, because it was so fair and even a tussle with Nature—and with Nature in no accommodating mood. We did our own work, and fairly earned for ourselves what measure of success we had. There is a fascination in this which outweighs all æsthetic considerations whatever."

The details of the climb need not be given. The route adopted led at first through pleasant woods to the base of a conspicuous buttress or shoulder separated by a great amphitheatre from the abortive southwestern arête running down from the summit. Climbing was easy. The cliffs were so broken down that they scarcely needed the help of their hands. Then steep shale gave place to snow patches for a while, then more of the interminable shale, until from shadow and steep stony slopes a single step lifted them above the edge of a plateau and into a new world. "In front, almost blinding from the reflected rays of the morning sun, there stretched a broad and almost level expanse of dazzling white; sinking very gradually to the northeast, rising as gradually to the southeast, and towards the south first rising slowly, and then suddenly lifting itself up in a splendid snow peak, nobly proportioned and very steep."

Up these snows they went, without special happenings of any kind, till a final scramble up 100 feet of rocks brought them to the apex—a little ridge of broken rocks—at half-past 12, and the vast panorama lay before their fascinated gaze.

Beyond Mt. Hector lies a trench-like valley by which a way can be made to Pipestone Pass, and farther still another tributary comes in from the Dolomite Pass, leading directly to the Siffleur River, an affluent of the North Saskatchewan. The first known to make this little pass were the Revs. H.P. Nichols and C.L. Noyes and Messrs. C.S. Thompson and G.M. Weed, all of the Appalachian Mountain Club. In 1898 they journeyed up the Pipestone River from Laggan to the Pipestone Pass; crossing the height of land, they travelled down the Siffleur River to its junction with a large stream from the southwest, which at first they thought might be the North Saskatchewan. So they crossed the Siffleur and proceeded up the new river, soon being quite undeceived as to its identity, but somewhat perplexed as to where it was to lead them. Eventually they emerged into the old Bow Valley after a most interesting trip. The character of the mountains along this newly traversed country being strikingly dolomitic, the pass and river received their present names. No real climbing, however, was undertaken, though one or two lesser eminences were ascended. Mt. Molar, a peak of most singular appearance and admirably named, is the most prominent altitude. The mountains of the Slate Range, lying to the east of the Bow Valley, with Mt. Hector and Mt. Molar as the chief summits, are far less alpine in character than those of the western side, and form an intermediate step between the latter and the ranges beyond, which are wholly devoid of glaciers. The icefields of the Waputik and Wapta, on the other hand, are most extensive, stretching in a magnificent curve from Mt. Daly, just north of Hector Pass, where the railroad crosses the Divide, encircling Mt. Olive and Mt. Gordon, sweeping round the bases of Mt. Collie and Mt. Habel, and terminating at the upper end of Yoho Valley, a distance of 25 to 30 miles.

A series of massive retaining walls girdles its outer edge, broken through here and there, where huge glacier tongues project between mighty portals into the vales beyond. As already indicated, this wall remains intact far up the Bow Valley, on the east, the first break of importance being where Balfour Glacier leads to Hector Lake, and by this gateway Mt. Balfour and the icefields were earliest approached. A few miles farther north comes the Bow Glacier, draining to Bow Lake, and this presents another noble entrance to the vast ice world. Both of these, with Peyto Glacier, at the head of the South Fork of the Saskatchewan, have been ascended to the Divide at least, and my expeditions to that point from the Yoho Valley side prove the feasibility of alpine passes being made across the watershed. As one swings round one faces less frequented regions; a glacier debouches between Mt. Baker and Mt. Collie, and another through the deep chasm separating the latter from Mt. Habel, but no one has yet been known to pass between these portals. From Mt. Habel the retaining wall continues unbroken to Signal 18 and the ridge beyond.

Upon the inner side, a minor tongue or two depend from the rocky sides of Mt. Balfour to the verge of the stupendous cliffs that line the eastern side of Yoho Valley, from one of them springing the Takakkaw Fall. But the two chief glaciers are the three-tongued Habel Glacier and the grand Yoho Glacier (which receives an affluent from Balfour Pass), both descending to the famous Yoho Valley.

The central peaks have all been climbed, as well as most of those upon the rim. Signal 18 (10,000 feet), to the west, was early taken as a survey point. Mt. Gordon (10,400 feet) fell on August 10th, 1897, before a party of nine, who climbed it by way of the Bow Glacier under the impression that it was Mt. Balfour. In 1898 Messrs. Collie, Stutfield and Woolley, on their return from an exploration trip to the headwaters of the Athabasca, ascended Thompson Peak (10,500 feet); and in 1901 Mt. Habel and Mt. Collie were climbed by Mr. Whymper and myself with three guides.

The highest mountain of the range is Mt. Balfour (10,875 feet), which was sought by the big party that ascended Mt. Gordon in 1897; and a second attempt, made by a section of them a few days later from Hector Lake, failed on account of bad weather. The following summer Professor Fay tried it from Sherbrooke Valley, a tributary of the Kicking Horse, and had a lengthy tramp across soft snow, which proved the undoing of Mr. R.F. Curtis, whose weight forced him to stop midway. Professor Fay and R. Campbell went some distance farther, when they too had to relinquish the attempt. This was on August 3rd, and on the 11th the summit was achieved by the Rev. C.L. Noyes and Messrs. Thompson and Weed. They were encamped at Hector Lake, familiar ground to all, especially to the two first, who had been members of the party that started from this spot with the same object just 12 months before.

"By rising at three," writes Mr. Noyes,[39] "we had time to prepare and eat a comfortable hot breakfast, oatmeal and chocolate, and get off by four. A diagonal course, slabbing up over the ridge intervening between this point and the outlet of Margaret, brought us to that lake by the easiest route. The sun had not yet touched its waters into beauty, and they lay a cold, sombre blue. It may have been six o'clock when we were climbing the screes at the head of the lake, and after seven when, by the one rock ladder, we scaled the wall above, and came over the outer rim of Lake Turquoise,—'a joy forever.' It was not far from eight when we stopped for lunch at the foot of the glacier above. ... The passage of the glacier was this year a delicate operation, taking some ingenious warping among crevasses, and light stepping over bridges, which needed but to melt a little more to almost cut off access to the névé above. This gained, full in view beyond it, broadside to us, rose the magnificent mass of Balfour. The difficulties of approach, which we had foreseen looking down from Vulture Col, by no means vanished. The final ridge, however, looked hopeful, promising us, if once on it, a clear way to the summit; but how to reach the ridge? Well to the south was the most encouraging route in view. Rising almost to the crest was a tongue of snow, but it was suspiciously gashed, and, once upon the ridge, there was no surety that the way would not be barred by cornices or precipitous breaks. The prospect was too doubtful to waste time in considering, and without slackening our steps we pressed on over the névé to the gateway at the south, which would let us through to the western side, where we had reason to hope we might find more level and stable snow, giving access to the final ridge. It was 11 o'clock when we broke over the Divide, and the change of worlds of vision, always thrilling in such a crossing, was grandly so in this case. To the south rose, near and imposing, Niles and Daly, like mammoth walruses, lifting their black heads above the ice, and thrusting their great snouts toward us; between them the névé sloped down to some glacier, and by them to the west rolled a vast snowfield toward the ravine of the Wapta, that enormous rent between the mountains, gathering into its bosom the immense volume of melted snow poured down from all the névés streaming off the western side of Balfour and Gordon, Collie and Habel, to the north; and over beyond, from the hither slopes of another system of mountains that filled the prospect to the horizon west and south. For all this we hardly had eyes at first; they were turned instantly toward our goal; and when they ran over a clear reach of snow leading to a ridge curving off from the main arête to the left, above which foreshortened could be seen the summit, as it seemed readily attainable, only the nonchalance of our tones betrayed our excitement as we remarked, 'We're going to make it.' We did make it, but it took four hours. The offshoot ridge once gained, there was along its curve an even, almost level, way to the backbone of the mountain. On this main arête there was more difficulty; a V-shaped cleft promised to block the passage altogether, but we circumvented it by slabbing down to the screes and snow below, and diagonally up again, over unstable and tricky footing, and with unreliable handholds on friable rock, all done without slip or danger, up to a depression in the ridge, where greeted us a reviving view Hector-ward, and a pool of water made by the snow shelf on the eastern side, melting against the warm rocks. This invited to a final lunch, refreshed by which we rose for our last hour's climb to a height much greater than Balfour,—the summit of our summer's adventure and success.

"Anyone who has walked the ridge of the Presidential Range will know the thrilling sensation of such a passage, as though one were moving on the backbone of the world. Suppose it is really a bit of the coping of the continent, lifted toward 11,000 feet, thinned down till it is no more than the fine edge of a wedge protruding through slopes of snow that cling to its sides high as the steepness will allow, flanked beyond stupendous gorges on either hand by a wilderness of mountains reaching everywhere to the skyline, rising in great steps along an untrodden way to an untouched peak,— that is what the final climb in the capture of Balfour meant for us. It tried tact, agility and care, but was not difficult or dangerous. By the time we had built our cairn and taken bearings with the prismatic compass, it was four o'clock."

The ultimate issue was a bivouac at treeline and a night out, and back to Laggan by seven o'clock next evening.

But to return to *our* camp. The site here is a well-known one, as the trail is fairly often travelled as far as the mouth of the Mistaya River and, less frequently, onward to the haunts of the wild sheep and goats near Wilcox Pass. At other times the march goes on until a suitable location turns up, the ordinary working day for a pack train being about six hours. By starting early, camp is generally reached by noon, and a busy scene develops.

Each rider first unsaddles his own steed and turns him loose, if his character will permit. My old "Nigger" [sic], unsurpassed as a trail horse, clever in fallen timber, excellent at fording streams, sure-footed on grassy slopes or rough, stony ground, dependable at all times when one is on his back, was utterly depraved when he was cast loose and would lead the other horses into mischief if any were practicable. So he, with Joby, Kootenay and Baldy, were usually hobbled, and on one or two sad occasions he even had to suffer the crowning indignity of picketing, thereby also having his evening meal considerably curtailed in quality and quantity.

Then all hands set to work to unload the pack horses, strip them and "shoo" them off for a roll and a good 18 hours' browse. The cook boxes are dumped in the "kitchen"; Fred gets his fire lit and hustles round for dinner; Christian cuts armfuls of spruce boughs, which we dispose expertly as a combination bed and carpet in the tents which we have just set up. The personal kit and blankets follow, and the balance of the packs are piled with the saddles close at hand and covered carefully with waterproof pack mantles. By this time Fred announces dinner, and we set to with ample appetites.

The afternoon is variously spent. Sometimes with Christian, often alone, I range round with camera, field glass, aneroid and sextant, making notes and observations, taking pictures, studying the routes for future expeditions, and so forth. Jim and Fred generally disport themselves in leisurely fashion, unless, in a new region, a trail has to be cut for the next day's journey, or some other need arises, and then they work like heroes. Two or three log cabins for winter use when trapping stand as memorials of afternoons off and days when Christian and I were on the heights.

Early to bed, we ordinarily sleep like tops till break of day calls us for a fresh start, and so *da capo*[40] while the march continues. The nights are usually cool, the freezing point being recorded on 11 nights out of 51 in July and August, and 46 was the highest minimum reading during that period. The coldest camps were those close to the streams, which are all of glacial origin, and a current of cold air accompanies them as they surge onward from their icy fountains. During our 54 days we pitched camp 34 times, eight of which were return visits to old localities. Our lowest camp was at the mouth of Bear Creek, 4,500 feet above the sea, our highest at the upper end of the West Branch Valley, about 6,000 feet; and, strange to say, this was the warmest of them all, thanks to its singularly sheltered position. On several occasions bivouacs were made at timberline (i.e., about 7,000 feet), and, as a rule, we were much warmer there than down in camp, being removed from the influence of the glacier streams.

Few regions could surpass the Canadian Rockies for the advantages of their camping grounds. Apart from the unvarying beauty of each spot, the three desiderata of an ideal camp are almost always abundantly in evidence. Fuel and water never fail, wherever you may wander, and pasture is very rarely lacking, though, fortunately, the Indian cayuse is not remarkably particular about his daily *menu*. Sometimes the day's journey may have to be extended or curtailed beyond the regulation distance, and at the Columbia camp the horses had to be taken three or four miles down the valley after the first day or two, but the rarity of these occasions brings them into prominence The addition of invariably excellent shelter under the lee of the lofty, close-set pines and balsams completes the tale of camping advantages and leaves nothing that the most exacting traveller could well demand.

Yet each spot has its own individuality, its special charm of scenery and location. One has a lake outspread in front, another is a garden of roses and asters, a third looks out upon a private waterfall, a fourth, from a proud eminence, dominates the whole surrounding landscape; each and all are of the universal genus "ideal."

Evening round the campfire is a pleasant time. The temperature is usually cool enough to make the blaze acceptable to more than the eye. Great logs are piled high, and there is cheerfulness and life. We sit round, each in his favourite attitude, narrate the individual experiences of the day, discuss our future plans, or, more commonly, "swap yarns." The varied lives of the five give scope for interesting episodes. The life of the cowboy, hunter, trapper, lumberman and pioneer of North America rubs shoulders with the experiences of the mountaineer and chamois-hunter of the Swiss guide, the traveller in almost all the European countries and one or two beyond, and the Canadian roughrider who has smelt powder on the veldt of the Transvaal.

Leaving Hector Lake behind us early in the morning, we traverse green timber for a while, the trees becoming smaller and more sparse as the valley rises. The outlets from the eastern valleys have to be forded, and we round Bow Peak, a massive promontory, jutting out north of Hector Lake, forming a conspicuous landmark all the length of the Bow Valley from Laggan to Bow Pass, and said to be visible as far as Wilcox Pass. An easy little pass for pedestrians lies behind, leading from the upper valley directly to the head of Hector Lake. Beyond its long rampart, where the valley narrows to nearly half its former width, a strikingly fine series of hanging glaciers appears on the dark, lofty cliffs that bound the Waputik snowfields, . and a tremendous cornice is conspicuous upon the summit of their southern outpost. At their base the glacier-green waters of Bow Lake gleam brilliantly below the moraine and stretch away to the north for about two miles, then, curving round the buttresses that push their way far into the angle, they sweep towards their source at the end of the Bow Glacier. A mighty obelisk, fallen from the heights, stands far out amidst the trees close to the southern shore—a fit monument to mark the memory of a bygone race. The trail being spongy and full of muskeg, we travelled in the water on the firm gravel of the lake bottom for a full mile to its northeast corner, then, turning westward along the shore, we crossed the creek to higher ground, where a large clump of timber makes an admirable camping place. Joby, always troublesome and obstinate, took it into his head to ford the creek at a point of his own selection, and, in attempting to climb the opposite bank at a bad place, lost his equilibrium and lay wallowing helplessly in the water, soaking both his pack and Peyto, who plunged to his rescue in a twinkling.

I spent the afternoon visiting a splendid gorge at the lake head, through which the outflow from the glacier descends with concentrated energy in a tortuous and turbulent torrent, pent up by the worn walls of the rocky chasm, so narrow that in places one could step across. At one point the deep ravine is crossed by a massive fallen boulder, 30 feet or so in length, which forms a natural bridge high above the rushing stream. The sides of the canyon are fantastically worn; twists and hollows mark its entire length, and numerous cascades and deep black pools alternate with foaming rapids, till the strait portals of the chasm are left behind, and the creek winds peacefully along a meandering course between queer promontories that alternate on either side of the valley for a considerable distance before the stony flats and finally the lake are reached. The glacier above is very broken, but easily ascended at the side, and has been used many times as a highway to the Wapta névé.

This is the main headwater of the Bow River (itself the principal source of the South Saskatchewan), though perhaps the longest branch is that which filters through the swampy tract from the Bow Pass, three miles beyond the lake.

Upon that pass the minor watershed is crossed that separates the basins of the North and South Saskatchewan, which thus have sources within a few feet of one another, if they do not indeed spring from the same morass, and, after a wide divergence that bears their waters fully 150 miles apart, their courses meet again some 350 miles from this spot where the infant streams mingle upon the broad bosom of Bow Pass.

The view from the tent door is exquisite: the broad lake sweeping round the rugged mass of mountains opposite, flanked by the wide, white expanse of icefield and glacier to the west, and the green vista of Bow Valley on the other side.

> "'Tis night upon the lake. Our bed of boughs
> Is built where—high above—the pine tree soughs.
> 'Tis still—and yet what woody noises loom
> Against the background of the silent gloom!
> One well might hear the opening of a flower
> If day were hushed as this."

CHAPTER XI

THE SOURCES OF
THE NORTH SASKATCHEWAN

ABOVE BOW LAKE THE VALLEY is fairly broad and open, rising gently over marshy ground to the wood-crowned summit of Bow Pass, about 6,700 feet above sea level, and, soon after six, Kaufmann and I were off, ahead of the outfit, armed with the larger camera, to endeavour to do something like justice to the entrancing view that opens out upon the northern side. In an hour and a half we reached the "height of land," and as the trees on the actual pass prevent one getting any view at all, we climbed the shoulder of the western hill, and, swinging round its grassy slope, we came abruptly to a magnificent viewpoint on a jutting spur of rock, and the long vista, of the South and North Parks of the North Saskatchewan suddenly opened out before us.

An almost vertical drop of more than 1,000 feet descends to the

"Silent sea of pines,"

which laves the bases of the precipitous cliffs on either side, throwing its tide of trees far up their lower slopes. Hemmed in by rugged ranges, whose broken summits pierce the sky, the view is limited to the single trench-like gorge that stretches away for 50 miles in a straight line to Wilcox Pass. Round to our left the strikingly pure Peyto Glacier descends in a fine icefall between grand cliffs from the northeast extremity of the Wapta névé, and forms by far the noblest and most attractive entry to those snowfields from the eastern side.[41] The stream, source of the South Fork, or Mistaya River, commonly known as Bear Creek, passing through Peyto Lake, a superb turquoise gem, and half a dozen other lakes (I counted nine in the valley altogether), is lost to view amidst the dark forests that are so marked a characteristic of the lower Bear Creek Valley.

The rival ranges that compress the narrow V-shaped valley are extremely picturesque. The western is the continuation of the Waputik Range, whose most conspicuous points are gabled Howse Peak, loftiest of them all, and the two Pyramids, the white and black. The latter, a remarkable and stupendous feature from end to end of the Mistaya Valley, is particularly impressive from every aspect: —

> "To the east
> Sheer to the vale go down the bare old cliffs,
> Huge pillars that in middle heaven uprear
> Their weather beaten capitals."

Opposite, the mountains culminate at their northern end in Mt. Murchison. This peak, estimated at first by Dr. Hector as 13,500 feet in altitude, and by another enthusiast as 15,781, has been, like almost all the mountains of this northern region, extremely disappointing in its actual elevation, as it only reaches 11,300 feet, and so far from being proudly preeminent, has been with difficulty identified, so many of the nearby peaks appearing, from a distance, just about level with it.[42]

The pass and all the slopes around amazed me by the marvellous profusion and variety of flowers, which were most luxuriant although almost at timberline. Painter's brush, of course, was there in plenty, and the beautiful yellow columbine, locally called the mountain lily, also red and white varieties of heather, dryas, anemones, etc. A beautiful wide-open little star, with pure white, wax-like petals, was particularly noticeable, also a delicate, white drooping bell, small and exquisitely veined, which I have not observed in any other spot during my wanderings.

The trail leads sharply downward on the northern side, rough and stony in places, with rocky steps and ledges and fallen trunks that tested the sure-footedness of our cayuses. Soon we found ourselves at the bottom of the steep descent. Fire, alas, has swept some portions of the upper valley, and the weird relics of tall, blackened poles and the accompaniment of tangled stems that lie in thick confusion amidst the rocky outcrops, sparse grass and bushes, and luxuriant fireweed, made the scene rather desolate and, with sundry mudholes and steep sidehills, added to the labours of our patient horses. Ere long the little cascading creek from the lofty pass falls into the larger stream that has its origin in Peyto Glacier and Lake, a swirling torrent of considerable volume. This is popularly called Bear Creek, officially Mistaya River, and geographically forms the South Fork of the North Saskatchewan, the Middle and North Forks of which possess no special name. By way of variety to the ordinary features of the trail, a creek from the eastern mountains, running for some miles almost parallel to the main river, required fording no less than five times, and we pitched our tents about half a mile above the junction, on a broad flat hemmed in by trees and bushes and affording excellent pasture for our 30 head of horses.

Crossing the creek on an improvised bridge formed by a felled tree, a few minutes through the woods brought me to a picturesque, but nameless, lake, fringed with trees which rise in thickly wooded slopes to splendid cliffs and crags above. This I explored in part. The lake is about four miles long, heading close to a tongue of glacier that descends a lateral valley from a pure snow peak to the southwest. A mile or so from the upper end Bear Creek flows in, issuing through a swampy tract at the northern extremity as a good-sized river.

July 13th gave us a long and rather tedious march of more than seven hours. The early scenery was magnificent: the valley fairly open and the trail skirting the shores of the pretty Waterfowl Lakes or following the windings of the creek. In the bottom the timber is just sufficient to give a park-like appearance whilst not interfering with the view. Right ahead, in the cleft of the narrow valley, Mt. Wilson fills in the vista grandly with its massive battlements: on either side forested slopes lead upward to the giant crags, frowning and sombre, with here and there a gleam of glacier or snow-capped peak beyond. The western mountains dominate the scene, closer and more precipitous than on the other side; the most splendid feature being the majestic steeps of Pyramid Peak, which brought Mt. Stephen constantly to mind, as it projected virtually sheer above the river; the whole was topped by an Italian sky, lit up by exquisite masses of cumulus clouds, a familiar condition in the Canadian Rockies which enhances their always lovely views. Occasional tenuous waterfalls drop from the rims of the upper cliffs, one especially, not very lofty but of considerable volume, commanding admiration as it leaped from its glacial source, high up upon our right, in the centre of a noble amphitheatre of rocks, flanked by dark precipices.

Then we enter the forest and remain in its cool and. pleasant depths for five and a half hours of travel. As we descend, the timber increases in size and density till it reminds one of the

> "forest primeval. The murmuring pines and the hemlocks,
> Bearded with moss and in garments green, indistinct in the twilight,
> Stand like Druids of eld, with voices sad and prophetic,
> Stand like harpers hoar, with beards that rest on their bosoms."

The stillness is remarkable,—a constant wonder of the Rockies is the scarcity of sound and life,—especially when one lingers behind the cavalcade and wanders alone amid these solemn aisles, the most inspiring and the fittest place of worship possible. For

> "The groves were God's first temples. Ere men learned
> To hew the shaft and lay the architrave,
> And spread the roof above them—ere he framed
> The lofty vault, to gather and roll back
> The sound of anthems, in the darkling wood,
> > Amidst the cool and silence he knelt down
> > And offered to the Mightiest solemn thanks
> > And supplication."

Nowhere perhaps could the sense of intimate communion with the everlasting Father be more exquisitely realized than among such lonely woods or on such solitary mountaintops as those of Canada. There may be found the long-sought sanctuary of the storm-tossed soul. The half-rebellious murmurings and questionings as to the justice and the love of God no longer dare to raise their voice. Burdens that seemed too heavy to be borne are rolled away. The throb of pain is stilled. The past and present merge in the vastness of eternal love. The world is lost in fellowship with God, its troubles matter not when once the heart is knit with His.

Anon the pack train is rejoined, halted perhaps whilst one or more of our men clear fallen timber from the path, or cut their way through the thick undergrowth when the trail is blocked beyond remedy. These halts were not infrequent in spite of the fact that Jim and Fred had, earlier in the season, cut through more than 300 trees to clear the route after the winter's ravages. Only the ring of the axe is heard, and the crash of the falling tree far ahead on the winding track. The beasts of burden rest in satisfaction, trying meanwhile to snatch a hasty lunch from the near bushes or the forest grass. Then on again, over many a smaller log, meandering hither and thither through the jungly brush, crushing between trees where the long-suffering packs are in great danger of immediate disruption; every now and then a wayward horse will make a dash through the timber at the side in a wild endeavour to gain pride of place in the long line, and either be hung up between two close-set trunks or have to be hunted back by one of the vigilant packers.

Sunny peeps open up here and there as we cross a lateral gorge, only to be lost again in a moment when the forest tunnel is reentered. These gave glimpses of the "Promised Land," the group of peaks west of the North Fork, where we hoped soon to be exploring the topmost heights and making the acquaintance of all the chief features of their deep-set environment The most noticeable point at first sight was the remarkable change in the stratification: the tilted, often almost vertical, formation found to the south of the Saskatchewan gives place to a massive series of perfectly horizontal layers, topped by thick, flat glaciers.

For some time we had wandered far from the creek, climbing well up on the eastern slopes, but as we neared the valley mouth, the trail suddenly emerged from the woods on the summit of a lofty bank, at whose base the brawling river raged along, and there before us, beyond the dark shoulder of Mt. Sarbach, appeared the cone of Mt. Forbes, attended by its miniature. This latter peak, on a spur of the big mountain jutting eastward, is absurdly like its big brother and is so placed that, although in reality about 2,000 feet less in altitude, from all the lower elevations to the east it dwarfs or hides the major point. Yet, even when dwarfed by distance, Mt. Forbes has a "personality" that thrills the inmost being of the mountaineer, particularly when, still unconquered, it rose before an enthusiast, one of whose chief objectives in a long expedition far from the haunts of men was to attempt the ascent of its untrodden heights.

The gateway of the South Fork lies between Mt. Sarbach and Mt. Murchison. The former (10,700 feet) was ascended on August 25th, 1897, by Mr. G.P. Baker, Professor Collie and the Swiss guide Peter Sarbach, whose name was given to the peak. The climb was principally marked by the looseness of the crumbling rock, until the summit ridge was reached, this being of a dark and harder limestone and very narrow and precipitous on both sides.

Mt. Murchison is a much finer mountain, about 11,300 feet high, and probably the loftiest peak east of the ranges of the Divide. The first attempt to reach its summit was made in 1898, when Professor Collie's party, on their return from the headwaters of the Athabasca River, climbed to an altitude of about 9,000 feet. It snowed steadily and the mountains were enveloped in mist, so they abandoned the climb at that point. The day was not, however, without its interesting and valuable features. Professor Collie tells us[43] that on the arête two remarkable phenomena attracted their attention. "The first was a tall column of rock that had become detached from the cliff, forming a slender pillar 400 or 500 feet in height, and tapering towards the summit and base. Much more extraordinary, however, was a group of rocks consisting, as it seemed, of petrified stems of pine trees that had been broken off about a foot from the ground, with numerous fossilized remains around their base. It has been suggested, however, that they are not trees at all, but the remains of some gigantic prehistoric seaweed. In any case, whatever they are, their existence at so great a height above sea level, and in so excellent a state of preservation, must be accounted very remarkable; and we could wish that they might be visited and examined by some geologist competent to give a thorough account of them."

Two of the same party, Professor Collie and Mr. H.E.M. Stutfield, with Mr. G.M. Weed and Hans Kaufmann, in July, 1902, reached the highest peak. A rest at the mouth of Bear Creek was necessary for the horses, so,[44] "by way of spending the time we arranged to attempt the ascent of the rocky pinnacle of Mt. Murchison which faces and, as it were, overhangs the valley where the tents were pitched. It was thought that the highest summit, or what we had always deemed to be such, lay too far to the east for us to climb it, at any rate in one day, from our present camping ground. . . .

"Leaving the trail about half an hour from the camp, we ascended the dry bed of a torrent that comes straight down the mountain side, some distance northwards of the route we followed in 1898 up to the arête where the fossil forest was found. In this way we avoided the long grind through the woods, which, after our experiences in the Bush Valley, we regarded with special aversion. The going proved excellent, and we soon found ourselves at timberline, ready to tackle Mt. Murchison with legs untired by log jumping or fighting our way through brushwood. As we were all more or less out of training this was a matter of no slight importance. Straight above us was a series of shale slopes leading up to a narrow snow couloir, which, though very steep and possibly somewhat risky owing to falling stones, looked quite feasible; and, as it obviously offered much the most direct way up the mountain, we determined to try it.... There was a good deal of ice at the bottom of the couloir, which in dry seasons is almost bare of snow, and to avoid the risk of falling stones we took to the rocks on our right. These were distinctly difficult in one or two places, and we soon had to put on the rope. Above the rocks we got onto the snow, which, though at a very steep angle, was in excellent condition....

"From the top of a rocky promontory, where we halted for our second meal, it was perceived for the first time that our objective rock peak was cut off from us by a mighty cleft, or notch, in the mountain, with perpendicular cliffs on either side some hundreds of feet in height. We were more than consoled, however, by the discovery that a snow-clad summit, invisible from Bear Creek, which rose straight in front of us and immediately to the right of the rock peak, was much higher; and we had no doubt of our being able to climb it. A long, but easy, scramble up alternate rock and shale slopes took us onto the final snow arête, which, as usual in these mountains, was very heavily corniced; and we had to traverse along the slope, which was excessively steep, a considerable distance from the edge.

"At four in the afternoon, more than seven hours from the start, we stood on the maiden crest of Mt. Murchison.... To our surprise, and great delight, we found we were on one of two peaks of about equal height—the clinometer made ours slightly the higher—which easily overtopped all the other numerous pinnacles of the Murchison group"

The bright and turbulent waters of Mistaya River mingle with the broad and muddy current of the North Saskatchewan in a wide valley bounded by mountain ranges. The Middle Fork, flowing from Howse Pass, a flat and marshy plateau less than 5,000 feet above the sea, between the Waputik and Freshfield Groups, first heads northward, receiving a considerable affluent from the Forbes and Freshfield Valleys; skirting the far-reaching buttresses of Mt. Forbes, it makes a sudden bend at right angles round the flanks of Mt. Sarbach, the northern outpost of the Waputiks, where it is joined by the stream from Glacier Lake. Five or six miles lower down, its principal tributary, the North Fork, largely augments its volume; two miles farther on, the South Fork enters, and the resultant river, already notable for size and strength, flows swiftly eastward, past the famous Kootanie Plain,—the ancient meeting ground of Indians from the western slopes and fur traders from the prairies, for annual market purposes,—through minor ranges, between each of which a new affluent comes down to swell the flood, and so on to the prairie and the sea.

Of the three forks that unite to form the main river, the southern is by far the smallest, but it is one of the most objectionable of streams to cross. The waters are very swift and its bed is filled with boulders, large and small, continually shifting beneath the pressure of the forceful current. Often it is unfordable for days together even in summertime, and at best it is a troublesome and sometimes dangerous undertaking to get across. We struck it in a favourable mood at the first attempt, though even then the swirling waters massed against the horses' flanks a full foot higher than on the sheltered side, and they had all their work cut out to keep their footing amongst the slippery, rolling boulders as they braced against the waves. A few weeks later Fred's horse got a hoof fast for a moment between two stones and horse and rider were engulfed. Fred, fortunately a fine swimmer, threw himself off to ease the pony, and swam to the nearer bank, happily only a few feet away. Toby, meanwhile, thus relieved, extricated himself and calmly proceeded on his way to the farther shore. Carried some way down the stream, he reached a small flat island and looked round with supercilious surprise and pity at his master, standing dripping on the bank from which he had just started. Fortunately a wetting was the worst penalty, but perhaps few, swimmers, even strong ones, would escape in safety if such an accident happened in mid-stream.

Our next water episode occurred about half an hour later in the Middle Fork. Ascending the right bank until above the junction with the North Fork, we selected a spot for crossing where a long spit of sand divided the river into two channels. Jim led the way, followed by the string of pack horses. Many of them, unused as yet to deep fords and some comparatively new to packs, balked when the depth necessitated swimming, and all the energy of Fred and Peyto failed to prevent them heading back to shore. So Peyto tried, as they were used to following his trusty mare; but they declined once more, and even the mare played Peyto false for the first time on record and ducked him most artistically when about halfway across. Finally Jim had to return, and eventually, by dint of drag and drive, the bunch was got across in detachments.

Peyto now bade us farewell and returned to Banff with three of the pack horses, as we had cached a portion of our provisions at Jim and Fred's trappers' hut at Bear Creek mouth, and ten horses were now sufficient for our needs. We next forded the North Fork, just escaping another swim, camped on a grassy knoll at the mouth of the river and spread our belongings out to dry in the hot sunshine.

It was a lovely spot, with the river foreground and entourage of majestic peaks, the castellated mass of Mt. Wilson at our back and vistas up or down four valleys, which here meet in an almost perfect cross.

A brilliant day wore to an evening marked by marvellous storm effects of lurid light and sweeping clouds, massed like a pall of deepest purple over the black mountains that surrounded us, and culminated in a wild night of thunder, lightning, rain and hurricane.

The Middle Fork we traversed nearly to its head at Howse Pass a few weeks later. The broad bed, flanked by sandy terraces or marshes, with a salt "lick" or two, beloved of mountain goats, is, during summer, cut by numerous winding channels, leaving stony flats between; but in spring the whole width is occupied by the rolling tide, swollen by the melting snows and quite impassable. At the bend under Mt. Sarbach we crossed and scaled the high clay banks that mark the mouth of Glacier Creek. Here there are traces of abundant game, Rocky Mountain sheep and goats, which come to lick the salty surfaces. Just beyond a pale-blue lake near the outlet the stream is jammed with logs, which form a solid bridge, known from Dr. Hector's time in 1858 as a highway for animals across the rushing river and still in constant use.

The trail required lots of chopping, but so numerous were the picturesque "bits" amongst the trees, upon the high cutbanks and more open slopes, that every step was fascinating and no wait too long. A few rods below Glacier Lake we turned up a game trail leading steeply upward, and found an ideal camping ground on the slopes about 300 feet above the lake. Mt. Forbes confronted us with its dark massif, the minor summit most imposing though the main peak lay out of sight: on each side of its series of huge buttresses an exquisite vista opened out; up the Middle Fork to the distant summits of Mt. Collie and Mt. Habel on the Pacific side of the Divide; and across the sweep of Glacier Lake to the icefalls of the Lyell Glacier and the ridge that marks the watershed.

In pursuance of my plan to map the watershed, Kaufmann and I made an expedition to a snowy peak,—for which the name of Mt. Kaufmann is suggested,—occupying a commanding position between Mt. Lyell and Mt. Forbes. Laden with instruments, large camera, blankets and commissariat, we had a rough and tiresome tramp along the north shore of the lake, with endless mazes of fallen and burnt logs to traverse, and a still worse fight beyond, where we were driven frequently to the swampy ground through which the glacier stream wanders by a score of channels. Wet and wearied, we bivouacked at dark about a mile from the glacier, beneath a patriarchal cedar. There is a charm unspeakable about a night in the open. As one lies beneath the dark, starlit canopy, cut fantastically by the tall and graceful spires of the forest trees, the grand solemnity of solitude and silence is unutterably impressive, and nowhere and at no other hour perhaps does communion with the Creator become so real, so intense, as in the untracked forests, amidst the everlasting hills, under the glittering lamps of heaven.

The Lyell Glacier, sweeping broadly from the triple peak of the mountain of that name, descends by one of the largest icefalls known in subarctic regions and exceeding any in the Alps. It was first visited by Dr. Hector and is some eight miles in length. Just at its termination it is joined by a smaller glacier, compressed between the spurs of Mt. Forbes and an isolated outcrop of bare, jagged rocks, protruding along the Continental watershed from an entourage of glaciers which encircle it completely. This smaller glacier—the Kaufmann Glacier—flows from a wide expanse of névé bounded by the Divide and receiving an affluent from the flank of Mt. Forbes' central pyramid.

Our way led up the Kaufmann Glacier, or, when icefalls barred our progress, by its steep left bank, and across a long stretch of névé directly to the base of our sharp, white, objective peak. It was uncanny work for two on a rope, for the huge crevasses were uncomfortably hidden by a thick snow mantle, soft enough to let us sink in deeply and render careful probing necessary every step. Many of these crevasses, too, were of the most objectionable type for an involuntary exploration. The ordinary form is of a V-shape, with more or less sloping walls narrowing towards the base. If the poor, hapless mountaineer falls into one of these, he can, while anchored by his comrade and dangling at the rope's extremity, cut a step with his ice axe in the icy surface, and from that resting-place proceed to carve a staircase to the upper world, aided by the support of his companion. But several of the crevasses we examined here were of an inverted character, widening from the great surface crack towards the hollowed caverns of its sides. In such a place one might as well hope to cut and climb a stairway on a vaulted roof, nothing but sheer muscle could bring him out again, and any one who has attempted to hoist unaided 190 pounds or more of man swinging beneath him in mid-air, will recognize how frail a hope exists for the victim of such an accident with but a single friend to lend his aid.

As we toiled along upward through the weary snow, heavily laden, scorched by sun and snow glare, we saw, careering lightly over the snowfield, 200 yards or so ahead, a full-grown marten. He seemed to hesitate awhile when first he saw us and stood still for some moments, enabling me to get a good look at him through the glass and to see what a fine specimen of his tribe he was. His graceful, agile figure was outlined against the pure white snow, which showed off his dark brown fur, with its rich paler markings, to the best effect. Then, in apparent unconcern, he continued his course, which was almost at right angles to our own, and, moving easily up the steep slopes of snow, disappeared over a projecting ridge about 10,000 feet above sea level, crossed the Divide and wandered down the rockier Pacific side into British Columbia, doubtless in search of a better *menu* than that provided by Alberta.

How, he made us moralize on the superior advantages of four feet over two and such a light and rapid tread! No need for him of rope and ice axe; no need for cautious sounding and a winding course; no heavy plodding through the soft snow for him. A beeline straight to his goal, without a thought of danger or fatigue: happy marten! Why do not we, human fanatics, of the so-called higher species, leave mountain climbing to those so infinitely better fitted for the task? And yet it is worthwhile. Yes, a thousandfold worthwhile to see Nature under the conditions that the mountaineer alone can witness; to understand and enter into its great heart; to triumph over obstacles and learn the value of the endowment which makes man the master of created things.

The final pinnacle of ice was excessively steep and hard, demanding much step-cutting and a ladder-like ascent to the tiny apex, some 10,200 feet above the sea. It is not one of the giant peaks of the Divide, but its position makes it a more important key to the topography than perhaps any other we ascended, with the exception of Mt. Lyell. The line of the watershed is most erratic, and Mt. Kaufmann stands like a bastion thrown out at an acute angle towards the west. Southward the line turns at right angles where Mt. Dent terminates the Freshfield Group, runs eastward to Bush Pass (visited later; see p. 229), thence again at nearly 90 degrees towards our pinnacle. Here its zigzag leads once more to the east as far as the sharp ridge of dark rocks rising like an island from the sea of glaciers, and, bending sharply northward, follows its crest and onward to the westernmost of the three Lyell peaks.

The next most interesting feature was the revelation of a new world of valleys on the Pacific slope, never before in all probability looked on by the eye of man. Beyond these towered the fine pyramid of Bush Peak, two other unnamed summits also calling for particular attention, whilst, in the far distance, the serrated outline of the Selkirks, in the midst of an atmosphere of haze, bounded the horizon.

A third notable outcome of the expedition, which stood us in good stead a fortnight later, was the close study we were enabled to make of the north side of Mt. Forbes, its ponderous buttresses and intervening glaciers, and the steep face of its imposing final pyramid, set proudly on a vast massive pedestal covering an enormous area, a ramp of stainless snow whose knife-edged ridges culminate in a sharp point that pierces the blue heavens like a javelin.

Night overtook us by the shores of Glacier Lake, and a second bivouac was forced upon us with a painfully restricted bill of fare, but by 4:40 next morning we were safe in camp and the culinary resources of our chef once more appreciated at their proper value.

The previous afternoon Professor Collie had "called," bringing the welcome news of the arrival of his party, with whom we had a rendezvous at Bear Creek that failed to materialize owing to sundry mishaps and heart-rending delays Meantime they had made the first ascent of Mt. Murchison, already chronicled (p. 195), and all were ready for the fray and eager to measure strength with the two chieftains of this neighbourhood, Mt. Freshfield and Mt. Forbes. In driving rain and sleet we took our way down Glacier Creek, forded the Middle Fork and followed our friends up the long flats to the mouth of Freshfield Creek, where we espied their camp just pitched on the borderland between the flat and forest on the southern side.

This meeting ushered in a most pleasant period of 11 days of climbing and companionship, sandwiched in between my two visits to the West Branch peaks. There were nine of them in the party: Professor Collie and Messrs. H.E.M. Stutfield and H. Woolley from good old England, Mr. G.M. Weed, an old climbing companion of mine, and a retinue headed by Fred Stephens, who shares with Peyto the reputation of being the best outfitter and leader in the Rockies, unsurpassed as a guide, philosopher and friend, always cheerful, always ready for anything, work or otherwise, and A1 in execution; whilst Hans Kaufmann, brother of my Swiss guide, completed the outfit.

Across the Middle Fork, here only three miles from its source on the pass beyond, the snowy triangle of Howse Peak, sharing with Mt. Balfour pride of place amongst the peaks of the Waputik Range, offered attractions to the mountaineer which led Professor Collie's party, after I had said farewell, to make the first ascent on August 14th, finding it a simple but laborious climb, with a delightful view. "Emerging from the woods after a tiring climb of over two hours,[45] we followed a rocky ridge leading straight up towards our peak. Presently, however, we found ourselves cut off by a couple of precipitous rock faces intersecting the ridge. The first was negotiated without much difficulty, but the second proved a more formidable affair. Hans and Woolley, after expending much time and labour and performing some really remarkable acrobatic feats, succeeded in getting down a perpendicular rock chimney about 50 feet high: the rest of the party, less avid of glory and doubtful if time would allow us all to follow in their wake, preferred the safer but more undignified course of descending into the valley and remounting to the ridge further on. The remainder of the climb was a long snow grind, with only a few crevasses here and there that required a certain amount of care; and we reached the top eight hours from the start. . . .

"The summit is formed of a most enormous snow cornice running along the ridge for a great distance, and overhanging the terrific precipices which line the western side of Bear Creek above Waterfowl Lake. Crawling on our stomachs one by one to the edge while the others held a firm grip of the rope, we looked over. The rocks fell absolutely sheer for some thousands of feet, and the valley, with its rolling pine-clad hills, and the river, a mere ribbon of pearly grey, winding between green meadows and dull drab shingle-flats, lay spread out immediately below us."

The principal motive for our meeting here was to attack Mt. Forbes, the king of the southern portion of the group that is bounded by the headwaters of the North Saskatchewan on the east, the Athabasca on the north, the Bush River on the west, and the Blaeberry on the south. Another objective was Mt. Freshfield, the chief peak of the group of the same name, lying southward from the massif of Mt. Forbes, and in order to give the big peak a better chance to shed some of its winter and more recent snow, we made our first move in the direction of the easier mountain.

Our "boys" spent the afternoon of August 1st cutting trail through the thick woods to the end of the Freshfield Glacier, and I took the opportunity of testing my three aneroids by Professor Collie's mercurial, and was agreeably satisfied with the results on this and subsequent occasions when comparisons with the standard were effected. The following morning, after making a large cache of provisions and unnecessary impedimenta we moved off in light order up the narrow canyon, getting some grand gorge views en route and in two hours reached the glacier tongue, camping amidst the trees only a few feet from its extremity, the altitude being about 5,250 feet.

That afternoon and the next were spent upon the glacier, the early morning of the 3rd being too wet to think of doing any climbing. The glacier is a magnificent river of solid ice, almost entirely "dry"[46] and wonderfully free from crevasses throughout the six miles or thereabouts up to the base of Mt. Freshfield, which rises to a sharp point right in the centre of the long icy vista. Two great fields of névé, each sweeping from an amphitheatre of comparatively low and insignificant points with wide connecting ridges, descend from the north and south for three or four miles directly facing one another; meeting under the cliffs of Mt. Freshfield, they turn suddenly at right angles to the eastward, and continue their stately course in a mingled flow for six or seven miles of much more rapid descent. Forty-four years before our visit, Dr. Hector explored the lower portion and commented upon the remarkably large and rectangular blocks of limestone that were scattered on the surface. The same feature is characteristic of it today. Many of the rocks are doubtless identical with those he saw, having travelled several miles during the period that has elapsed.

August 4th broke with a few fleecy clouds encircling Mt. Freshfield's summit, but we started at 4:20 and they cleared away as we proceeded. The party was a formidable one: five "Herren" and the two guides composed the climbing force, and Robson, who had never set foot on a glacier before, accompanied us to the base of our peak, a two-hour tramp. Thus far we had already a thorough acquaintance with the route, and Professor Collie had been within 1,000 feet or so of the summit years before, when, in 1897, with Mr. G.P. Baker and Peter Sarbach, he reached the steep ridge leading directly to the top, where a halt for plane-table and photographic work led to the abandonment of the ascent; but, as a momentous result, the wide view of the giant peaks in the far north led him to return next year and seek their heights, with consequences that every lover of the mountains rejoices in.

Bidding good-bye to Robson, we commenced the climb soon after seven, up cliffs and hard snow to an upper glacier where concealed crevasses in profuse abundance called for the rope to be brought into requisition, and a brief halt for this purpose was made as we faced the shapely form of Mt. Pilkington, radiantly beautiful with its shining curtain of pure snow. A good deal of tortuous meandering amongst the fine crevasses ensued as we swung round a cliff-base and worked upward, past a couple of huge schrunds, to a rocky outcrop on the main east arête. Here we halted for a second breakfast and a lazy rest, for we had plenty of time and no doubts about a fairly easy and successful issue. The rest of the ascent was chiefly on rocks; some interesting corners, where we overhung a glorious precipice while clinging to the ice-bound fragments of a none too stable cliff, one or two chimney-like scrambles up narrow icy gullies, some awkward traverses and an occasional acrobatic effort, gave us a pleasant and varied climb, and the sharp little summit, crested, of course, with a heavy cornice, was attained at 12:25, eight hours of leisurely going from the start.

Unfortunately the wind was very strong and keen, a characteristic of the summer of 1902, when scarcely one ascent was made in calm weather, whereas the previous year wind and cold were rare exceptions. This and the altitude were, however, the only disappointments. We could not make the aneroids allow us more than 10,900 feet of elevation, and perhaps 10,800 is a more likely figure. This was much below former estimates, and though we had expected some reduction, we were not prepared for such a drop as this. The view was simply wonderful, and extremely instructive to those of us who were students of the topography, though some of the higher peaks were capped with clouds.

The zigzag course of the Divide was again a topic of special interest. After following the heights of the Waputik Range in an almost straight line, on reaching the apex of Howse Peak it suddenly becomes disgracefully erratic, turning off at right angles to cross the low plateau, where the Middle Fork and Blaeberry commence their divergent courses, an abrupt drop of 6,000 feet. Beyond Howse Pass it rises to the crests and ridges of the "Alpine Club" group, where it takes in Mt. Conway, and runs along the low range that curves to the main peaks which celebrate the names of Walker, Pilkington, Freshfield and Dent, all closely approximating the 11,000 feet mark. Another low retaining wall bends to the east again from Mt. Dent, completing the horseshoe within which the huge expanse of névé of the Freshfield Glacier is contained.

Most fascinating also was the view to the unknown west, where, just at our feet beneath the precipitous cliffs of our mountain, a large icefield, with a long glacier tongue, formed the head of the South Fork of the Bush River. A fine vista opened up along the valley, which is almost straight, between fine peaks and battlements, with numerous glaciers and resultant tributaries on either side, those on the flanks of the Continental watershed being particularly noticeable. Far in the distance, at the base of sheer Mt. Bryce, could be seen its junction with the North Fork, born of the snows of Mt. Columbia, and in the middle distance Bush Peak and a nameless vis-à-vis stood guard above the stream. Southward a smaller glacier trends towards the Blaeberry under the shadow of Mt. Mummery.

Parboiled by the intense August sun, par-frozen by the arctic wind, the majority were early driven downward, but Mr. Weed and Christian, who were on the rope with me, charitably braved the unpleasant climatic conditions and gave me a longer licence for photography and observations, for I had borne the larger camera to the top to try for a complete panorama. But 50 minutes marked the limit, and we crossed the summit, descending the steep snows of this attenuated peak to a rocky outcrop, where, sheltered from the wind, we had a merry lunch in full view of Mt. Pilkington—a noble vision—directly opposite. A picturesque gap, broken abruptly in the narrow western wall connecting the two peaks, afforded a strikingly framed peep of the green lower world from our immediate entourage of ice and snow and bleak, bare precipice.

Being thrust into the lead, my long legs set a tremendous pace down the snowslopes, and though the intricacies of the crevassed névé required care and many a turn and twist, the big strides covered ground so rapidly that my unfortunate successor, Mr. Weed, whose sturdy limbs were fashioned less generously as to elongation, had a hard time of it to reach the tracks ahead, when I forgot they had to serve for those behind. No time was wasted anyway, and, freed from the rope at 3:15, we scrambled by any route down the final rocks and debris to the big glacier and back to camp soon after six.

Next morning saw us back on the Freshfield flats, an hour sufficing for the journey down, and the tents were pitched beside Forbes Creek at a short distance from our previous location. A lazy, hazy afternoon was succeeded by a marvellous sunset. Sharply defined against a brilliant background of the richest, deepest blue, Howse Peak and the Pyramid stood out dead white upon the eastern side. Westward, above the sombre wooded canyon, threaded by the cold, dancing waters of the creek, Mt. Forbes reared its huge crest, jet black against a gorgeous sky, where tints of sea green merged in pale and richer blue, the whole ethereal expanse embossed with fleecy, flying clouds of every hue conceivable, from darker slate to jade, pale sulphur deepening to orange, delicate pink to vivid crimson, as the dying rays flashed their "Good night" to our rest-seeking world: there, in the centre of this grand illumination, that seemed to have been kindled for its glorious display, the mighty mountain

> "Like a monarch stands,
> Crowned with a single star."

Five days later seven mortals had the impertinence to set their feet upon this regal summit, but the king demands a separate chapter for the narrative of this adventure, and we must pass down the Middle Fork again and seek the northern affluent. The 12th of August saw our little party bid farewell to our late associates and turn its back upon Howse Pass and its beyond. The pass used to be a highway for the Indians, but fires and other deadly elements have wrought havoc in the valley of the Blaeberry, and it is now impassable for horses and would require a vast amount of labour to clear a way to the Columbia. Beyond the base of Mt. Habel, however, Peyto, when in charge of Professor Collie's outfit in 1897, managed to find a rough and terrifically steep way up the southern barrier and led his horses over Baker Pass in triumph to the Amiskwi Valley and thus down to Field.

Twice we ascended the North Fork, once on either bank and had considerable work to get the trail through to the western side. The regular road is good, but the valley is by far the most monotonous and least impressive of the three Forks that go to form the North Saskatchewan. The frowning ramparts of Mt. Wilson are imposing, but 15 miles of them pall eventually upon the most enthusiastic, and, except for a fine cascade, high up in a deeply recessed upper gorge, and a few glimpses up the lateral valleys on the other side, there is but little to attract. The river is swift and of considerable volume, with a picturesque fall about a mile above its mouth, and until the West Branch is reached fording is possible at only one or two places and difficult even at the height of summer. Cottonwood trees, willows and alders mingle with the evergreens, and the thick bark of the cottonwoods under the skilful jackknives of Jim and Fred was transformed into a variety of beautifully carved book-rests, frames and other souvenir articles both useful and ornamental.

Our first approach was under somewhat gloomy conditions; a heavy pall of clouds oppressed the mountaintops, damp and mist exuded everywhere, the trees and bushes reeked with moisture, and as the exigencies of the route drove us frequently from the open ground beside the swirling river and cutbanks forced detours through masses of fallen timber and into the green forests and thickets of tall willows, saturated with the rain of a stormy night, there were additional features of discomfort besides the usual monotony of the scene. Four hours that day and two on the next brought us to the mouth of what is called the West Branch of the North Fork. To me it seemed a larger stream than the so-called main river, besides being undoubtedly of greater length and I am of opinion that it is the true North Fork, and that the supposed main stream is in reality the tributary, though, as the latter occupies the direct valley while the other comes in at a right angle, there is something in favour of the existing nomenclature.[47]

The weather had again been dull with heavy clouds, but as we proceeded on our way and neared the valley from the west, whither we were bound and where the bulk of our season's work was centred, far away at its head appeared a gleam of light, the only bright spot in the whole expanse of gloom, and I hailed it at once as an omen of success. Another amusing augury, pointing to a safe and successful issue to our climbing plans, in spite of the undesirable two-on-a-rope conditions, lay in the happy and convincing fact that Kaufmann's and my initials formed the cipher "o.k.," and who could dream of misadventure in the face of that?

Fording the river, we camped in a pleasant spot upon a knoll some 30 feet above the flats, in the angle between the two streams. Our explorations in this vicinity lay entirely amongst the peaks and passes reached from the West Branch, and a separate chapter must be devoted to this region. The other valley has been a highway for many a long year to the headwaters of the Athabasca River. The earliest published record, however, seems to be that of Mr. Wilcox, who, in 1895, outfitted by Tom Wilson, with Tom Lusk and Fred Stephens as packers, ascended to the pass that now bears his name, on his way to Fortress Lake. There was a trail, but it was ancient and much blocked, and the difficulties of the narrow valley were innumerable.

It is deeply set between high precipices and it was necessary to cross and recross the river very frequently. Near the head the scenery becomes very grand, waterfalls are numerous, lofty peaks come into view, and finally, the long, straight tongue of the Saskatchewan Glacier, which supplies the greater part of the river's source, opens out to the west, pointing the way to the enormous Columbia icefield (the extent of which, however, was not dreamt of for three years to come), and dominated by the grand mass of Athabasca Peak.

In 1898 Professor Collie and Messrs. Stutfield and Woolley journeyed thither in a search after the truth concerning the mysterious altitudes of Mt. Hooker and Mt. Brown. From a camp just on the northern side of Wilcox Pass, an ascent of the great peak (Mt. Athabasca) was accomplished by Professor Collie and Mr. Woolley, while Mr. Stutfield ranged the eastern hills in a triumphantly successful hunt for big game, as the larder had shown that the party stood in imminent danger of starvation. A late start and subsequent delay occasioned by the pursuit and bagging of a brace of ptarmigan by stone-throw militated against the interests of the climbing party, but they had a splendid time. First a small glacier was traversed, then a rotten ridge so disagreeable that they crossed to the western glacier and worked their way up into a great basin just beneath the summit. An ice-slope next had to be ascended to the northeastern ridge, and this was rapidly accomplished. Here, writes Professor Collie,[48] "a very narrow and steep ice arête lay before us. At first was sufficient snow to enable us to ascend by kicking steps, but soon Woolley was hard at work with the axe. For two hours almost without intermission was he cutting, and the ridge was almost too steep to allow us to change places. Finally we arrived at a small platform just underneath the precipitous rocks that guard the summit, only to find that they were perpendicular. By carefully skirting round their base to the right a narrow chimney was discovered. It was our last chance: either it had to be climbed, or we should return beaten. Owing to the excessively broken state of the limestone rock, produced probably by the great extremes of heat and cold, the climbing was not difficult; but there were many loose rocks that to avoid needed exceeding care. With much caution bit by bit we managed to climb up this narrow chimney, expecting to come out within easy reach of the summit; but, as we gained the ridge, a wall of overhanging rock 15 feet high seemed to bar further progress. After what we had gone through down below, 15 feet, even though it did overhang, was not going to keep us from the top. How it was surmounted I have forgotten, but, I remember how we saw the summit almost within a stone's throw of us, and how at 5:15 P.M. we stepped onto it. By mercurial barometer its height is 11,900 feet."

This was the greatest height attained up to that date in Canada, and, in addition to that proud accomplishment, they had the boundless satisfaction of obtaining a view of new peaks and new glaciers such as has never greeted any other climbers in that land of wondrous mountain scenes.[49]

Descending in haste by the northwest arête, in ever deepening shadow, they reached the more or less level ice just as the sunset hues were fading from the sky and, after stumbling along stony slopes and struggling through muskegs, fallen trunks and tangled brushwood finally got back to camp at 11 o'clock, to find that Mr. Stutfield had been equally successful in his quest and had secured three splendid Bighorn sheep, not to mention several ptarmigan.

On our return from the West Branch, Kaufmann and I rounded off our season's work by the traverse of Mt. Wilson from end to end, whilst our camp outfit followed the trail to the mouth of the North Fork. This long-cherished scheme of mine gave me the opportunity to look into all the tributary valleys on the west side of the valley below the West Branch, especially an interesting one studded with lakes, which had been observed for the first time on the occasion of our ascent of Mt. Lyell.

Another desire was to ascertain the contour of the mountain and the configuration of the country to the east, besides getting observations of the long line of Divide peaks from a new angle.

Starting on the 26th of August, at 4:45, from an old Indian camping ground at the foot of Pinto Pass, an hour's walk down the valley of the North Fork brought us to the outlet of a narrow and lofty valley north of the massif of Mt. Wilson. A steep scramble of 1,000 feet, along the line of a barely indicated Indian trail of some antiquity, led to the upland vale, whose slopes, jewelled with quite an array of flowers even at that late date, were traversed to the foot of a fine waterfall that leaps from the crest of a transverse wall of rock some 300 feet in height. Crossing to the left bank (a very troublesome job), we climbed the barrier, traversed a barren valley, and ascended a long ridge running northeast from the northern peak of the mountain, following in the wake of a disturbed he-goat. When high up we discovered that this route was not so advantageous as had at first sight appeared, and we were confronted by the alternatives of having to return, and double the end of the arête, or find a way down the almost vertical cliffs to the long glacier on the farther side. A sporting little climb resulted from the adoption of the latter method, the 300 feet occupying 50 minutes. Gaining the glacier at 11:15, it was ascended to its head, between Mt. Wilson proper and the northern peak, and a grand view towards Mt. Lyell opened out as we stood above a tremendous gorge, walled in precipitously on either side. A traverse on snow and debris led to the northeast ridge of our mountain, and, keeping along its crest, an easy task on firm, hard snow, at 2 P M we reached the summit, 11,000 feet above the sea.

On it we built our first cairn of the season! No other peak of the ten big ones climbed that summer, except one ascended in the dark, had stones upon its top The view was one of the most delightful of the year. Besides the new country now displayed towards the north and east, the panorama furnished a complete résumé of our entire trip, and no other mountain could have offered so perfect an ideal for a consummation of the summer's mountaineering. Mt. Temple, in the far distant south, marked our starting-point at Laggan; then Bow Pass led to the long, narrow trench of the South Fork, and the eye followed up the Middle Fork to Glacier Lake and Kaufmann Peak, Mt. Freshfield and magnificent Mt. Forbes; the North Fork, glistening at our feet, 6,000 feet below, was traced mile by mile to its farthest source at the head of West Branch Valley, hemmed in by Mts. Lyell, Alexandra, Consolation, Turret, Bryce and finally Columbia.

What memories those peaks and passes, streams and valleys, conjured up! Toils and fatigues, dangers and difficulties, certainly; but oh, what crowning joys and satisfying conquests. A thousand times worthwhile to have fought with Nature's forces in their strongest holds, even had Nature proved victorious. But victory was ours. Those proud crests had yielded to the skill, training and experience of man, and from their matchless vantage grounds secrets of Nature, hidden for centuries, had been revealed; and the vast sea of mountains, in all their majesty of might, the attendant valleys filled with treasures of most perfect beauty, glacier and forest depth, sparkling stream and flower-decked glade, have graven with imperishable strokes upon my memory a record that will be a never-ceasing joy through life.

A descent over soft snow and a fine piece of rock work, undertaken to avoid the dangers of an abominably crevassed and thickly covered glacier, terminated in our arrival at a sharp little nick in the otherwise impregnable southern wall at half-past four, almost two hours from the summit. Another half-hour was occupied by a most welcome lunch, and then we romped down a steep gully of scree and grassy slopes (2,500 feet in 25 minutes), from which point a tedious tramp ensued, through tall grass and underbrush, forests and dense thickets, all strewn with fallen logs, both large and small, burnt and decayed, till our pleasant camp on the banks of the Saskatchewan was reached at half-past six.

Next day the swim across the big river was accomplished without any of the trouble that marked our first essay, and two days later we crossed Bow Pass and bade farewell to the enchanting region of the headwaters of the North Saskatchewan.

CHAPTER XII

MOUNT FORBES

FOR 47 YEARS MT. FORBES has borne the reputation of being one of the grandest and most lofty peaks of the Canadian Rockies, and though in our latter day it has been necessary for us to reduce the number of prosaic feet above sea level which had during all these years been ascribed to it, yet nothing can reduce its claim to admiration and respect. It still remains the monarch of the region, where it rears its splendid forehead far into the skies, more than 1,000 feet above its neighbours, and without a rival save Mt. Columbia, 30 miles away, and far Mt. Robson, 60 miles beyond.

This magnificent three-sided pyramid rises from a mass of mighty spurs and buttresses, with narrow ridges and stupendous cliffs. The splendid monolith, combining (like Mt. Assiniboine, which it in many ways conspicuously resembles) the appearance of the Dent Blanche and the Matterhorn, was named by Dr. Hector in 1858, and has always evoked the admiration of all who have had the privilege of seeing it from far or near. To the mountaineer it is particularly fascinating, offering an absolutely first-class problem in rock work, and the great desire of both Professor Collie and myself to try conclusions with it in the year 1902 led us to arrange in London a meeting at the base of the great mountain in the latter portion of July.

Professor Collie was no stranger to its neighbourhood. In 1897, with Peter Sarbach, he ascended to the shoulder, but heavy rain drove them back when little beyond timberline, having barely seen the peak itself, enveloped as it was in a dense shroud of mist. So it remained virtually untouched and unexplored. On the day following our return from the Freshfield region the weather was so exquisite, that, to utilize its perfection to the best advantage, we determined to ascend a lofty ridge opposite our camp, and spend our time in prospecting Mt. Forbes, in preparation for the serious climb that lay before us, that we might study at close quarters its approaches and its character; and, besides reconnoitring the peak itself, examine the topography of the spurs and valleys on the eastern side of the massif.

Our men were all busy labouring in the forest, hewing out a trail through the thick timber that clothes the valley leading to the mountain's base, and it was well on in the morning before we set out leisurely. As with the "ten little niggers," [sic] events combined to thin our numbers by degrees. The first episode was more amusing than tragic. A swift, icy stream, three or four feet in depth and rushing turbulently along, intervened between us and our goal. A tree had been felled across it to form a bridge,—the customary practice in these parts,—but it was rather slim and very slippery, and we were not Blondins by any means. Two members of the party solved the problem by getting astride the trunk, hooking their toes upon it to keep them out of the swirling water only a few inches below; then they worked their passage to the other side with much labour and not to the conspicuous improvement of certain articles of apparel, but greatly to the entertainment of the rest of us, who, however, did not feel equal to a more upright course of procedure. A happy thought suddenly struck an ingenious mind, and a long pole was obtained, one end planted firmly in the shingle, the other gripped by the performer; this acting as a support, we could maintain our equilibrium fairly well as far as about the middle of the bridge; its length then gave out, but a few hasty, wobbling steps effected the transit without catastrophe, and in turn we gave a gratuitous and entertaining exhibition on the tightrope. But one still remained unwilling. He had a precious rifle and no wish for a bath for it, however little he might mind it for himself; the chances *per contra* loomed too large, and thus it happened that, when the biggest herd of goats we ever saw was strolling about the mountainside within easy range of the other six, the sportsman par excellence of the party and the only one who thought of bringing a rifle was far away. Which was so much better for our friends the goats.

Our course now lay through a fragrant forest of spruce, balsam and pine. The going was pretty easy: fallen trunks were few; the undergrowth comparatively light; the trees were not too densely packed together; and a slight breeze tempered the heat of the cloudless morning. Ascending gently over the mossy turf spangled with myriads of white, starry blossoms, we soon struck more sharply upward along a swathe of open ground, cut by a snowslide from the lofty cliffs overhead. A rich carpet of brilliant flowers lay outspread beneath our feet, the gorgeous scarlet of the painter's brush particularly resplendent. On either side of this flower-strewn aisle the tall, straight stems and waving, feathery boughs of fir and pine were ranged majestically; up the steeps in front rocky bands of limestone cropped out between the masses of green foliage and many-tinted blossoms; and, far above, a rampart of dark cliffs crowned the upland slopes, outlined like steel against the radiant blue of the summer sky.

After a brief halt midway, each followed his own devices in the line of ascent: some fast, some slow; one this way and another that; and soon I found myself alone, passing through the sparse, stunted trees that verge the timber limit, and approaching a wide, verdant upland, where heather, red and white, dryas, anemones, yellow mountain lilies, painter's-brush of many hues, great purple and yellow asters, and masses of exquisite forget-me-nots, with countless less conspicuous flowers, grew in wild profusion. Behind, across the deep valley, over whose dark abyss a golden eagle hovered lazily, its plumage radiant in the clear sunlight, stood a shapely snow-crowned peak, encircling a beautiful, pure glacier; farther away a host of mountains girdled the horizon, and in the purple depths the various streams that form the headwaters of the North Saskatchewan shimmered in a haze of heat.

Away to the west, the scene was entirely monopolized by the tremendous mass of Mt. Forbes; the precipices facing me across a much-crevassed glacier loomed black and threatening; the abrupt northeast ridge was infinitely steep and broken with rocky needles and sheer buttresses; the south arête was longer and set at a less fearsome angle, and was evidently the most promising, if not the only, line of ascent from the Forbes Valley, but it displayed at least three very awkward cliffs for the ambitious climber to negotiate; rugged spurs stretched out from the main pyramid, holding glaciers deep down in every cleft, and, above all, soft, fleecy clouds floated in the still air, their purity contrasted exquisitely with the brilliancy of the azure sky and the dark gloom of each enshadowed precipice.

To the north the alp sloped steeply to a long and almost level ridge, the bare gray of whose shaley side was broken by frequent large patches of winter snow: on its far side a vertical wall, 1,000 to 1,200 feet in height, crested by overhanging cornices of snow, dropped to a fine glacier, whose mighty fissures opened wide their deep blue caverns immediately below. But the most delightful feature of the scene was the appearance of three herds of Rocky Mountain goats.

A peripatetic group of ten was wandering along the scree above an amphitheatre of rocks, where a small green valley headed. A little to the right another bunch of perhaps a dozen was browsing leisurely on the sparse grass that grows amongst the debris, so scantily that from a short distance its identity is merged in the universal gray of the prevailing shale and boulders. These, too, were trending slowly in the same easterly direction, towards the spot where the main tribe was gathered. Here more than 30 goats were scattered over a small area—goats of all sizes and apparently all ages, from shaggy patriarchs to tiny kids only a few weeks old.

It was a fascinating occupation to watch them through the glass, while waiting for my friends to join me. Here, a little group of mothers, with timid babies nestling close to their protecting sides and trotting spasmodically along when the parents changed their ground; one or two were blissfully engaged in drawing their mid-day meal from the maternal fount; others, somewhat older and more independent, frolicked around in youthful gambols or wandered away a little distance on their own account; and one such, frightened by his too distant solitude, came tearing headlong to his dam in wildest perturbation, leaving a trail of dust and flying stones behind him, and terminating his mad career by a terrific somersault.

The stalwart, full-grown animals strode solemnly along, intent for the most part on the seemingly universal and all-important business of dinner; occasionally halting to throw up their massive heads and stand with noble pose, gazing around them like monarchs surveying the entire world as their domain.

The three groups ere long merged in one strikingly picturesque herd, more than 50 strong, and, following the lead of a magnificent he-goat with splendid shaggy limbs and a huge pair of horns, moved quietly towards the topmost ridge. No order was observed, but, straggling up the slope by twos and threes, they shortly disappeared behind a projecting shoulder of the mountainside.

Three or four hours later, after a long reconnaissance towards Mt. Forbes and thence along the summit of the ridge for a considerable distance, I was descending over the same flower-decked alp to rejoin the other members of the party, who had not made so long a round, when, lifting my eyes to the great cliffs continuing the ridge towards the east, my steps were suddenly arrested by a wonderful sight. Above the rugged walls, now blushing with a softer glow as the setting sun intimated his early disappearance behind the near mountain ranges in the west, a long line of my acquaintances were standing immovable upon the topmost heights, in sharpest outline against the pale blue of the evening sky. I counted them as they paused there like statues, each limb and head clearly defined in the brilliant light. There were 27 in all, almost everyone full-grown, apparently engaged in watching eagerly, with interest equal to my own, from the security of their castled refuge, the human intruders who had ventured thus unbidden into their ancestral solitudes. There I left them, long, I trust, to enjoy, immune from accident, starvation or the deadly rifle, the active life, carefree amid these mountain fastnesses, for which they were created and in which they surely have a right to live in peace.

Two days later our trail was ready, and on a bright morning, after a vivid display of lightning overnight and some heavy rain, our cavalcade was once more set in motion for the great attempt upon Mt. Forbes. Crossing the creek, we plunged into the forest and made our way up the left bank. Side streams with steep and rugged banks cut across our route, and Fred Stephens' warning that the horses would have to stand occasionally on their heads was wonderfully near a literal accomplishment; but though the trail was rough and showed evidences of tremendous axe work, all went well and in less than two hours we emerged at a broad open space cleared in some bygone year by a mighty avalanche, that crossed the stream, bearing its debris of wrecked timber some distance up the opposing slope, and piled it in a huge bulwark against the sturdy trunks of their more fortunate brethren. Our tents were pitched in the green bosom of the narrow valley, which heads right under the frowning precipices of the great peak. Huge firs encircled the open grassy meadow, an eddying glacier stream sparkled amongst the boulders and bushes that line its course, and nearly 7,000 feet above towered the lofty summit.

The forests here were more luxuriant than are usually found upon the eastern slopes of the Divide. The rainfall round the Forbes and Freshfield Groups appears to be heavier, and the mossy carpet, dense undergrowth and larger timber approximated more closely to the conditions on the Pacific side. I also came across more flowers in the Forbes Creek valley than anywhere else in all my wanderings, both in variety and luxuriant abundance. On the high "Golden Eagle" alp, the shoulder of Mt. Forbes, and, above all, at the upper end below Bush Pass, the masses of rich, variegated colouring more nearly resembled a cultivated nursery garden than a wild mountainside.

The afternoon was showery again and not much exercise was taken. Off days and half days nevertheless have their value, besides giving often a much-needed rest. They afford opportunity for writing up notes and making calculations; laundry work has to be attended to occasionally, and the demands upon the needle are numerous The sharp, serrated edges of the limestone crags, the wicked spikes with which the pines are armed, the ambushed broken limbs of fallen logs, besides the ordinary wear and tear, are hard on clothing, and the long tramps test the endurance even of home-knitted Scotch yarn stockings.

A cold night was a good omen, a quarter of an inch of ice forming in the buckets. Bright sun and masses of exquisite cumulus clouds gleamed overhead, as at 2 P.M. our party moved out of camp to bivouac at timberline on the shoulder of Mt. Forbes, the climbers being reinforced by Stephens and Robson, who kindly came along to help us with our impedimenta of blankets and two days' provisions. All nature was at its loveliest (except for a slightly undue supply of heat, mosquitoes and horseflies), and the weather promised the very best for our success, as the long string of hopeful but perspiring mortals threaded its way under heavy burdens through trackless wastes of forest trees and undergrowth up the steep flanks of the huge outlying buttress of our mountain. We got separated into several sections early in the march, and the subdivision to which I belonged had an amusing time crossing an ancient log that spanned a deep ravine above a raging torrent and this precarious means of transit called for a good head and steady foot to achieve a dignified passage in an upright position. We arrived first, however, and found a charming spot to bivouac, where a warm and comfortable night was spent. Right opposite the camp was the grand snow peak conspicuous across the valley from the alp of our reconnaissance, and, as it was the Coronation Day of King Edward and Queen Alexandra, we gave it the name of "Coronation Peak."

Next morning, the 10th of August, we were astir by three o'clock, and started on our climb shortly before half past four A long and narrow ridge projects to the southwest from the snow-crowned summit of Mt. Forbes, rough and jagged throughout almost its entire length It was of the customary disintegrated limestone of the Canadian Rockies and broken near the top by three formidable cliffs, which from a distance appeared quite inaccessible and made the prospect of a successful ascent extremely doubtful But the more numerous and serious the difficulties, the greater the attraction for the true mountaineer, and the greater the satisfaction if skill and patience can surmount the obstacles and win a way to the desired goal.

The earlier approaches to this ridge were over green slopes carpeted with flowers. These soon gave place to barren wastes of debris, and a tiresome pull ensued over its sliding scree until the rocks came to our relief, and a more rapid and agreeable progress was possible. Then a long stretch of snow-covered glacier was reached, sweeping from the crest of the arête to an icy basin just above our bivouac. Up to this point we had proceeded leisurely and in loose order, while keeping within hail of one another. Now the rope became necessary as the more serious work commenced, requiring caution, discipline and order. We tied up in two parties, Christian, Mr. Weed and I leading, and the remaining quartet, headed by Hans, forming the second contingent. The snow was firm after the frosts of night, and all was plain sailing except for a few crevasses that had to be turned; so in less than half an hour we were again on rocks, making our way up loose, angular stones and easy ledges to the ridge, which was to form our general line of ascent thenceforward to the summit.

A narrow ridge it was, too, with frequent precipices on one or both sides, which increased in steepness with their altitude, until the sheer black ramparts fell almost vertically to the distant glaciers that swept their bases. From a distance there had been little hint of anything but quick and simple progress up the first part of the arête, but closer acquaintance revealed the existence of a more troublesome state of affairs than we had anticipated. The ridge was very jagged, and the cliffs steeper and smoother than they had appeared to be. The substance, being of friable limestone, disintegrated and eroded by the alternate influence of heat and frost, was weathered, loose, and treacherous in the extreme. Sometimes we were clambering up the broken, indented rocks right on the skyline; at others, forced to make excursions onto the eastern face, a ledge of varying size but never of striking width would be our pathway for a short distance, overlooking a sharp descent of rock and snow; patches of hardened snow or loosened scree occasionally took the place of ledges as we worked along from gully to gully in the scored face of a succession of escarpments, and by their means pursued an ever upward course. These gullies furnished many a disagreeable experience for the unfortunate hinder man. Most of them seemed to be a natural track for all the loose stones and debris from the rocks above. Small fragments rested on every available projection, and had to be dislodged or came down of their own accord as the leader scrambled up. The rotten walls were studded with insecure excrescences, a majority of which failed to stand the strain when tested by the guide, and broke away beneath his foot or in his hand. The last man's lot is, therefore, not a happy one. He has to bear with meekness all the hail of debris, often sharp and weighty, and does not have the satisfaction of kicking down his share upon the head of someone else.

Under a raking fire these ramparts had to be stormed in turn, but scaled they were at last without serious damage, and by ten o'clock we stood upon a minor elevation on the arête (compared by Professor Collie to the Pic Tyndall on the Matterhorn, and corresponding to the "Lost Peak" on Mt. Assiniboine), at an altitude of about 10,800 feet, and separated from the main peak by a slight depression. Meanwhile a second breakfast had been done ample justice to, sheltered from the keen and blustering wind a little way below the topmost edge, where we spent a pleasant hour seated on blocks of quartzite in our lofty eyrie above the precipices of the eastern face.

From the detached pinnacle we scanned with intense interest and much anxiety the cliffs upon the farther side of the small gap. They were the crux of the whole enterprise. Our observations of the mountain had revealed three formidable obstacles, barring the approach by this southwestern route, in the shape of three very upright cliffs, two close together just beyond our present situation, and the third still higher and not far from the actual summit. Our powerful field glasses had left the problem still uncertain. Undoubtedly no possibility existed of escaping them, for the wall on either side rose sheer and the advance was restricted practically to the ridge itself. The fate of the expedition hung on the condition of the rocks. Provided there were a few excrescences firm enough to rely upon and not too far apart, or even roughnesses sufficient to supply friction in the most critical and awkward stages, and thus aid the struggling climber when more desirable assistance failed, we believed that the steepness would be no fatal hindrance. But for these details the glasses proved inadequate at such a distance. Now we stood face to face with the two lower cliffs, and our eager eyes examined foot by foot the smooth, straight battlements. The weathering of the face, some tiny transverse cracks and a tiny cleft or two gave ground for hope, and our spirits rose accordingly. With such a fine rock-climber as Christian Kaufmann to lead the way, if there were any possibility of a human being scaling those heights, our success was, I felt confident, assured. But it was going to be no child's play to gain the lofty eminence that made our necks ache as we looked so straight up to its dizzy pinnacles, whilst on either side the black, rough precipices, seamed by gullies filled with glassy ice or hardened snow, fell away abruptly to the white glaciers thousands of feet below.

Unfortunately our supply of ropes was rather inadequate for such work as here confronted us. Our trio possessed a 60-foot length, and the other party had 80 feet among the four, neither of them nearly long enough for comfort, considering the difficulty of the rocks. For ordinary purposes, 15 or 18 feet is the allotted distance between each pair of climbers, but on tremendous cliffs like those of Mt. Forbes, with a scarcity of proper holds and resting-places, such an allowance is most insufficient. Seldom within so short a space can solid and large enough footholds be found to enable the leader to stand secure and render any needful assistance to the man behind, or be in a position to hold him or to prevent himself being jerked down also should a slip occur. With 30 or 40 feet he could attain some firm location and be able to counteract the effects of any contretemps to the next climber on the rope. In the same way, again, has No. 2 to cling in a precarious position whilst the guide moves upward for another spell. Moreover, the more there are in a direct line, the greater the chance of accident from falling stones.

Three hundred feet or more of cliff had thus to be negotiated, the greater part of it of the most interesting and exciting nature, all nerves at the utmost tension. Not a moment of slackness or cessation of watchfulness and care is possible. Whether himself engaged in climbing onward, or intent upon the progress of a comrade, a keen lookout is constantly imperative, a readiness for any possible emergency, however seemingly unlikely its occurrence may appear, a knowledge and forewarnedness of what to do if that emergency should suddenly arise; these thoughts must dominate one's whole attention. Lives may depend upon the action of a single moment. A second's relaxation on the part of one individual may be fatal to the entire party. The practised forethought that grasps the possible contingency, the quickness of eye that notes the sudden need, the instant application of the proper remedy in the immediate correspondence of hand and foot, may prove the safety of all in time of danger. No true mountaineer takes anything for granted in such a place, except the fact that everything is unreliable, and that he must live in expectation of an accident. To those who climb like this there rarely if ever comes the realization. In mountaineering, as in many other things, to despise is criminal, to relax is dangerous; and it is to those who do not expect an accident that it will come.

In these circumstances, after our trio had embarked upon the climb, Professor Collie detached himself from the other rope, disinterestedly preferring to abandon the ascent rather than increase the risk of his companions by the presence of a fourth member; and he retired to the minor peak to watch our upward progress. When both parties had successfully achieved the apex of the second cliff, Christian and Hans, with their habitual good nature and enthusiasm, responded cordially to my suggestion to go down again and accompany Professor Collie, who deserved more than all the rest the gratification and honour of being the first to conquer Mt. Forbes, since he was the pioneer climber in the region and had already been disappointed, by reason of bad weather, in a previous attempt.

The actual climb was a continuous call to brain and body to exercise their powers and energies to the fullest possible extent. Gymnastics entered largely into the long and varied climb. Sometimes five, six or seven feet up a decent hold is found, and all below is glassy; or perhaps the upper portion overhangs. A pull up then is necessary; or far away a little foot rest may be discovered about the level of the shoulder, and the climber swings across to get a moment's purchase which enables him to plant his other knee upon the tiny rocky shelf that he is gripping tightly with his straining hands. Perhaps a comrade's back, a lusty push or an impromptu step formed by an ice axe held securely by No. 2 is needed to hoist the leader within reach of a specially lofty and difficult ledge or crack, by which he pulls himself up by an acrobatic effort. Another time we find ourselves in a sort of chimney, with one side open, and force our way up largely by pressure against the slippery parallel walls and by the aid of any cracks or protruding fragments that may happen to turn up. Again, we are swarming up a rugged buttress, with arms and legs embracing its opposite sides, hugging it painfully with every portion of the body that can get some grip. Knees and arms cling to the roughened surface when holds for hands and feet are absent, and here, as on many a slab and steeply inclined face of rock, friction affords assistance which is astonishingly valuable. Once we were reduced to progress by the hands alone, on a section of the second cliff, where, on the rapidly descending ridge, precipitous on either side, our bodies spread upon the western slabs of rock, our fingers clutching the sharp knife-edge that formed the sky-line, we hang and cling as we work sideways and upward foot by foot until at last our feet again find somewhat of a ledge to stand upon. Traversing, in another place, along a narrow ledge, face inward, rounding a buttress to reach a more accessible piece of the rock face, the art of balancing is brought into play, and this feature is one of the most notable tests of an expert climber The marvellous results obtained with comparative ease and small output of strength and energy by the skilled mountaineer by means of a perfect equipoise are most astounding to the novice; speed, safety and success are the rewards of mastery in balancing.

And it was, upon the face of a stupendous precipice that all this climbing was encountered. There was not much opportunity to enjoy the wonderful effects and striking details suggested by a fleeting glance down the sheer mountainside up which we climbed so tediously. Every attention had to be paid to the work before us, if we desired to escape the risk of a still more fleeting glimpse of these details in a hurried and involuntary descent to the white glaciers that gleamed so suggestively below, apparently so close, but in reality thousands of feet away. Such visions as we got of vertical escarpments, jagged points of broken rock, icy gullies and tremendous drops into the far abyss, were thrilling enough as we clung to the treacherous cliff like flies on the wall of a house.

At length, a strenuous effort landed us on the pinnacle which crowns the upper wall. We stood as it were in mid-air! On two sides, nothingness for many thousand feet; in front, 300 feet of cliff, so steep we wondered how we ever managed to ascend, dropping to the narrow ridge of our approach, that stretched away to the distant forest valley, where our tents were glistening in the sunlight. Beyond was a vast alpine panorama, upon whose countless ranges, with scarcely an exception, we could even then look down. From this sharp rocky apex we passed along a narrow causeway, with a marvellous polished precipice straight below us on the left, and gained a temporary resting-place, where we were joined soon after 12 by Professor Collie and the guides.

A few minutes later we were all once more en route, the pure white, corniced crest right before us, close at hand, and only one remaining problem between us and victory. This was cliff No. 3, the base of which we speedily attained by easy slopes of snow and scree, to find it abominably rotten: loose fragments lay on every available resting-place, and holds were scarce and most unreliable. Though dozens of pieces were hurled into the abysses below, there was still considerable inconvenience from the chance of falling stones. This trouble is, of course, exaggerated on a first ascent. If a dozen parties were to climb Mt. Forbes, each doing its share of clearing away the debris and eliminating the unsubstantial holds, all danger and much of the present difficulty would be removed, and a far more rapid and congenial climb result. Despite the fusillade of falling stones, however, our storming of the fortress proceeded satisfactorily; on the same lines as previously, the final battlement was won.

But on our arrival at its top an unexpected difficulty was encountered, which proved one of the most trying and certainly one of the most hazardous pieces of work in the ascent. A very narrow causeway, perhaps 18 inches wide, between two fine precipices, connected the head of the cliff with the final snowy mass of the summit. It as composed of rock in the last stage of disintegration, topped by a loose agglomeration of strange plaques of stone, from 12 to 20 inches long, two to four in width, and about half an inch in thickness, piled in wild confusion. This was backed by a wall of winter snow, fully as rotten as the rock, ready to shear off at the slightest touch and avalanche in one tremendous leap to the mountain's base. Whether the rock held up the snow or vice versa, or the support was mutual, seemed a moot point, both looked so frail and tottering. A violent wind, moreover, which had been a supplementary difficulty to contend with all the morning caused the entire place to quiver and did not aid our equilibrium or the stability of this fragile pathway. Happily the distance was not great and Christian warily advanced. The snow one dared not even touch; the rattling stones scarcely allowed of any pressure without sliding underfoot. With catlike tread each balanced step was taken, till he gained a firmer stand upon the farther side, though even there the prospects of an avalanche were not convincingly remote. Then Mr. Weed's turn came, and, as he stepped from the worst place, a huge mass of rock detached itself from the main ridge, and, with a rattling accompaniment of loosened fragments, thundered down the western precipice, leaving a shelving slope of rotten debris even more awkward to traverse than the original narrow and shaky path. However, an elongated stride and a convulsive effort accomplished the most treacherous portion of the undertaking in safety, and, after a little journey along a sharp snow arête and up a steep face of rather doubtful consistency, a few hundred feet of firm and easy snow brought us in triumph to the sharp-pointed summit, about 12,100 feet above the sea.

The wind was boisterous and piercingly cold, and we huddled together, a frigid group, on the exposed white cap that crowns the apex of the lofty pyramid. A heavy cornice overhung the black eastern precipice: on the west, the slopes trended sharply to a grand wall of cliffs; and to the north, the pure white face tilts downward at a tremendous angle to the glaciers and buttresses that overlook the still, dark depths of Glacier Lake. The panorama was magnificent. Our mountaintop, preeminently higher than any of its neighbours, has no peer until Columbia's snowy head rises from the mighty sweep of its grand icefields 30 miles away. In the pure atmosphere, mountains far and near stood forth with clear-cut outline in all directions to the horizon, a full 100 miles distant, and the line of the Continental watershed could be traced for scores of miles, a vast section of its complicated valley system lying map-like at our feet. Deep, wooded ravines intersect the countless broken ranges, whose bold escarpments, battered towers and jagged pinnacles present a splendid contrast to the enormous areas of ice and snow. Such a vision is alone worth far more than all the toil and effort expended in gaining the summit of this peerless natural observatory.

It was one o'clock when we arrived, so we only allowed ourselves a little more than half an hour to enjoy the landscape and attend to photographic requirements. A little Union Jack was then unfurled and planted in the topmost snows, and we made ready to depart. Finding that the snow upon the northern face was in magnificent condition, thanks to its shaded aspect and the icy breeze from that direction, we resolved to return that way, as this plan had the double advantage of avoiding objectionable places on the southwest arête and of enabling us to cross the mountain, acquaint ourselves more thoroughly with its character and environment, and have the interest of an entirely new route exactly opposite in its nature from that of the ascent.

For greater security in case of slips, or footsteps giving way, or possibly a minor avalanche, both parties roped together during the descent. It proved a long and tedious affair. The face was terrifically steep, and steps had to be cut with the ice axe in the hard snow or ice almost the whole way down. After a detour to avoid the cliffs that form one side of a narrow glacial gateway terminating the western ridge of Mt. Forbes, a swift glissade down the steep snow between these portals to the névé on the southern side was quite a luxury; and then came a steady tramp for 40 minutes across the snow beneath the heights of the western wall, sinking frequently well above our ankles, and traversing more than once the hard, rough debris of a recent avalanche. Bearing gently upward we struck the ridge of our approach at its lowest point, and soon after six unroped at the spot where we had tied up nearly 12 hours before. An hour later we straggled back to bivouac and spent a second night in our snug retreat, a very much warmer location, as it proved, than the main camp 2,000 feet below.

Being particularly anxious to get a further observation of the watershed and the headwaters of Bush River, in order to fill in a small hiatus between Mt. Freshfield and Mt. Kaufmann, I suggested a digression to explore Bush Pass next day. This was in line with Professor Collie's topographical desires, and Mr. Weed's energetic interest in all things appertaining to the mountains brought him along too.

After another warm night and a good long rest, it was eight o'clock before we were off, leaving to our obliging friends our share of blankets, etc., which they most kindly carried back to camp. Rounding Mt. Forbes's shoulder, we gradually descended towards the valley bed, first across grassy and flowery alps, where wild geranium was particularly prominent, later through forest, till in an hour we found ourselves on the banks of the main stream, just below its junction with a good-sized tributary. This latter is the outlet of the glacier south of Mt. Forbes, which we had crossed on our return journey after traversing the peak. We had to ford it knee-deep, and then took to the shingle flats, sometimes driven into the water for a short spell to avoid sundry obstacles, and in half an hour of good going arrived at the foot of the pass.

We rested and cooled off for a few minutes under the shelter of an enormous mass of detached rock, its base draped with ferns and mosses, and its crest ornamented by a little spruce growing in a tiny crevice high above. It lies beside the stream, with a picturesque waterfall hard by, and surrounded by a garden of flowers clustered in bewildering profusion and blazing brilliantly with richest colouring. I gathered 32 distinct kinds of flowers during the morning's tramp, without wandering from the direct line of march. The painter's-brush was gorgeous in a variety of shades from yellowish white and palest pink to flaming scarlet, the "flame-flower" of Thoreau, whose

"Scarlet tufts
Are glowing in the green like flakes of fire."

Mingled with these prevailing sunset hues, masses of purple and gold, pure white and vivid blue, combined to form a matchless harmony of colour.

Then upward, over stony slopes and well-packed snow to easy rocks, and the broad summit of the pass was gained. Professor Collie had long hoped to find it practicable for a pack train, but glacier and belts of rock preclude the possibility and, though disappointed in the result, we were able to set at rest the question of the existence of a feasible route for animals between Howse and Thompson Passes, and the matter of timber on the Pacific side in both of these cases is a most formidable obstacle to their use. The pass is about 7,800 feet above the sea, situated just north of the angle where the Divide leaves the circle of the Freshfield horseshoe and trends towards the western offshoot of Mt. Forbes. The valley beyond falls easily to meet the principal source of the South Fork of Bush River, a short distance below the South Fork Glacier.

More than an hour was pleasantly and profitably spent, and then with frequent glissades a rapid descent was made to our "garden rock" in about half an hour; thence by flats and forest, with occasional wading and the traverse of a huge mass of avalanche snow, which had blocked the valley and still lay unmelted right across the river, tunnelled through by the obstructed stream, we made our way to camp at 4 P.M.

CHAPTER XIII

THE MOUNTAINS OF THE
WEST BRANCH

THE HISTORY OF THE WEST Branch is singularly brief. Indians
used it in ancient times as a highway across the Divide, coming up
the North Fork or by way of Pinto Pass from the Cataract Valley
east of Mt. Wilson. In 1896 Mr. Wilcox climbed a spur of Mt.
Saskatchewan, situated in the angle where the streams meet and
obtained a view over half the valley, concluding, most naturally, that
it headed in the glaciers at the foot of Mt. Alexandra, a dozen miles
away. Four years later Mr. C.S. Thompson traversed the valley almost
to its head, and, striking westward, ascended to a pass between Mt.
Bryce and Watchman Peak, leading over to a source of Bush River.
This has been named Thompson Pass.

No ascents were made, and, as the trip was very brief—little
more than a dash to the pass and back,—numerous details still
remained uncertain or unknown, whilst all the peaks were absolutely
new. The regions both to the north and to the south, seen from their
outer edges by Messrs. Collie, Wilcox and Habel, during various
exploratory expeditions, were practically untrodden. The estimates
of enormous altitudes and sundry questions of identification, which
remained unsolved, assured a most interesting geographical problem;
plenty of grand scenery and the probability of first-class climbing
completed a list of inducements to investigate that section which
would appeal to any mountaineer.

The West Branch divides the great block of mountains lying
between the headwaters of the Saskatchewan, Blaeberry, Bush and
Athabasca rivers into two almost exactly equal parts, and strikes into

its very heart. Mt. Lyell, occupying the centre of the mountain mass, seemed the key peak from which to get a comprehensive survey of the entire system; Mt. Columbia, the monarch of the northern section, I hoped to be able to reach from the valley head; several glacier passes and prominent peaks on the Divide appeared to offer opportunities for a thorough acquaintance with the whole line of the watershed, and, supplemented by our projected expeditions to Glacier Lake and the Forbes and Freshfield district, promised to complete the chain of evidence which was wanted to map the range in its entirety.

This ample programme I was fortunately able to carry out successfully. During the trip ten new peaks over 10,000 feet were conquered, almost all of them on the Divide, and four new passes were investigated: the chief questions of identification were set at rest, the position of Mt. Lyell rectified, numerous unknown valleys brought to light, and the matter of altitudes fairly determined. This was the only disappointment of the summer, as from 1,000 to 1,500 feet had to be deducted from the earlier estimates in the case of almost all the higher mountains, the loftiest of which is probably no more than about 12,500 feet, instead of approximating 14,000. Nevertheless they are splendid peaks, and as the valleys are almost uniformly low, especially upon the western side, an abrupt rise of 8,000 feet or more is not uncommon. The structure is, as usual, mainly limestone, extremely friable and wearing into many striking forms.

Our first afternoon was spent in a training climb to the spur of Mt. Saskatchewan, whence Mr. Wilcox had obtained the first glimpse of the valley and its surroundings. The early clouds had lifted and the outlook was hopeful enough to make the prospect of securing some more valuable results than mere exercise quite encouraging. While Kaufmann and I started upward, the others occupied themselves with the no light task of cutting a trail for service on the morrow. Our route lay through the woods and we soon struck a well-marked game trail, which we followed to the timberline, and advanced along the rocky ridge of the outlying spur as far as Mr. Wilcox's cairn, about 8,400 feet above the sea.

The view was most interesting and inspiring—a foretaste of the good things in store for us. The billowy clouds that seemed reluctant to leave the loftier summits eventually lifted, and revealed one by one the peaks that we had come to pit our strength and skill against, besides a host of minor satellites. In the forefront was Mt. Saskatchewan, presenting to us a face absolutely precipitous, great horizontal belts of limestone stretching from end to end in splendid cliffs and its arête and outlying northern spur broken by pinnacles and needles of shattered rock, of quaint, fantastic appearance, some of them 200 or 300 feet at least in height. Across the deep valley impressive walls of the prevailing horizontal strata, crowned with an icy mass of level glacier of immense thickness, curved like a titanic amphitheatre round a huge basin filled with pure white névé from which a crystal stream cascaded to the wooded slopes below. At our feet the tortuous river meandered through the stony flats by a variety of channels, large and small, and we could trace it for several miles as far as a right-angled bend, where three grand glaciers unite at the base of a fine range of peaks; farther to the right the three sharp points of Mt. Bryce loomed dark beneath the luminous masses of lifting clouds, and then the shadowed peak of Mt. Saskatchewan cut off the distant view.

As Mt. Lyell was regarded as the pivot point for topographical research, its whereabouts and character were naturally the first questions that we sought to solve. Previous suspicions concerning the correctness of Mr. Thompson's surmise as to its identity, which had arisen in my mind from a study of his and Dr. Hector's narratives and maps, gave place to serious perplexity when confronted by the physical conditions as they appeared in actual fact. It was impossible to make the Mt. Lyell of the one coincide with the Mt. Lyell of the other. Dr. Hector, who named the peak,[50] saw it from a low elevation to the southeast; Mr. Thompson viewed the range only from the depths of the valley lying to the north, and very naturally selected the most prominent peak in sight as the one to identify with the most prominent as seen from the other side. Hence the trouble. From our vantage point the peak that has for some years been designated as Mt. Lyell by all explorers from the south was clearly recognized, standing a few miles west of Mr. Thompson's peak, from which it is separated by a gabled mountain with considerable gaps on either side. The peak, thus shorn of its imputed name, has been called Mt. Alexandra; it stands conspicuously above the triple-headed glacier already mentioned and dominates the valley as one approaches the great bend. One more objective mountain was thus added to our original programme.

We descended into the valley of the North Fork, returning to camp drenched by the shower baths conferred upon us by the rain-soaked brush. Next morning we started by the newly cut trail through the woods that edge the swamps, which cover the entire valley floor for some little distance above the mouth of the stream. Then for a time we continued along a series of strange, grass-covered causeways that provide a solid road between the river and the swamps 20 feet or more in width; next came long stretches of shingle flats, varied by numerous fordings of the stream, whole or in part, until a convenient camping place was found about a mile below the junction of the waters from the triple glacier and the main stream. The view of the dominating Mt. Alexandra, flanked by forest slopes and bare escarpments, with its central icefall shining in brilliant contrast to the belt of trees into whose depths it plunged, was most entrancing all the way along, gaining in beauty and grandeur as we approached its base.

The afternoon's programme was a repetition of the previous one. A long section of timber lay ahead, and both Jim and Fred went off to make a trail. Christian and I, meanwhile, climbed to the summit of a barren ridge in the angle of the valley about 9,000 feet high, to get a nearer view of the big peaks, conclusive evidence as to the Lyell problem, and a bird's-eye view of the upper portion of the valley, which might help us in our attempt to reach the head in a single day, horses never having been taken farther up, at any rate within the knowledge of any white man. Clouds were again prevalent in certain quarters, but we got splendid visions of Mt. Forbes's pure, sharp pyramid, the triple-headed mass of Mt. Lyell, Mt. Bryce's narrow, three-pointed ridge and the several intervening peaks. Mt. Columbia, the giant of the region, reputed to be 14,000 feet above the sea, and on that account the most interesting summit of them all to reach, remained persistently enveloped till nearly sunset, when, just as we were turning homeward, the white mists rolled away and the great dome appeared in all the golden radiance of the evening glow.

> "Round its breast the rolling clouds are spread;
> Eternal sunshine settles on its head."

It was a most dramatic first appearance, and immediately laid us under its most potent spell and determined us to take the very earliest opportunity of attempting the ascent of its grand slopes.

The good work done by our two axemen enabled us to traverse the thick forest with ease, and in two hours we emerged upon the banks of the river again, having cut off a very lengthy corner, and, right in front, gleamed the snowy summit of Mt. Columbia, dazzlingly bright against an azure sky that fairly rivalled Italy for richness and depth of colouring.

It was a trying march thenceforward. The large boulders on the flats were terribly hard on the horses; the river, swirling along, icy cold and very turbulent, made fording neither easy nor agreeable; the banks narrowed frequently and drove us to the woods, through which our leader piloted us skilfully, albeit a good deal of heavy axe work was demanded from both packers before we finally descended to a broad expanse of rough stones and shingle, where the river broke tumultuously from a deep and rugged canyon, and it was evident that there was no use in trying to take our camping outfit any farther that day. So we pitched our tents just within the border of the trees, in a sheltered, sunny spot, close to a splendid waterfall, which, like a smaller one a few yards distant, sprang from a subterranean channel.

The new camp was inaugurated by a most exciting episode. The packs had just been unloaded and their contents were lying scattered all around; Kaufmann and I were busy putting up one of the tents, and Fred was engaged in preparing a well-earned dinner, when suddenly a crackling sound was heard and I looked up to see the lowest branch of a young balsam fir close to the fire ablaze. In an instant a sheet of flame swept to the topmost bough with a rushing hiss and crackle like a monster rocket, and the entire tree became a blazing pillar of fire. Another and another caught, the lurid flames shot up like fireworks, and thousands of burning spines fell all around in showers. A general rush was made to rescue our belongings from the circle of fiery rain, whilst the prospect of a raging forest fire, devastating this beautiful virgin valley, was imminent. Fortunately the breeze, whose variable eddies blew first this way and then that in our secluded corner, veered just at this crisis and set steadily towards the boulder-covered flat. The flames died down, and the trees, dry as tinder, that circled the three other sides, were spared. Water was close at hand, and soon the smouldering blankets, tents, pack mantles, garments and saddlery were safe from further destruction, although riddled with holes from the fall of blazing sparks and looking rather dilapidated during the remainder of the trip.

All this made dinner rather late, and it was three o'clock before Christian, Jim and I moved on to make a reconnaissance of Mt. Columbia and ascertain if it were possible or advisable to make a higher camp. Our present elevation was almost exactly 6,000 feet and the glacier snout about 500 feet higher. Between the two a spell of trackless forest intervened. Going very fast in half an hour the trees were left behind and we crossed a bare, rocky slope, composed chiefly of terraced ledges, often strewn with stones, descending abruptly to the riverbed. In front is the steep glacier tongue, which forms the source of the West Branch, and is an outlying portion of the great Columbia icefield. We took to the ice at once and climbed the rather steep, dry glacier until snow was reached, when we roped up and continued to ascend as far as the flattened summit of the névé some 8,200 feet above the sea. Here we crossed the Divide, which makes a wide circuit from the eastern spurs of Mt. Bryce, on our left, to the centre of the immense Columbia snowfield, stretching for miles in a northerly direction and then turning sharply westward to Mt. Columbia and the peaks beyond. From a better viewpoint, a few hundred yards down the western slope, we were well pleased to note that nothing but distance and soft snow seemed likely to prevent a successful ascent of the big mountain. The expanse of icefield was enormous, though only a section of it was visible from where we stood. Between us and the peak lay a deep and narrow valley, into the upper part of which three glaciers poured their broken masses: one from our névé; one opposite, descending from the steeps of Mt. Columbia; and the central, passing through a narrow rocky gateway far below the lofty level of the sweeping expanse of ice, which forms the vast reservoir from which the three tongues issue: this snowfield, circling round the valley head, extends for many miles towards the north and east, where numerous other tongues descend to form the sources of various branches of the Saskatchewan and Athabasca Rivers. The stream below us flowed beneath the stupendous walls of Mt. Bryce, which rose precipitously to a narrow, corniced crest. In consequence of this deep valley and its encircling glaciers, a long detour was obviously necessary to reach the far-off base of the peak, and our reconnaissance was invaluable in enabling us to plan a somewhat shorter route than we should otherwise have taken. The height of Mt. Columbia did not seem to approach the former estimates, and the distance more than the altitude evoked forebodings of difficulty in gaining the coveted goal. Only a few minutes could be spared to take in these salient features of the scene, and then we turned and hurried back to camp at racing speed to make our preparations for a very early start next day.

We were now at the southern extremity of that monster ice world discovered by Professor Collie and Mr. Woolley on the occasion of their eventful ascent of Mt. Athabasca, on the eastern verge. Such a discovery cannot be described in other words than those of the discoverer.[51] "The view that lay before us in the evening light was one that does not often fall to the lot of modern mountaineers. A new world was spread at our feet; to the westward stretched a vast icefield probably never before seen by human eye, and surrounded by entirely unknown, unnamed and unclimbed peaks. From its vast expanse of snows the Saskatchewan Glacier takes its rise, and it also supplies the headwaters of the Athabasca; while far away to the west, bending over in those unknown valleys glowing with the evening light, the level snows stretched, to finally melt and flow down more than one channel into the Columbia River, and thence to the Pacific Ocean. Beyond the Saskatchewan Glacier to the southeast, a high peak (which we have named Mt. Saskatchewan) lay between this glacier and the west branch of the North Fork, flat-topped and covered with snow, on its eastern face a precipitous wall of rock. Mt. Lyell and Mt. Forbes could be seen far off in the haze. But it was towards the west and northwest that the chief interest lay. From this great snowfield rose solemnly, like 'lonely sea-stacks in mid-ocean,' two magnificent peaks, which we imagined to be 13,000 or 14,000 feet high, keeping guard over those unknown western fields of ice. One of these, which reminded us of the Finsteraarhorn, we have ventured to name after the Right Honourable James Bryce, the then President of the Alpine Club. A little to the north of this peak, and directly to the west of Peak Athabasca, rose probably the highest summit in this region of the Rocky Mountains. Chisel-shaped at the head, covered with glaciers and snow, it also stood alone, and I at once recognized the great peak I was in search of; moreover, a short distance to the northeast of this mountain, another, almost as high, also flat-topped, but ringed round with sheer precipices, reared its head into the sky above all its fellows. At once I concluded that these might be the two lost mountains, Brown and Hooker."

This hope proved vain (see p. 272), and the peaks were subsequently christened Mt. Columbia and Mt. Alberta. The same climbers, accompanied by Mr. Stutfield, were, a few days later, the first to set foot on this enormous icefield. In the hope of climbing Mt.

Columbia, they bivouacked as far up the right bank of the Athabasca Glacier as possible and were up at 1:30, starting by lantern light. "Dawn broke at length in a dark and lowering sky.[52] The glacier was easy enough to begin with, but gradually the crevasses, growing wider and more numerous, kept us dodging about backwards and forwards without making much progress, until we almost fancied we were threading the ice maze of the Col du Géant. The Athabasca Glacier descends from the upper snowfields in three successive icefalls, the highest one being very much crevassed. Through the mazes of this upper icefall we slowly made our way, zigzagging between the séracs or ice pinnacles, and innumerable crevasses. The latter were unsurpassably fine. Huge chasms of immense depth yawned beneath us on every side, branching out below into mysterious caverns and long, winding grottoes, their sides tinged with that strangely beautiful glacial blue, and festooned with enormous icicles.

"We had been going nearly five hours when we emerged onto the upper glacier, and the wonders of that vast region of snow and ice were unfolded to our view. …We stood on the edge of an immense icefield, bigger than the biggest in Switzerland—that is to say, than the Ewige Schneefeld and the Aletsch Glacier combined—which stretched mile upon mile before us like a rolling snow-covered prairie. … The weather was very sultry, and thunder was in the air; for several hours we tramped steadily on over the almost level icefield, but Mt. Columbia proved to be much further off than it looked. The ascent, we saw, would be quite easy—merely a long snow grind—but we were still a long way even from its base. The weather was very threatening—it was now past noon, and we had already been going nine hours—so we decided to give it up. …

"To the eastward of where we stood, and almost on our way home, rose a great white dome, and we determined to ascend it. After a hot and very tiring climb through snow that broke under our feet at every step, we finally reached the summit at 3:15 P.M. We have named this peak The Dome (11,650 feet). …The Dome is not a very striking mountain in itself, but hydrographically regarded, it is of great interest. Viewed in this light it is the apex, as it were, of the Rocky Mountain Range, for the meltings of its snows descend into three great river systems, flowing into three different oceans— to the Columbia and thence to the Pacific; to Hudson's Bay via the Saskatchewan; and by the Athabasca to the Arctic Ocean."

Mindful of the fate of this expedition we were up at one o'clock, in anticipation of a snow tramp so lengthy as possibly to prove too much for us, although we had the immense advantage of having no obstacles to compare with the intricate icefall which so delayed their progress. The moment it was light enough to thread our way amongst the trees and forest tangle (2:20 A.M., July 19th) we set out. So long a snow tramp, with the certainty of softness and consequently extremely heavy going, was sufficient, without any extra troubles, to make success at the first essay very problematical, and a hot night and troubled sky at dawn did not tend to reassure our minds. In 50 minutes we were enjoying the cooler atmosphere of the glacier after the closeness and toil of the rough forest ascent. For a short time we diverged to some grassy terraces that lined the glacier on our right, but soon returned to the snow-covered ice and made steady progress over its hard surface until we found ourselves trapped in a chaos of huge crevasses, wide chasms and large, crater-like depressions seamed with smaller fissures. So at five we roped. We had by this time attained an altitude of about 8,000 feet and the snow remained firm and good; but covered crevasses were numerous and some bridges we were forced to cross called for the utmost care, and were fragile enough even at this early hour to make us wish for a better way of escape from the maze in which we were entangled. Kaufmann's skill was, as always, equal to every emergency, and we soon crossed the bad bit in the hollow of the glacier and commenced to traverse the less broken surface of the nearer of the two high snowy ridges that tower above the icefall of the central tongue.

From its summit the outlook was fascinating in the extreme, though Mt. Columbia rose before us apparently as far away as ever. We were now almost at the centre of the main plateau of névé, the snowfields sloping gently downward in almost all directions from our elevation of about 10,000 feet. Towards the north, above a sharp depression and beyond a magnificent cirque of rocks and glacier, which separates them from Mt. Columbia, were the Twins, the loftier pure white and its brother darkly impressive; then the immense area of snowfield sweeps upward to Mt. Douglas and the Dome on the one side and dips to the green valleys of the West Branch and the Bush River on the other. Between these two rose the imposing walls of Mt. Bryce, whose appearance is particularly striking from the north, whilst Mts. Athabasca and Saskatchewan stood guard over the long, icy avenue to the headwaters of the North Fork of the Saskatchewan.

Much to our relief we noticed that, by swinging round considerably on the return journey, we could keep above the broken section lately crossed, and avoid by a slight increase of distance its objectionable features; for bridges, delicate at 6 A.M., are apt to be impassable after a day of July sun. Just beyond the ridge, at 7:20, we made a 50-minute halt for breakfast,—well satisfied with our progress so far, but somewhat appalled at the way in which our peak appeared to retrograde as we approached, and at the growing softness of the snow. *Per contra*, the clouds that in the early morning overcast the sky had gradually risen, and after massing rather heavily were dissipating rapidly, and a clear panorama was assured.

Resuming our long snow tramp, we circled round the head of the central western glacier and ascended the farther ridge in ever deepening snow. We were now nearer Mt. Columbia than the point where Professor Collie's party had been obliged to turn back, and being some hours ahead of their time were fairly confident that we should get there, though thus early equally assured of an abnormally lengthy and laborious grind and a probable arrival at our camp well after dark. The going for the next three hours was most monotonous; two or three great undulations in the mighty sea of névé had to be traversed, and we sank deeper and deeper as the hot sun increased in power. At last, however, the final billow was surmounted, the base of the mountain proper was attained, and the steep slopes of the last 2,000 feet were nigh at hand. This gradual rising of the outlying glaciers to the main level of the enormous icefield (about 10,000 feet), and thence still gradually to within 2,000 feet of the actual summit, detracts considerably from the real height and grandeur of the mountain; and from a scenic point of view it is a great mistake to approach Mt. Columbia from the eastern side. The finest aspect is unquestionably from the depths of the low valley of the West Fork of the Athabasca River, whence its great altitude and imposing form are seen to the best advantage. The summit there is 8,000 feet above the river flat, but its appearance is so totally unlike the views that had been obtained previously from other points of the compass, that, when Mr. Habel observed and photographed his mighty "Gamma" from the north, it was hardly deemed possible to establish its identity without further evidence. This it was our endeavour to supply.

Another brief halt was made at 11:30 just below the bergschrund and our food supplies and all the impedimenta we could do without were left there to await our return. The open portion of the schrund was easily circumvented at this season, scarcely any of the winter snow having yet disappeared, and we were soon engaged in pounding up a ladder-like arête of soft snow on a hard, slippery substratum, very likely under the scorching sun to avalanche. It was breathless work. We were both terribly out of condition, it being the first climb of the season, and the long, toilsome trudge, under our packs, on a hot summer day, told on our unaccustomed limbs and lungs. Some 1,200 feet up, the gradient became easier and we moved with less fatigue, until a very sheer and icy escarpment confronted us at the junction of the southeast and southwest ridges. This brought the axe into play; but in a few minutes the crest was gained, and we shook hands in mutual congratulation on the summit of Mt. Columbia.

What the feelings of the Governor-General may be on his appointment I am not prepared to state, but I know we felt a thrill of exultation when we occupied (though for only one short hour) the highest position in the Dominion of Canada! As we anticipated, the previous estimates of altitude were far astray, and I believe that 12,500 feet will prove to be not very far from the true figure. Nevertheless, we appeared to stand well above all the neighbouring mountains, of which the White Twin seemed to be the loftiest, and the next in altitude probably is Mt. Alberta.[53]

The panorama was simply marvellous. The vast extent of these mountaintop views is extremely striking, especially in such untrodden regions as the Canadian Rockies freely offer. The charm of the unknown is mingled with the pleasure of recognition. The climber knows not—no one living knows—what awaits him on the summit of a peak or pass. Bewildering hosts of splendid mountains, many unviewed by anyone before; new valleys with their glaciers and foaming torrents, hitherto undreamt-of tributaries of familiar rivers; the now revealed line of the erratic watershed, laid down by guesswork in the past,—these are some of the more fascinating revelations of the hour. And equally enjoyable, amid this world of the unknown, is the tracing of the journey's course over yonder pass and along those now familiar valleys to the spot far below where the white tents convey to you a fancied congratulation and welcome back again. Pleasant, too, is the recognition of old friends among the near or distant summits, from whence the present vantage ground was perhaps observed and reconnoitred in the hope of the closer acquaintance that has now been consummated. They are friends indeed, and happy is the man who has many such. But, alas, one cannot always linger in the company even of friends, and the sublime landscape, the nerve-restoring air, the quiet of the far-uplifted solitudes, must be reluctantly forsaken till a further opportunity arises of renewing our acquaintance, simultaneously with the addition of yet another intimate to the growing circle.

Thirty miles to the southeast Mt. Forbes (as yet unconquered) towered high above everything in that direction, and alone challenged comparison with our elevation. But at twice that distance to the northwest Mt. Robson showed up grandly and is perhaps the one mountain in the Canadian Rockies that exceeds 13,000 feet.

It was interesting and satisfactory to ascertain beyond a doubt that Mr. Habel's "Gamma," despite its difference in form and character from Professor Collie's Mt. Columbia, was nevertheless the identical mountain, and much of Mr. Habel's description of the western Athabasca and its vicinity was followed step by step as we looked down upon the valleys and the minor heights trodden by him in 1901.

We were 60 miles north of any summit either of us had previously ascended, which lent enormous additional interest to a panorama which, even if familiar in every detail, would be quite entrancing. But, while most of it was entirely new to the eye, the excellent and graphic descriptions and pictures of Messrs. Wilcox, Collie and Habel made almost all the chief features of the landscape recognizable at the first glance. Some old friends in the distant south, fully 80 miles away, Mts. Temple, Goodsir, Hungabee, Dawson and Sir Donald, and more recent acquaintances of the past fortnight, gave one great pleasure to recognize amongst the myriads of peaks of every shape and size. But the crowning feature of the panorama was the survey of the immense area of the Columbia icefield, possibly the largest known outside the arctic regions and their fringe. It covers about 200 square miles, being upwards of 30 miles in length from the head of the névé to the tongue of the Saskatchewan Glacier, protrudes its glacial ramifications to every point of the compass, and occupies the geographical centre of the water system of a quarter of the Continent of North America.

I planted the Union Jack upon the broad, white platform that crowns the summit, the highest point in Canada from which the British flag has ever floated, and set to work with camera, plane-table, sextant and clinometer, until the hour warned us that we must depart. So, at 3:20, we bade a reluctant farewell to the grand peak and its inspiring view, and commenced to retrace our steps. The descent was more agreeable than the tedious ascent, and we plunged gayly down the steep, soft slopes, until in half an hour we stopped again for some refreshment at the point where we had left our things. Twenty minutes later we embarked on the long journey over the interminable expanse of weary snow. Soon we were both thoroughly tired out. At every step we sank in well above the ankles and usually to the knees, and, as we tramped monotonously onward, a sort of mirage formed upon the undulating surface of white snow. Towards evening the fierce heat abated, and the conditions of both air and snow improved as we swung round the wide detour above the lower névé. The glow of sunset flooded peak and glacier with a golden radiance, merging here and there into the most delicate tints of rosy pink and culminating in a blaze of richest crimson glory.

Long before we reached the limit of the snows the sun had disappeared, but a full moon gave ample light until dark belts of cloud came up and partially or entirely obscured its soft, clear rays. At nine o'clock we reached the rocky terraces and could dispense with the rope that had bound us together for 16 hours; and our parched throats rejoiced in an ample drink of pure, cold water.

An hour's traverse of the dry glacier in the half light and then we entered on the worst part of all the day's proceedings To travel through a forest full of undergrowth and strewn with trunks of fallen trees is no easy task in broad daylight, but at night, without a moon, with limbs so tired that they would scarcely obey the orders of the will, it was as tough a job as ever fell to our lot to undertake. Stumbling over stumps and stones, tumbling into holes and gullies, swinging across fallen logs, and fighting through the tangled brush, we dragged our weary way for two awful hours. And then we missed the camp and wound up with a chilly fording of the icy torrent, nearly waist-deep, before the welcome tents appeared in sight, and, shortly after midnight, all our toils were ended. A grand hot supper, prepared in a magically short space of time by our awakened chef set us speedily to rights, and the joy of bed after our 22-hour expedition is quite beyond the powers of any pen to tell.

Sunday was a day of rest, well earned and thoroughly appreciated; and the following day we were fit for almost anything and went up to Thompson Pass to reconnoitre Mt. Bryce and the neighbourhood generally. The snow conditions of Mt. Bryce, combined with threatening weather, caused us to postpone our meditated attack upon that peak, and, instead, we moved our camp down to the bend, where we had such comfortable quarters that we named it "Camp Content."

Clouds hung about the peaks all the following day and climbing was useless; so Christian and I spent our time exploring the triple glacier, which is a splendid one, and for which the name "Trident Glacier" is suggested.[54] About a mile below the ice-tongue the glacial stream unites with the main waters of the West Branch as they emerge from a magnificent canyon, rivalling the famous Gorge of Pfäffers. The lower portion of the glacier is remarkable for the contrast between its eastern and western halves. The former, coming from a narrow gap between Mt. Lyell and the adjacent Gable Peak, descends in a fine icefall to join the sweep of the combined masses of the other two. It is intensely pure and free from debris and carries its characteristics to the end. A lofty ridge of ice, covered with debris, forms the dividing line between it and the western half, seeming to have been forced up into a distinct crest by the pressure of the rival forces. The western part is strewn from end to end with stones both large and small, and has its origin at the head of a lofty glacial pass[55] in the Mt. Bryce direction, and, after a very steep icefall, flows evenly along the base of the ridge that culminates in Mt. Alexandra, the ice almost completely hidden by the accumulation of rubbish. Just as it reaches the steep and broken central glacier it swings round at right angles, and together they descend to meet their confrère from the east. We clambered also up the spur that separates the western glacier from the upper valley of the West Branch, and from its angle obtained fine views of the glaciers and the encircling peaks, with Mt. Columbia appearing beyond the valley head. A route up Mt. Lyell, which faced us to the east, was also prospected, and plans were laid to try that mountain on the morrow.

On the 24th an early start was made, and its important geographical position caused heavy packs to be in order. A 5 × 7 camera with 18 plates, theodolite, plane table, aneroids and other paraphernalia, besides necessary extra garments and provisions, composed two weighty loads for a climb of 7,000 feet. Our camp being for pasture's sake on the wrong side of the river, we had to ford the stream on horseback, and Jim went off at half-past one to hunt the ponies in the dark. By three o'clock we had crossed and were making our way through woods to the flats beyond. On reaching the glacier, we kept along its right bank till we came to the eastern fall, and then faced the steep cliff upon our left, which looked extremely nasty in places, but promised greater rapidity than dodging crevasses and séracs and cutting up the icefall.

Our distended rucksacks hampered us considerably, and in one particular chimney caused each of us in turn to stick so fast that it was only with extreme difficulty that we could extricate ourselves. At the top of the cliff a fight through dense dwarf spruces resulted in our gaining the high lateral moraine close to the head of the icefall. Proceeding along its crest a flatter expanse of glacier opened out and gave us a spell of easier going, and we roped up just below the bergschrund at Mt. Lyell's base. As we threaded our way amongst the crevasses here, an icy wind struck us and gave the first unpleasant intimation that the top would be a somewhat arctic locality, although a clear sky and hot sun reigned above. Breakfast was taken among the rocks a little later, and at 8:30 we assailed the steep slopes of rock and snow, where the axe had to be freely used, till we came to a deep hollow lying sheltered between the central peak and the spurs from the eastern and western summits.

Here we were roasted by the scorching heat of the sun and snow glare as we plunged through knee-deep snow, winding hither and thither to avoid the numerous crevasses. Ascending directly between the central and western peaks the surface grew harder, and, in an icy gale that whirled the sharp, frozen particles of snow in a thick cloud across our path, we gained the col, a lofty one nearly 11,500 feet up, and looked down upon a long and easy slope of névé stretching away before us in unbroken purity almost to the head of Glacier Lake, with the grand, regal pyramid of Mt. Forbes piercing the heavens above.

Then in a chilling hurricane, amidst the driving turmoil of the snow, we hastened up the ridge towards the central peak, which seemed—as it proved later by a few feet—to be the highest of the three.

It was, as I had long anticipated, the key peak of this great mountain group, 70 miles by 25, comprised within the limits of the upper waters of the Athabasca, Bush, Blaeberry and Saskatchewan rivers. Situated almost in the centre of this section, and little short of 12,000 feet in altitude, it forms a natural observatory from which a marvellous outlook is obtained. The eye sweeps round to the far horizon in a circle 150 to 200 miles in diameter, and is caught here and there as it wanders over the bewildering sea of mountains, glaciers and valleys, by the more prominent summits of the distant Selkirks or the far-reaching Rockies. But, first in importance, almost exactly at the opposite poles of vision, the two greatest and grandest of them all command our admiration and attention: Mt. Forbes, a snow-white cone, alone in its supremacy, towering above its fellows in the south; and Mt. Columbia, likewise pure and preeminent, but surrounded by an entourage of peaks of marked distinction,—the Twins, Alberta, Athabasca, Bryce and others,—that rise above or almost to the height of 12,000 feet. Although Mt. Robson, still farther northward, may surpass in altitude any of these summits, yet the general system there is far less lofty and indubitably of far less geographical distinction than this region, which contains the greatest aggregate of mighty peaks and sweeping icefields in the Canadian Rockies, yet, strange to say, remains without a special name.

An interesting feature was the discovery of the extent of one of the western tributaries of the North Fork, hitherto mapped as short and of very minor rank. It now appeared as a deep enshadowed trough, jewelled with a host of little lakes, and fed by a considerable glacier which descends apparently from Mt. Lyell's eastern peak, between two splendid walls of rock that sever it from the great Lyell Glacier on the south and the West Branch Valley on the other side. This valley has been named the "Valley of Lakes."

In spite of the keen and violent wind and a temperature 20 degrees below the freezing point, it was necessary to try to vindicate the bringing of the big camera and transit to the top. The snow was soft, and the tripod had to be sunk almost to the head to get any pretence of steadiness. Even then so great was the vibration that only a rapid exposure could be made, and when it came to the turn of the theodolite, the acme of tribulation was experienced. Prone upon the snow, with fingers numbed, I endeavoured time after time to fix the quivering telescope upon the apex of the desired mountain and turn the ice-cold screws to a true adjustment; but with all one's trying the wind and cold had certainly the upper hand, and I should be very loath to stake my reputation for accuracy on the results obtained upon the summit of Mt. Lyell. For three mortal hours these trials of an amateur attempt at scientific work were thus prolonged, considerably aggravated by the knowledge that Christian had dug himself a cozy shelter in the snow at the southern edge, and was comfortably reposing in his sunny niche, where not a breath of wind disturbed his peace.

At last my chilly task was over, and at 2:15 we raced down the hard slopes, trudged more carefully and laboriously across the crevassed hollow, crept cautiously down the steps which had to be cut in the steeps below, and, after a much-needed lunch, a quick glissade landed us on the level glacier. Traversing the moraine, we descended the steep cliff by a varied route, which turned out more difficult than the way we were avoiding, and finally arrived in sight of camp at half-past seven, as thoroughly satisfied as we were tired. Our shouts were answered speedily by Jim, who brought our horses over for us, and in a very few minutes we were once more in "Camp Content," enjoying a good supper round the blazing fire and more content than ever.

The next three weeks were spent in carrying out my plan for joining forces with Professor Collie and his companions, and on August 10th we were back at "Camp Content." Two wet days were spent in exploring the immediate neighbourhood, including the magnificent gorge of the West Branch, a splendid deep and very narrow flume through which the little river foams and thunders, its waters frequently hidden from view even from the extreme verge of the cliffs, owing to the worn caves and hollows left in the winding walls by the action of the harassed current that has cleft its way in the long centuries through the barrier of solid rock. Then commenced the last week of mountain work.

I had three objects in view for my next expedition—most ambitious programme: first, to ascend Mt. Alexandra; then to investigate the pass at the head of the western glacier; and, finally, to make a way thence to Thompson Pass: thus exploring the whole section between Mt. Alexandra and Mt. Bryce. To this end, I burned my boats and sent the outfit to the Columbia camp whilst Kaufmann and I set out at 6 A.M. on the 19th in the hope of achieving at least two of these projects and gaining the shelter of the camp ere nightfall. ·

The horses were again requisitioned to cross the river, which had completely changed its course during our absence, and we made good time to the glacier. Taking our way up the centre, we swung round to the western affluent, which was covered with debris, amongst which we picked up numbers of iron cubes, some of considerable size. A noteworthy incident was the discovery of a large cascade almost in the middle of the glacier. A turbulent stream flowed far across its undulating surface in a deep-worn channel, till it pitched headlong into a huge circular chasm and disappeared beneath the solid ice, fully 60 feet in thickness, continuing its hidden course till it emerged into the light once more three miles farther down.

Our desire was to attempt the peak by the northwest arête. Previous observation showed that probably three sides were inaccessible, but we hoped that a closer inspection might reveal a way to escape the difficulties of the sheer or overhanging cliffs of the skyline, and save the long detour required to reach the easy but most distant side. So we intended to try the long arête that stretches westward from the secondary peak, an almost exact duplicate of the larger one. This could probably in ordinary years be gained directly from the glacier by scaling the cliffs beyond the precipices in the angle of the west and central glaciers; but above these extended a cornice two or three miles long, so large and seemingly unbroken, that, with our camp removed, we did not deem it worthwhile to risk the chance of failing to get through it, and therefore determined to continue by the much longer glacier route.

The icefall, which is extremely sheer and broken, forced us to the rocks on the north side, and they were so awkward in places that the rope was put on as a precaution. Eighty minutes' scramble took us high enough to try the ice again, and after skilful turning and twisting among the large and numerous crevasses, crossing several startling bridges, a safer but softer part was reached, and a steep and rather disagreeable finish brought us to the narrow glacial pass at 11 o'clock, about 10,000 feet above sea-level.

A lofty ridge separated us from Thompson Pass and the valley running from it to the west; in front, a glacier descended into a tributary valley, with a conspicuous unnamed mountain in the background. On our left rose the arête parallel to the glacier of our approach, and after lunch we commenced work in that direction. Steep at first, it soon became comparatively easy in gradient, and we kept mainly to the skyline; some short and interesting bits of rock work gave variety, and the universal looseness of the structure and occasional perpendicular drops of many hundred feet demanded caution, but we ascended rapidly, traversed several low eminences on the ridge and in an hour and a half reached the culminating point west of Mt. Alexandra and its miniature. This was over 11,000 feet in altitude and commanded a fine prospect.

But the chief interest lay in the peaks ahead. The wet weather of the past few days had left fresh snow upon the rocks, and many a glassy film and slope of ice made things look troublesome. But the secondary peak, which would have to be traversed first, appeared practicable. Most formidable, however, was the main ridge of the larger mountain. The actual arête was perfectly impossible, being broken in at least two places by canopied masses of overhanging rock some scores of feet in height. The north side is absolutely sheer, and we could see no way up the face before us which, under the existing conditions, looked available. Nevertheless we went on, to try to get a closer and clearer view before declaring it wholly inaccessible. But so distant was it still that by 2:30 we were only at the lower peak, and it was obvious that with the extreme difficulties presented by the fresh snow and verglas there was no time to think of an ascent, and even to climb the nearer point would probably involve us in serious troubles, for a long and untried tract lay between us and our camp, and the days were getting short.

So we retraced our steps, set up the usual Union Jack—my mountaineering visiting-card—upon the summit of the ridge peak, which we nicknamed "Consolation Peak," had another snack of lunch, and hurried to the glacier pass, where we arrived at 5:15. Our way now lay along the hard snow slopes below the ridge on the Thompson Pass side. We knew that there was nothing like a pass in this direction, for we had already scanned the long and lofty wall that rises with almost unbroken perpendicularity for miles above the farther valley; but we had hopes that we could work along the crest and, traversing a rocky peak crowned by two shattered towers, eventually descend by slopes of scree to Thompson Pass.

This we succeeded in doing after some eerie experiences. The first was the breaking away of a huge mass of rock, down which I was clambering on the verge of a fine precipice. And this adventure illustrates the peculiar need for caution which is imposed by the friable nature of the limestone of the Canadian Rockies, causing difficulties and delays which would be unknown on peaks of solid character. Kaufmann had preceded me and felt no insecurity, but when my full weight was hanging from its upper edge and I was groping for a lower ledge to aid me in the precarious descent, a tremor, followed by a distinct yielding, warned me of danger. Instantly swinging to the inner side, I dropped the few remaining feet to a fortunately fairly ample standing place, and Christian's firm and ready grip steadied me as a ton or so of rock went crashing to the base of the precipice, 1,500 feet below, leaving a great, jagged hole above.

The edge of the ridge, to which our progress was confined, became intensely steep, often vertical and in places overhanging, and it took slow and cautious climbing, with plenty of gymnastic work, to effect a safe descent. The dusk was deepening as we reached the foot, and we scrambled up the 600 feet of arête to the towered pinnacles beyond with the assistance of the fitful moonlight. The long shadows and uncertain light made it very difficult to judge distances or steepness, and on the icefield beyond especial care was needed, but fortunately the ridge was fairly simple and our progress steady. The peak itself, for which the name "Turret Peak" is suggested (10,200 feet), was crossed at eight o'clock, and in three-quarters of an hour more we were unroped and scurrying wildly down the loose scree, glissading wherever a patch of snow appeared. At ten o'clock we threw ourselves at last upon a grassy couch beneath the sweeping spruces that border the lakelet on the summit of the pass.

It was so late and dark that Christian did not at all relish the idea of another midnight tussle with the dense jungle and mass of fallen timber that separated us from the camp, and proposed to stay where we were until daylight. I was of opinion that even a repetition of our Columbia finish was preferable to a night in the high open, with little shelter, no blankets, and no food. But as Christian steadily refused to let me leave him and go down alone as I desired, I consented to remain. In less than an hour my teeth were chattering and I announced that I was not prepared to endure five more hours of such conditions, but begged him to stay, as I knew I could easily find my way. This he declined to do; so on we went, and found things infinitely better than even I expected, less than two hours sufficing for the journey; and again we roused our admirable chef from his post-midnight slumbers at this fated Columbia camp, and in a few minutes were revelling in the delights of a roaring fire, delicious soup, hot tea, and bannocks, prepared à l'instant by his willing hands. I, for one, as I crept into a comfortable sleeping bag, after this excellent meal, did not regret the extra journey, and rejoiced that I had insisted on leaving the cold and hungry summit of the cheerless pass.

Next afternoon we returned to spend the night up there, equipped with necessaries for a bivouac, and successfully achieved the conquest of Mt. Bryce, whose thrilling experiences deserve a chapter to themselves. That night we had a third finish after midnight, and it was certainly a strange coincidence that all our troubles of this nature on the trip should have occurred at the head of the West Branch, on the occasions of the only expeditions that we undertook in that locality.

On our return from Mt. Bryce, we stayed once more at "Camp Content" to make another effort to reach the top of Mt. Alexandra, determined that we would not again be baffled, as it was a necessary link—the only one remaining—to complete acquaintance with the valley system on the Pacific slope between Mt. Freshfield and Mt. Columbia.

Our start, on August 23rd, involved, as heretofore, a ford on horseback, and we followed our previous route at a slightly faster gait to the high glacier col, 10,000 feet up, in five hours, noticing some striking changes in the upper glacier since traversing it four days before. Many bridges used that day had wholly disappeared, and the zigzags through the maze of fissures were in lines entirely different from the former route and more erratic and heart-rending as well as more perilous than ever. Crossing the pass, we traversed an expanse of névé, close under the rocks of the sharp ridge, upon the crest of which our previous attempt was made. Soon we arrived at a small nick in a long spur from "Consolation Peak," which divides the glacier just crossed and its sequent valley from a much larger amphitheatre of snow and ice, walled in by rugged cliffs, above which rose the crests of Mt. Alexandra and its miniature in front of us, and "Consolation Peak" to our left. This glacier, aided by some minor ones, supplies another stream, whose valley, sweeping westward, joins that above-mentioned, and both unite with the affluent of the Bush River which has its source at Thompson Pass. Descending into the great basin, we steered straight across its ruddy surface,[56] fantastically marked with geometric patterns, to the base of the long, easily sloping back of Mt. Alexandra. Here, on another tiny col, we stopped for lunch and spent a delightful hour revelling in the new landscape of this western world.

Beyond the notch the grand sweep of another glacier-headed valley stretched from Mt. Lyell and its western spur right to our feet, trending to the South Fork of Bush River. We got new views of several of the prominent unnamed peaks of this untraversed land, several of them closely rivalling Bush Peak, the only one at present honoured with a designation. Rocks of many varied hues surrounded us; red, yellow and orange predominated, set off by dark green and purple, and a magnificent icewall, pierced by caverns dazzling in their brilliancy of glacial blue and hung with arctic tracery and giant icicles, faced us across the gap.

An easy climb, mainly over snow of a fair steepness, brought us by a steady pull to the top in 80 minutes, the elevation being estimated at 11,650 feet. Of course, in accordance with our unvaried happy fate (due somewhat to careful weather watching and waiting), we had a practically perfect view. An unbroken panorama of the glorious galaxy of northern peaks was spread before our eyes, and all the final details of the long stretch of previously undetermined watershed, with its adjacent valleys, was unfolded. All the peaks ascended during the past weeks were in full sight, as well as our familiar friends amongst the Rockies and the Selkirks in the vicinity of the railroad belt. One of the finest "effects" was the glance over the huge cornice edge, an overhanging shelf of a vast thickness and protruding more than a score of feet beyond the wall of the great precipice. Crawling to the rim, I lay as it were suspended in space, gazing into the abyss. The black cliff fell away sheer to the central icefall of the glacier, and even at its base scarcely appeared to have reached forward far enough to equal my position, thrust forward on this far-projecting crest of snow. Six thousand feet below, the ice-stream flowed in mighty volume to the depths of the green valley, where the river wound like a silver-gray ribbon through the distant flats.

An hour was all too little for what I longed to do and see; but camp, though near enough in a direct line over the cornice, was far away by the route we had to take, so by 2:30 we were glissading gayly down delightful slopes of admirable snow; and, returning exactly as we came, with a brief halt for some refreshment by the way, the camp was reached in wonderfully respectable time for us at half-past seven.

This climb concluded most successfully the programme I had outlined and, after a Sunday's rest, we resumed our march towards civilization. The enormous mass of Mt. Wilson was traversed from end to end on our way home, and from its summit, about 11,000 feet, we bade a last farewell to the West Branch and its noble mountains, amongst which, besides two smaller peaks, we had been fortunate enough to make the first ascents of the four loftiest.

Chapter xiv

MOUNT BRYCE

Darkness was gathering apace. The sun had set nearly an hour ago. A piercing wind from a world of glaciers was whistling by on its wild course; and the rising moon, shining feebly athwart a mist of clouds, revealed two shivering human forms silhouetted upon the skyline of a rocky ridge 10,000 feet above the sea.

One, perched on the apex of a cliff some 70 feet in height, a precipice on either hand, watches intently the painful progress of his companion in adversity, who, in the dim, shadowy distance, is clinging with chilled fingers to the vertical face of rock by handholds of the tiniest dimensions, and wildly waving first one leg and then the other in a blind search for some small broken ledge or scant projection which may bear his weight, and form another step in the slow, difficult descent.

The mountain was Mt. Bryce, named in 1898 after the well-known British statesman who then held office as President of the Alpine Club. Projecting westward from the Continental watershed, the mountain rises in splendid isolation from a massive base to a long and extremely narrow ridge, crowned by overhanging cornices of snow, and culminating in three sharp peaks of increasing elevation in the direction of the ever deepening valleys, till the final, sudden precipice of the main summit looms almost vertically above the timbered slopes and foaming torrent of the Bush River, more than 8,000 feet below. Its rugged flanks present a long expanse of rocky walls, frequently sheer and always inaccessible, scored here and there by icy gullies, or hung with a glistening mantle of ice and snow, rendering access to the highest, or western, peak possible only by traversing the long ridge almost from end to end.

Mt. Bryce was first brought to notice by Professor Collie and Mr. Woolley, when they climbed Mt. Athabasca and subsequently explored the great Columbia icefield. In 1900 Messrs. Collie, Spencer and Stutfield forced their way from the west along the valley of Bush River, in the hope of reaching the three great peaks that rise preeminently in that vicinity, Mt. Columbia, Mt. Bryce and Bush Peak; but so dense were the forests on the Pacific slope, and so untoward the weather conditions, that they were compelled to return without achieving the main objects of the expedition. Obviously the line of least resistance was by the North Fork, and on that account I had selected the West Branch as the centre of operations, it being not only the simplest approach to Mt. Columbia and Mt. Bryce, but also a key position to the general topography.

The second day after our Columbia climb, July 21st, Christian and I ascended to Thompson Pass for a reconnaissance of the other big peak from that side, as the northern precipices had been seen to be out of the question. Felling a big spruce, we obtained a bridge across the swift glacial torrent and entered the woods beyond. The usual forest experiences of fallen trees and tangled brushwood marked the fairly steep ascent for three-quarters of an hour, till we emerged upon the shores of a delightful lake; a splendid rocky pinnacle, which I called Watchman Peak, towers like a sentinel 4,000 feet above the vivid blue-green waters, which are fringed on three sides by firs and pines; a lofty rampart, massed with trees, rises to the pass, 6,800 feet above the sea, where lies a second lakelet still more attractive, with indented shores, clothed with brilliant greenery of every shade, grasses and moss and undergrowth, relieved by the dark trees and broken here and there by rocky outcrops. On the far side a tributary of the Bush River runs sparkling down a narrow, rapidly descending valley, sombre with heavy forests and frowning precipices, Mt. Bryce on one side and a long range of snow-capped mountains opposite.

We clambered up the rugged slopes and ledges to the south, and, from an altitude of about 8,000 feet, obtained a fairly comprehensive survey of Mt. Bryce and its approaches. Perhaps, strictly speaking, I should say "approach," as we could see but one that seemed to offer any prospect of success—and that was an inordinately long and trying one. Great cliffs girdled the base, as far as our view extended, and even with strong field glasses we could detect no break sufficient to afford any inducement to make a journey far enough down the valley to find out for certain. A considerable overhang was evident in places, but, it is quite possible that a closer inspection may reveal at least one line of ascent whereby a scramble may effect the desired result, and, if so, that will prove by far the easiest and quickest route. Failing this, the one remaining chance was by the long ridge over the eastern, and possibly also the central, peak. But the character of the peak involved a serious problem besides length. Almost the entire ridge from end to end was corniced heavily. These huge cornices hung sometimes on one side, sometimes on the other. The arête was everywhere extremely narrow and the sides then hideously steep. Vast mantles of the winter's snows, as yet unmelted and evidently awaiting the slightest pretext to avalanche, were massed upon the upper slopes; and away in the distance, at the head of the final peak, a weird, indistinguishable pile of broken glacier, buried in snow, hung beneath the summit and looked to be a most appalling barrier in its then condition. Remembering that we were but two, these dazzling possibilities of a first-class avalanche appealed strongly to our bumps of discretion and self-preservation, so reluctantly but valiantly we came to the conclusion that it would be wiser to postpone the climb until a greater portion of the fresh snow should have had time to disappear. A drop in the barometer and several thundershowers confirmed the wisdom of this decision. Next morning our camp was shifted down the valley, and it was not until the 20th of August that we were again in quest of victory over the fascinating difficulties of Mt. Bryce.

Having proved quite unequal to the task of persuading Professor Collie's party to travel up the West Branch and share in the interests of the undertaking, Kaufmann and I were once again left to our own devices; and in the afternoon we wandered through the trackless forest from our Columbia camp to bivouac somewhere above Thompson Pass. In two hours we found a snug spot under a clump of balsams, in a hollow on the flanks of the massif of Mt. Bryce. A clear stream gurgled through the rich grass close at hand; the abundant heather and spruce boughs, chopped with our ice axes, provided material for most comfortable beds. Dry wood for fuel was collected and we looked forward to a good hot supper, when, to our dismay, it was discovered that we were matchless! Christian, probably for the first time in his career, had omitted to bring a single one,—a doubly reprehensible oversight for a habitual smoker,—and every last one of my supply had been jerked from my pocket during the forceful struggle through the forest tangle. Every corner was ransacked without avail. Not a solitary match rewarded our united search. Ruefully the inevitable was accepted. Kicking the pile of firewood away, I subsided in chill despair, and Christian deposited a "billy" full of ice-cold water on the grass before me and solemnly announced "Supper is ready." We tried cold-water bovril, but cannot warmly recommend it, and the chill of evening at our elevation of more than 7,000 feet, combined with a plague of mosquitoes and yellow stinging flies, drove us betimes to the recesses of our sleeping bags. We tried to slumber, ineffectually for long, and then, of course, we overslept, and, having no fire, decided to wait for breakfast till we got into sunlight, hung up our blankets on the trees to preserve them from voracious marmots, cached our spare provisions, and started at 4:40 on our journey round the steep shoulder that intervened between the bivouac and the main ridge of Mt. Bryce.

Crossing the Divide, we skirted along slopes of loose scree, which gave place later to heather and coarse grass, where flowers blossomed in wonderful profusion, driven upward by the advancing season, and stunted spruces reached an altitude several hundred feet higher than on the Atlantic side. Ascending steadily, we soon arrived at the little glacier that nestles in a rock-bound hollow at the mountain's base, and, crossing the high bank of lateral moraine, found pleasant going on the hard surface of ice and snow, towards the rocky face of a subsidiary point just to the east of the main mass of the mountain. On one of the lower ledges we halted for breakfast, and then by snow and slippery slabs clambered up to the connecting ridge above. Striking this at its lowest point we encountered the first really awkward obstacle. A snow wall about ten feet in height, and crowned by a small overhanging cornice, faced us across a yawning chasm in the hanging glacier on which we stood. The snow was soft in the extreme and gave way at each attempt to form a step in its vertical surface, pouring like dry sand into the crevasse below. By dint of care and patience, however, two or three sufficient holes were excavated, and Christian, breaking through the cornice and planting his ice axe in the firmer snow above, drew himself up to solid ground once more.

We were now at the east end of a long slope of névé trending gently down to a tongue of the Columbia icefield on our right, and ending abruptly on the side of our ascent in a large cornice surmounting a rugged precipice. Beyond it rose the steep ridge along which we had to travel, comparatively broken and easy at first, but narrowing rapidly till the southern wall grew perpendicular and the northern slopes tilted at a tremendous angle, leaving but a razor edge of jagged rock between, or crested by a great overhanging shelf of frozen snow.

The weather, to our satisfaction, gave more hope than at the start, when clouds, clustered low on every lofty peak, augured ill for a clear view, without which any climbing success would count for comparatively nothing. A breeze had sprung up and the clouds lifted gradually; several summits already were emerging from the gloom, and Mt. Columbia, with its pure snowy dome wreathed in trailing mists, appeared like an ethereal vision against the pale azure of the sky, aglow with radiant dawn, and at its feet swept the broad snows of its vast icefield.

But we were obliged to hasten on, for we were only 9,500 feet above sea level (about 2,500 feet above the bivouac), it was already half-past seven, and many difficulties lay ahead. The route, of course, was quite untried and all we knew about it was that it would be very long, and that there must be several exceedingly troublesome bits of climbing, certain to test our powers to the full, if not impossible to overcome. We had roped together before tackling the snow wall, and continued thus throughout the day. Advancing rapidly over the level surface, steps had to be cut up the steep icy slopes to the rock base, where ledges large and small, scarred rock-faces or rugged buttresses, with now and then a scramble on the skyline, provided for the most part an easy and rapid progress, the customary rotten rock being the only drawback. Later on, the traversing of occasional icy or snow-filled gullies gave variety, with their alternative opportunities for us to slip on them or for them to slide with us. The southern precipices were getting very sheer; those opposite, increasing in sharpness to rugged escarpments, scored by narrow gullies and. ribbed with minor buttresses, plunged downward some 6,000 or 7,000 feet, with no halting-places on the way, to the great glacier below.

Eventually, near the apex of the rock arête, well over 10,000 feet above the sea, we came to a bit of cliff, about 70 feet high, which appeared so serious a problem as to threaten a summary defeat. We stood on the edge of the arête and it towered above us as a narrow buttress, smooth, nearly perpendicular, with few excrescences to grip or place even the corner of a boot upon, and of a consistency so rotten that only a small percentage of the existing few would probably be reliable. The only relief was the existence of a tiny rift extending part of the way up, which broke the face in some degree We peered round the angle on our left and discovered that we were about midway along a great bare wall, without a vestige of foothold as a rule, sheer in its drop of 2,000 to 3,000 feet to the glacier at its base, There was no escape in that direction. Then to the right. A narrow gully broke the directness of the rocky face, descending abruptly, with occasional wicked-looking spikes of jagged limestone protruding from the surface and swept by showers of debris from the cliffs above. Beyond this, more buttresses as steep and uninviting as the one confronting us.

So there was nothing for it but to try to scale the escarpment straight ahead, and Christian immediately led the way. Perhaps it might prove easier than it appeared; oftentimes when things look absolutely beyond all hope it turns out a case of *solvitur ambulando*;[57] and though we knew the shortness of our rope was a serious drawback, we hoped that 50 or 60 feet up more favourable conditions might develop. The first dozen feet were fairly broken and not particularly vertical, but then commenced a strenuous conflict with the difficulties of this natural outpost, set to bar approach to the stronghold's central tower. Hold after hold gave way as the guide tried them one by one, and fragments rattled down the gully and leapt from rock to rock in ever growing bounds till, lost to sight and sound, they dashed to final rest upon the glacier 6,000 feet beneath—a most suggestive journey to those who were engaged in an attempt to climb that selfsame cliff by means of very slightly more reliable supports.

Fortunately Kaufmann is a magnificent rock-climber, and it was a treat to watch the skill and science he displayed in his advance slowly and cautiously towards the goal. Now he was clinging to the rounded surface of the buttress edge, now swinging into the narrow cleft at its side. Sometimes with arms and legs outstretched, like a gigantic starfish, in a wild endeavour to grasp a possible support; or bunched together after a huge step upward, where no intervening foothold offered in an expanse of a yard or more. A tiny resting-place, perhaps an inch in width and two or three in length, on which a portion of a nailed boot-edge can maintain a transitory grip, is hailed with delight and looked on as a luxury. The least projection, if happily not slippery, suffices for a hold, and one slow gymnastic effort succeeds another as the climber gently draws himself upward foot by foot. As little spring or jerk as possible is the invariable rule, lest it detach one of the treacherous supports, and leave him hanging precariously on a fragile remnant, or hurl him in an instant on the cruel rocks that line the gully at his feet.

For the rope is practically of no advantage to the leader under such circumstances. Though his companion may be firmly planted at the cliff base, the rope clutched in an iron grasp or anchored round a solid mass of rock, yet should the first man fall, a drop of twice the length of rope paid out must follow, and the chances of escape from, at the least, considerable injuries are small. Christian, however, is equal to almost anything one can encounter on the mountains, and certainly to all that gives a possibility of overcoming it; so, little by little, he made his way higher and higher till the rope was taut between us. Above him still nearly 20 feet remained of the bad bit, perhaps the worst section of it all. His situation was not of the most secure; the slightest slip or jerk on my part would possibly be enough to drag him from his hold and so precipitate us both into the abyss, where the white glacier gleamed apparently so close beneath our feet, yet really more than 6,000 feet away. But I must come on or give up the expedition.

And the future! It is an axiom that in nine cases out of ten descent is far more trying than ascending on a difficult rock climb. If we could only just achieve success by dint of all the skill and energy we possessed, how about coming down late in the day, most likely thoroughly tired, with all the additional dangers of a descent? However, the result of our deliberations was that, in the circumstances, there was an overwhelming preponderance of reasons in favour of success; so on we went. Soon I could halt, and Christian clambered to the top, where, anchored firmly, he could have held me or even hauled me up if all my holds had gone at once and left me dangling in the air. Nothing of this sort happened, nor was the rope needed even as an aid, though it was a climb that taxed my powers to the full, and some of the scant projections and occasional spells where in shifting holds one learns the wonderful properties of friction as an almost sole support, brought me nearly to their utmost limit.

In due time the tension was over and the victory was won. A total change in the character of the climb appeared before us now. The gradient of the ridge became quite easy; rocks gave place almost entirely to snow; but the southern precipices were crowned by enormous cornices, to which a wide berth had to be given, necessitating a traverse of the steep snowslopes that fell away at an alarming angle till they ended in a "jump off," beyond which only the valley bed, some 7,000 feet below, could be seen. For a short distance the going was delightful, and we had visions of a quick and easy finish, but soon the snow became very hard, solid ice succeeded, the axe was requisitioned and severe step-cutting followed for awhile. Several strange transverse fissures had to be avoided, and another snow wall, this time frozen solid, had to be climbed across a wide crevasse, close to the edge of the projecting mass of cornice. Thence rapid progress along the broken, narrow ridge ended in our arrival at 11:50 at the sharp summit of Mt. Bryce's eastern peak.

Here, seated on the pile of loose rocks that forms the tiny apex, we enjoyed a well-earned rest for half an hour and an acceptable lunch, meantime taking in with much appreciation the extensive views from our advantageous elevation of 11,000 feet. The chief interest lay ahead. To our relief, the hopes of escaping the tedious and dangerous traverse of the central peak were confirmed. As it was, we had presentiments already of a night out upon the mountain. But nothing short of absolute impossibility was going to deter us from achieving the purpose on which we had embarked, and we were glad to find a shorter route by descending 600 or 700 feet to a wide glacier that swept along the bases of the three summits, skirting the central cliffs and striking the ridge again at a narrow gap between the, two highest peaks.

Down rocks and snow we hurried, carefully leaving a substantial staircase in the latter for use on our return, then across the glacier, covered with snow, save where the suggestive lines of huge crevasses showed dark upon the universal whiteness of the otherwise unbroken surface. The snow was soft and we sank deeply in at every step, but before long we were plodding laboriously up the farther steeps, and in an hour and a quarter stood in the little dip where the descending ridges of the main and central peaks converge.

Only 900 feet remained for us to scale, but the prospect was not at all inviting. The lower part of the arête was simple enough, though so knife-edged that, as we trod the snowy crest, both toes and heels projected into space, one on each side. Then came a cornice, hanging as before towards the south, with the slope frozen hard, presenting a safe and solid substance in which to cut steps. But beyond this lay the worst of all our difficulties. The crest of the cornice was suddenly reversed and topped the northern precipice. The slope, on which we were obliged to move in order to avoid the danger of the cornice giving way, now faced the south and was exposed to the full blaze of the summer sunshine. So steep was it that it seemed marvellous how the glistening curtain of soft and yielding snow, massed on a slippery substratum of glare ice, could cling at such an angle. It looked as though the slightest touch would tear the treacherous mantle from the shoulder of the peak and in an instant sweep its rude disturbers in the whirling volume of a seething avalanche into the distant depths. Yet at the same time the situation was not without its compensations. Had the configuration of the mountain been reversed, there would be no present record of any conquest of Mt. Bryce, for to dream of attempting the traverse of such a slope, when the failure of a single foothold might mean a fall of nearly 8,000 feet, would be sheer madness. Fortunately when this grand abyss was yawning at our feet, the sheltered snow, congealed by an icy wind, was firm, and, though the labour of continuous step-cutting was involved, there was perfect safety. Now that the sunny side was forced upon us as a route, the mountainside, though steep, was never perpendicular, but covered by a pure expanse of snow, that, unbroken save in its earliest stages by protruding rocks, swept smoothly down to the broad surface of the southern glacier only 1,200 or 1,500 feet below. Even should we take a sudden ride in this unusual kind of automobile, there would be little likelihood of any further damage than the abandonment of our attempt.

After long inspection and deliberation, the same old argument that turned the scale upon the first occasion of hesitancy again prevailed, and, in the firm conviction that skill and care could overcome, we decided on giving the snow a thorough test at least. It was a period of intense strain and watchfulness. Of course but one moved at a time. A jerk or spring would probably send us swiftly hurtling downward in an eddying hurricane of snow. Scarcely a word was spoken and not a needless movement was allowed. Even the hole made by the leader's ice axe had to be utilized by his companion, lest any undue shaking or splitting of the crust might start a slide.

With cat-like tread, face inward towards the slope, Christian would make a cautious sidelong step knee-deep in the soft, powdery snow, his ice axe planted firmly and securely grasped; gently and patiently he trod a fairly solid resting-place for one foot, then quietly drew the other leg to the same hole and carefully trampled a moderately stable little platform there. Another planting of the ice axe and a further step was gingerly negotiated in the long, slow advance. After ten or a dozen were thus laboriously accomplished, he would halt and I as cautiously move forward to his side; and so *da capo*. It was exhilarating work. At almost each fresh step a patch of crust, perhaps as large as a man's hand, would break away and, sliding downward with an ominous hiss, in a few yards gouge out a trench some 18 inches wide and six or seven deep, and, gathering strength and volume as it sped along, form a fine specimen of a miniature avalanche and thunder to the glacier below.

Two on a rope is a wee bit uncanny for such an undertaking, but foot by foot we made our way in safety until the worst was over and we took a welcome rest upon an island of projecting rock. Beyond this was yet another of the vertical snow walls which were a peculiar feature of the climb. First came a traverse on a narrow ledge under a canopy of dripping snow, so low that a most uncomfortably constrained position was necessitated. Keeping one's balance was not easy, and so unstable was the snow that a mere touch might readily displace the mass above, and our weight alone suffice to loosen the ledge and shoot us down the icy, snow-swept gully at our feet. Then the usual patient striving to gain a foothold in the sliding snow was resumed, and the usual ultimate success achieved, and solid ground once more rewarded us. All our toils were now forgotten. The long-desired summit rose quite close above, and eagerly we hastened towards the goal. A splendid hanging glacier clings to the northern flank of the mountain's topmost pinnacle; a wild chaos of gaping fissures, ice towers and séracs. We threaded our way through its weird arctic jumble, climbed a short, sharp arête, and, breaking through a little cornice, stood at last upon the mountaintop.

A platform of unblemished snow crowns the great peak, a matchless natural observatory. The mighty walls are sheer or almost sheer on every side, save where the narrow ridge of our approach connects the bastion outpost with the rest of the upland world. Except for this, we seemed to be severed from earth and isolated in the realms of space. In front, to right, to left, over the brink of the rocky ramparts, we gazed into the heart of the green forest depths more than 8,000 feet below. Above these wooded chasms

"Hills peep o'er hills, and Alps on Alps arise"

in most bewildering complexity, rugged and desolate; huge, fantastic piles, with frowning precipices and jagged pinnacles, and vast, majestic domes, whose shapely forms are clothed in snowy splendour.

The altitude was about 11,750 feet, the time 3:40, exactly 11 hours from the start, with only 4,700 feet of actual ascent, which reveals the character of the climb better than much description. With Christian continually hurrying me up, I could only allow a bare half-hour for photography and observations, and at ten minutes after four we turned our faces homeward. The descent was fairly rapid. The sunlight had passed from the snow slope, and the cool of evening, aided by a keen wind, hardened it sufficiently to enable us to move with greater freedom than we expected. In spite of some photographic halts, we reached the eastern peak by 6:20 and snatched five minutes for rest and a mouthful of chocolate before hurrying on along the upper portion of the east arête. Throughout, the steps made in the morning were of great assistance, and there were no delays beyond especial care at some of the most difficult places.

It was almost dark when we approached the well-remembered cliff, which had been continually on our minds, and to reach which before nightfall had been the object of our hasty, foodless march. But we arrived too late. And now the question arose as to the wisest course to take. We were on the horns of a dilemma. To go on meant descending practically in the dark a cliff which we had deemed so difficult by daylight as almost to be deterred from undertaking it at all. But on the other hand, a night out 10,000 feet above the sea, without the smallest vestige of shelter, on the exposed skyline of a ridge swept by an arctic wind, with boots and stockings saturated and certain to freeze (and possibly the feet inside as well) before the dawn could aid us on our way, and almost destitute of food, offered a prospect particularly uninviting. I left the decision entirely to Kaufmann. The risk was practically his alone. For me, descending first, with the good rope in his trusty grasp, there was no danger, even should I slip or fail to find a hold, except for the short distance when both would be upon the face at the same time. For him, a slip, a lost grip or a broken hold might mean destruction. But again he voted for advance, and at any rate I could make a trial and report upon my personal sensations before his turn arrived. So I turned my face towards the rock, slipped over the edge, and entered on the fateful climb.

It will be long before I lose the recollection of those 70 feet of cliff. Drawn out for one long hour of concentrated tension were the successive experiences of helpless groping in the dark depths for something to rest a foot upon, of blind search all over the chilled rocky surface for a knob or tiny crack where the numbed fingers might find another hold, of agonizing doubt as to their stability when found, of eerie thrill and sickening sensation when the long-sought support crumbled beneath the stress and hurtled downward into the blackness of space, whilst the hollow reverberations of its fall re-echoed through the silence. Then the strain of waiting on the best, but very questionable, protuberances for several tense minutes of motionless suspense, whilst the exigencies of the rope compelled Christian to climb down 15 or 20 feet, and I could move again. At long last came the marvellous relief of feeling solid and sufficient standing room once more, followed by the still more trying period of inactivity, the patient intensity of watching and hauling in the slack as the rope came slowly and spasmodically down, telling of Christian's gradual descent, the strained anxiety lest any accident should happen to my comrade, and, finally, the thankfulness of seeing his figure looming close above and in a few moments standing by my side, and we could breathe again.

In the dim light we poked on slowly down gullies, walls and ledges, tracts of loose debris, patches of snow and ice, to the broad névé where the mountain proper ends. It was past ten when we emerged from the gloom and difficulties of the rocks and allowed ourselves a few minutes' rest before commencing the final portion of the journey. To avoid several awkward places, a variation from the line of our approach was made by taking a wide detour, probably to our advantage, but involving more trouble than we anticipated in the negotiation of a steep, corniced ridge, which in the dark had to be descended backwards with a good deal of labour in making steps in the hard snow. The lower glacier reached, with staggering and unsteady gait we swung along the rough, uneven surface in the deceptive light, until about midnight we left the snow behind and could unloose the rope that had bound us together during nearly 17 hours of adventurous companionship.

Rough scree and boulders, thickets of dwarf spruce and tangled heather, were our next experience, but eventually at 1 A.M. we sighted the clump of firs that marked our cheerless bivouac. Though nothing but a little chocolate had been our sustenance since noon, it was too dark and we were too tired to enjoy cold bovril and canned mutton at this dismal hour. The blankets appealed most strongly to us, and we crept into our sleeping bags and slept the sleep of the just till dawn. Off again at 4:30, we arrived in camp by six, and soon were seated before a glorious fire, enjoying the luxury of a hot meal once more, and doing ample justice to a varied menu. A few hours later the "outfit" commenced the return journey from these mountain solitudes to prosaic civilization, and a last farewell was said to this strangely fated camping-ground, where all three expeditions had involved us in post-midnight returns from more than 20-hour climbs.

CHAPTER XV

FARTHER NORTH

THE EARLIEST EXPLORERS CROSSED THE Continental watershed north of the limits of the territory which forms the subject of this volume, and the nearest pass then known was the Athabasca Pass, reached in 1817 by the ill-starred remnant of Ross Cox's expedition, and described ten years later by David Douglas, the well-known botanist. Two striking mountains, which stood guard above the pass, he named Mts. Brown and Hooker, and estimated their altitudes at the stupendous figures of not less than 16,000 to 17,000 feet, the pass itself being 5,710 feet above the sea. All the geographies and atlases since then have given currency to these elevations, although for some years doubt has been cast upon their authenticity, and the existence of peaks of that magnitude so near the railway belt was a matter about which many were extremely skeptical.

In 1893 Professor Coleman and Mr. Stuart made a journey to that region with the express purpose of settling the question. Starting from Edmonton, they ascended the Brazeau River to the headwaters of the eastern branch of the Athabasca River, only a few miles from the upper end of the North Fork of the North Saskatchewan. Following down the Athabasca to its junction with a tributary from the southwest, they ascended the latter and rediscovered the pass of Mr. Douglas with its historic tarn, called "The Committee's Punchbowl." But where were the tremendous giant peaks that have masqueraded on our maps for all these years? The northern summit, the Mt. Brown climbed by Douglas, was ascended, and careful measurement showed it to be only a little over 9,000 feet, whilst Mt. Hooker, to the south, is scarcely so exalted! Provided there was no mistake about the identity of the pass, which hardly admitted of a doubt, these famous mountains were thus proved to be little more than half the height they had so long received credit for.

In 1896 Messrs. W.D. Wilcox and R.L. Barrett crossed the pass now known by the name of the former from the Saskatchewan North Fork to the Athabasca basin; they struck Professor Coleman's trail, which they followed for a while, and finally turned up the western branch of the Athabasca as far as a fine lake (named Fortress Lake) towards the west, which proved on exploration to be on the Divide and to possess outlets from the opposite ends flowing to the rival oceans. Its height is only 4,200 feet above the sea. From the shore and from a minor elevation on the north bank, about 8,450 feet, Mr. Wilcox took triangulations of the most imposing peak to the west, supposed to be Mt. Hooker, from which he deduced an elevation of 10,505 feet, and also of an impressive mountain south of the lake, which measured 11,450 feet, and seemed to be the highest within a radius of many miles.

It seemed now almost indisputable that the true pass and peaks had been identified, and that all the spurious glory the latter had enjoyed for seven decades must be finally swept away. The only barely possible alternative was that Mts. Brown and Hooker guarded some other pass, and that Mr. Douglas had in some way mixed his descriptions, though the clear and detailed narrative practically precluded such a supposition, and his itinerary scarcely permits of the exploration of a second pass.

However, in 1898, Professor Collie, with Messrs. Stutfield and Woolley, planned an extensive mountaineering trip in that direction, with the particular object of setting at rest for all time any doubts whatever on the subject. Other explorers had kept to valleys and lesser spurs; they hoped, by climbing several of the giant peaks of the Columbia group, to get such information from "the highest sources" as would solve the difficulty. Owing to various unavoidable delays and, finally, a serious shortage of provisions, they were unable to go as far as they had hoped, though, by the ascent of three very lofty and commanding peaks, they practically assured themselves that no such alternative pass exists, and that there are no mountains that approach the altitudes in question.

But after his return to England, Professor Collie, while hunting up all the data on the subject, came across an ancient periodical (*The Companion to the Botanical Magazine*, by Dr. W.T. Hooker, vol. II, pp. 134–137), in which the original journal of David Douglas was published, and the following statement of the discoverer was brought to light. He writes: "Being well rested by one o'clock, I set out with the view of ascending what seemed to be the highest peak on the north. Its height does not appear to be less than 16,000 or 17,000 feet above the level of the sea. After passing over the lower ridge I came to about 1,200 feet of by far the most difficult and fatiguing walking I have ever experienced, and the utmost care was required to tread safely over the crust of snow. A few mosses and lichens are observable, but at an elevation of 4,800 feet (sic) vegetation no longer exists. The view from the summit is of too awful a cast to afford pleasure. Nothing can be seen, in every direction far as the eye can reach, except mountains towering above each other, rugged beyond description. ... The majestic but terrible avalanches hurling themselves from the more exposed southerly rocks produced a crash, and groaned through the distant valleys with a sound only equalled by that of an earthquake. Such scenes give a sense of the stupendous and wonderful works of the Creator. This peak, the highest yet known in the northern continent of America, I feel a sincere pleasure in naming 'Mt. Brown,' in honour of R. Brown, Esq., the illustrious botanist."

Had this document ever been studied thoughtfully, the absurdity must have been at once apparent of an unskilled climber (or any climber at all) ascending, after 1 P.M., by a route "far the most difficult, and fatiguing he had ever experienced," a mountain 11,000 feet above his starting point and returning before nightfall at the early date of May 1st, since he makes no mention of darkness overtaking him! And so we chant with deep regret the requiem of these once famed but now dethroned monarchs.

Neither Professor Coleman nor Mr. Wilcox aimed at mountaineering during these northern travels, though doing immensely valuable pioneer work and adding greatly to our knowledge of the mountains there. A somewhat similar expedition was made in 1901 by Mr. J. Habel, of Berlin, to investigate the headwaters of the Athabasca more closely and completely. Following Mr. Wilcox's route to Fortress Lake, he penetrated much farther up the valley south of its eastern end, and also the middle one of the three streams which go to make up the main river. The easternmost, coming from Wilcox Pass, is called the Whirlpool, or Sun Wapta, indiscriminately. The central stream has no specific name, and Mr. Habel refers to it as the West Fork, calling its western tributary the Chaba River. These latter unite a short distance below Fortress Lake. At the head of the Chaba Valley are two forks, each springing from a glacier surmounted by considerable peaks. The left-hand one was called the Coleman Glacier, and its peaks the Coleman Range; the other with its chief summit received the name of Eden. An attempt was made to climb Mt. Eden, and a little col, 9,245 feet in altitude, was reached between the mountain and its eastern neighbour. The latter, Mt. Chaba, was then ascended instead, and found to be 10,300 feet above the sea. The West Fork was next explored to its head right under the magnificent pyramid of Mt. Columbia, here rising 8,000 feet above the valley flats. The glaciers northwest of the peak were visited, and a pass (9,845 feet) was reached (but not crossed) on the ridge dividing this valley from that of the Sun Wapta.

From the point of view of the alpinist, Professor Collie's expedition in 1898 stands a head and shoulders above any other to the Athabasca region; and from the observations made from the great altitudes attained, the topographical results surpassed in many ways those obtained from lower elevations. The first ascent made by the party during the trip was Mt. Athabasca (11,900 feet), which belongs to the Saskatchewan domain. Then the Dome (11,650 feet), on the Divide, was ascended from the Columbia névé and finally Diadem Peak (11,500 feet), a lofty point upon the range that projects from the Columbia mass between the East and West Forks of the Athabasca River.

This last climb was made from a bivouac, 7,000 feet above sea level, at the foot of the Diadem Glacier. Diadem Peak is the northernmost of three that form a minor group encircling a small valley on the left side of the Sun Wapta. The highest summit has been named Peak Woolley (11,700 feet), and the third, Peak Stutfield (11,400 feet). A tremendous rock fall from the ugly, bare limestone cliffs of the two latter has covered the whole valley, nearly half a mile wide, with boulders and debris to a depth of some hundreds of feet "What had happened, apparently, was this.[58] The immense amount of rock that had fallen on the glacier below Peak Stutfield had prevented the ice from melting. Consequently the glacier, filling up the valley to a depth of at least 200 feet, had moved bodily down; and its snout, a couple of hundred feet high, covered with blocks of stone the size of small houses, was playing havoc with the pine woods before it and on either side. In our united experiences, extending over the Alps, the Caucasus, the Himalaya and other mountain ranges, we had never seen indications of a landslide on so colossal a scale. Note.—The remains of a similar landslide were afterwards noticed blocking the outlet to Moraine Lake in Desolation Valley."

The intention of the party was to try Mt. Woolley, but the dawn was unpropitious, and, soon after starting, heavy rain drove them to temporary shelter under a friendly rock when they had reached the foot of a formidable icefall that descends between that mountain and Diadem Peak. "In five minutes it cleared; but the brief delay was possibly our salvation.[59] We were just putting on the rope to ascend the icefall, when, with a roar and a clatter, some tons of ice that had broken off near the summit came tumbling down, splintering into fragments in their descent. We took the friendly hint and left that icefall alone. The only alternative peak was Diadem, so we turned aside and began climbing its face.

"At first we had to make our way up slopes of loose shale and ice, and we kept fairly near the arête to avoid falling stones. This involved us in a scramble up some rather diverting rock chimneys; after which a sort of miniature rock-rib gave us safety from stones, and we followed it up to the summit. The rocks were very steep in places, and, as usual, terribly insecure and splintered, and one had to be very careful. The 'diadem' of snow proved to be about 100 feet high, set on the nearly flat top of the rocks. From the summit a wonderful panorama burst upon us, in spite of the murky atmosphere. Standing as we were, near the Great Divide, we looked down on a marvellous complexity of peak and glacier, of low-lying valley, shaggy forest, and shining stream, with here and there a blue lake nestling in the recesses of the hills. Quite close, as it seemed, the overpowering mass of the supposed Mt. Brown (Alberta) towered frowning many hundreds of feet above us. It is a superb peak, like a gigantic castle in shape, with terrific black cliffs falling sheer on three sides. A great wall of dark thundercloud loomed up over its summit; and there was a sublime aloofness, an air of grim inaccessibility, about it that was most impressive. To the west we could dimly discern the outline of another high peak, with a large grey cloud floating like a canopy over it. Northwards the mountains were all much lower; and it was evident that the Columbia group formed the culmination of, at any rate, this region of the Rockies. In these northern districts the landscape, as was to be expected, presented a sterner and more forbidding aspect: indeed, the softer and more homely features of Alpine scenery were everywhere absent from these higher valleys of the western Athabasca. One missed the tiny green pastures dotted about with brown chalets, the terraced cornfields and vineyards; and the familiar tinkle of the cowbells would have sounded more musical than ever in our ears, for, as Mr. Leslie Stephen observes in 'The Playground of Europe,' these evidences of civilization tend to improve rather than spoil mountain scenery.

"It was bitterly cold on the top. . . . All day long there had been a growling of distant thunder in the west, and as we turned to go down the storm burst upon us with a vengeance. It grew very dark, a white driving scud of sleet and hail swept by on the whistling wind, making our ears and faces tingle. The thunder rattled and roared in grand style among the crags; the air was aboil with eddying twisting vapours; and the lightning leaping, as it were, from peak to peak, zigzagged merrily athwart the sky. More than once we were constrained to stop and take shelter from the drift and sweep of the storm, throwing aside our ice axes for fear of the lightning, which seemed to be playing all round us. We took the easiest way down the face, taking chances with falling stones; and it was with a feeling of relief that we ultimately got onto the glacier below. In the woods another bad storm struck us, with hailstones as big as—well, of the usual travellers' size—anyhow they hurt very much when they hit you, and again we ran down into camp like three drowned rats. During the night there were more thunderstorms,—we had five in 24 hours,—and the drippings from our leaky tent soaked our already damp sleeping bags; but we slept soundly through it all."

Here, with the account of the ascent of the most northerly important peak yet climbed, we must part from our friends the Canadian Rockies. From Mt. Assiniboine to Mt. Columbia and Diadem Peak, we have traced them in all their unsurpassed and varied majesty. Although few peaks of the first magnitude and alpine difficulty remain unconquered by the ever advancing pioneer of mountaineering, the grandeur of these mountain monarchs, rising superbly from an unrivalled setting, is still the same and always must command the awe and admiration of the nature lover, and, whilst those of us who have been privileged to lead the way to their untrodden summits will possess lastingly a double portion of love and reverence for these companions of our hours of solitude and meditation, of strenuous struggle and of final triumph over every obstacle, perhaps this humble record of some of these memories, however haltingly expressed, may influence some to visit and to know and love these noblest of God's monuments; and, in the contemplation of His handiwork, be led to love the everlasting Maker of the everlasting hills, and not only find in Him the source of power in the might of His marvellous creative works, but also reach the "heart of the Eternal" which is so "wonderfully kind."

No words perhaps can better sum up the picture of these glorious mountains and their truest influence, than those of Sir Edwin Arnold: only, while transposing the scene from polytheistic India to Christian Canada, I would fain plead the privilege of altering the final word, and trust that that name—the "finis" of this attempt to tell of a little part of His wonderful world—may be the goal of all our thoughts and aims through life and our reward hereafter.

> "Northward soared
> The stainless ramps, ...
> Ranged in white ranks against the blue—untrod,
> Infinite, wonderful—whose uplands vast,
> And lifted universe of crest and crag,
> Shoulder and shelf green slope and icy horn,
> Riven ravine and splintered precipice,
> Led climbing thought higher and higher, until
> It seemed to stand in heaven and speak with 'God.'"

Appendix a

THE SELKIRK MOUNTAINS

A MOST INTERESTING AND EXHAUSTIVE little work on the Selkirk
Range, by Mr. A.O. Wheeler, of the Dominion Land Survey, is about
to be published by the Canadian Government, and, in order to avoid
conflicting with any of the most recent authoritative observations
and deductions contained therein, only a very brief and general note
is here made relative to that range and its mountaineering history.

The Selkirk and Purcell Ranges, commonly referred to under
the general name of the Selkirks, cover an area roughly oblong in
form, running parallel to the Continental watershed on its western
side, and severed from it by the deep valley of the Columbia River.
This area is about 250 miles in length (dipping into the States at
its southeastern extremity), and 100 miles wide near the borderline,
though not more than 50 where it is crossed by the railroad. It is
remarkable for being completely surrounded by two rivers, the
Columbia and the Kootenay, which form an enormous trench or
moat all round the group, never exceeding an elevation of 3,000 feet
and scarcely reaching half that height during the greater part of its
extent. The Columbia lakes and marshes supply the headwaters of
both rivers, which flow in opposite directions till 250 miles apart;
then each turns with a sudden bend and doubles on its former course,
and, after passing through the Arrow and Kootenay lakes, they unite
just before entering the States.

The character of this isolated group igneous, hard schists and
shales affording good holds for the climber, and the southern sections
are alive with mining camps. The culminating portion lies just south
of where the railroad cuts the range at Rogers Pass. Here is the

Illecillewaet Glacier, the nearest large glacier to a railway track to be found in America and perhaps the world, the famous Grindelwald Glacier excepted. Its crevassed tongue is only a half hour's walk from Glacier House station, and leads to the Illecillewaet névé, a considerable snowfield, from the neighbourhood of which rise the loftiest known peaks, Mt. Selwyn (11,038 feet), Mt. Wheeler (11,023 feet), Mt. Dawson (10,692 feet), and others closely approaching that altitude. But the most striking perhaps of all is Mt. Sir Donald (10,806 feet), which rises 6,500 feet above the railroad track as a fine rock pyramid. Northward the Hermit Range is set with several picturesque peaks, of which the highest are the Swiss Peaks. Farther north the region is scarcely known at all, but two fine mountains, one white, the other black, are quite conspicuous and greeted us in every view we had of the Selkirks from our points of vantage in the Forbes and Columbia districts of the adjacent Rockies.

The precipitation is very great in this vicinity, and consequently the vegetation is infinitely richer and more luxuriant than on the bigger range; cedars and hemlocks especially attain great size, and I have measured cedars over 20 feet in girth at altitudes of upwards of 4,000 feet. The deciduous trees also are found in far greater variety and splendour, and animal and bird life is more abundant.

The principal mountain centre is Glacier House, situated in a charming lateral valley of the Illecillewaet, almost at the head of the main valley. The Illecillewaet Glacier and Mt. Sir Donald form a magnificent background, and both are easily accessible. The chief gem of the district is the Asulkan Valley, named after the mountain goats which used to haunt its solitudes, a truly exquisite spot, richly wooded, with fine waterfalls and sparkling stream and a grand entourage of glacier and peak. The glacier is well worth a visit as far as the Asulkan Pass, which presents a view of singular grandeur, with Mt. Dawson and its attendant mountains facing us across the tremendous cleft of the Fish River Valley, nearly 8,000 feet below the highest crest.

Climbing, although the rocks are infinitely better adapted for safety and comfort, is not nearly so attractive as in the Rocky

Mountains proper. The peaks for the most part are absolutely simple, and the ruggedness, grandeur and difficulties of the main range summits are to a large degree wanting. Nevertheless, the Selkirks were five years ahead of the Rockies as a field for the mountaineer, and almost all of the peaks have been ascended, by a variety of climbers and at all sorts of dates. Foremost in time stand Messrs. Green and Swanzy, then Messrs. Huber and Sulzer, Topham and Forster, and hosts of lesser names with one or two first ascents apiece. By far the largest and most important share has been accomplished by Mr. A.O. Wheeler in his work for the Dominion Land Survey, and, as I know from personal experience, he is as fine a mountaineer as he is a surveyor, and one of the keenest for the work of exploration, observation and mountaineering that ever lived.

The most popular and most frequently ascended peak is Mt. Sir Donald, named after the present Lord Strathcona, which occupies the same position with regard to Glacier that Mt. Stephen (named after the other great railway magnate of the early days of the construction of the Canadian Pacific Railway) bears to Field. The first ascent in 1890, by Messrs. Huber and Sulzer, was for some reason long considered mythical, and was not finally established beyond cavil until M. Le Prince Ringuet found their cards on the summit exactly nine years later to a day. Since then numerous parties have made the climb, Mrs. Berens, an English lady, being the first of her sex to reach the top (in 1901).

It presents no difficulty whatever to a good amateur or a well-guided party, but affords specimens of most of the different varieties of rock and ice work and an extensive view, and it is a really interesting climb.

All sorts of walks and scrambles, mountain expeditions of varied extent and calibre, and opportunities for studying the characteristics of the marvellous ice world, make the attractions of Glacier House, situated at the very heart of the group, a most delightful spot and the best place from which to gain a knowledge of the interests and beauties of the Selkirk Range.

APPENDIX B:

ACCIDENT ON THE
GLACIERS OF MT. GORDON

THE DANGERS OF TRAVERSING A glacier unroped could hardly be more startlingly exemplified than by the accident to Mr. C.S. Thompson near the summit of Mt. Gordon. It is safe to say that in 99 cases out of 100 a fatal termination would result from such a fall. This, most fortunately, proved to be the exceptional instance. By a happy combination of unwonted circumstances, when the hour arrived the means and the man for the emergency were both forthcoming. The ample supply of rope, occasioned by the abnormal number of nine climbers in the party, was the first requisite: the presence of a man of Professor J.N. Collie's rare calibre and physique, to turn the means to good account, supplied the culminating factor of success. Those who read between the lines of the modest, yet graphic and thrilling, narrative of the chief actor, quoted from "Climbs and Exploration in the Canadian Rockies" (p. 29) will realize that only the combination of remarkable skill, judgment and resourcefulness displayed by the rescuer could have brought to a successful issue an adventure which in ordinary circumstances must have resulted in a fatal tragedy.

"Some time was spent on the top [of Mt. Gordon], but, as there was another summit about a third of a mile to the westward, several of the party started off for it. It was dome-shaped and covered with snow, the first peak consisting of an outcrop of limestone rocks. It was near the top of the second peak that Thompson very nearly ended his mountaineering experiences. Not far from this second summit a huge crevasse partially covered with snow had to be crossed. All the party had passed over but Thompson, who unfortunately broke through and at once disappeared headlong into the great crack that ran perpendicularly down into the depths of the glacier. Those of the party who were still on the first peak saw their friends gesticulating in the far distance, but did not take much notice until Sarbach drew their attention to the fact that there were only four people instead of five to be seen: someone, therefore, must have fallen down a crevasse. A race across the almost level snow then took place, Sarbach being easily first. Although Thompson was too far down to be seen, yet he could be heard calling for help and saying that, although he was not hurt, he would be extremely grateful to us if we would make haste and extricate him from the awkward position he was in, for he could not move and was almost upside down, jammed between the two opposing sides of the crevasse.

"It was obvious that every second was of importance; a stirrup was made in a rope, and Collie, being the lightest member of the party—and, withal, unmarried—was told to put his foot into it, whilst he was also carefully roped round the waist as well. Then he was pushed over the edge of the abyss, and swung in mid-air. To quote his description: 'I was then lowered into the gaping hole. On one side the ice fell sheer, on the other it was rather undercut, but again, bulged outwards about 18 feet below the surface, making the crevasse at that point not much more than two feet wide. Then it widened again, and went down into dim twilight. It was not till I had descended 60 feet, almost the whole available length of an 80-foot rope, that at last I became tightly wedged between the two walls of the crevasse, and was absolutely incapable of moving my body. My feet were close to Thompson's, but his head was further away, and about three feet lower than his heels. Face downwards, and covered with fallen snow, he could not see me. But, after he had explained that it was entirely his own fault that he was there, I told him we would have him out in no time. At the moment I must say I hardly expected to be able to accomplish anything. For, jammed between two slippery walls of ice, and only able to move my arms, cudgel my brains as I would, I could not think what was to be done. I shouted for another rope. When it came down I managed to throw one end to Thompson's left hand, which was waved about, till he caught it. But, when pulled, it merely dragged out of his hand. Then with some difficulty I managed to tie a noose on the rope by putting both my hands above my head. With this I lassoed that poor pathetic arm which was the only part of Thompson that could be seen. Then came the tug-of-war. If he refused to move, I could do nothing more to help him; moreover I was afraid that at any moment he might faint. If that had occurred I do not believe he could have been got out at all, for the force of the fall had jammed him further down than it was possible to follow. Slowly the rope tightened, as it was cautiously pulled by those above. I could hear my heart thumping in the ghastly stillness of the place, but at last Thompson began to shift, and after some short time he was pulled into an upright position by my side. To get a rope round his body was of course hopeless. Partly by wriggling and pulling on my own rope I so shifted that by straining one arm over my head I could get my two hands together, and then tied the best and tightest jamming knot I could think of round his arm, just above the elbow. A shout to the rest of the party, and Thompson went rapidly upwards till he disappeared round the bulge of ice 40 feet or more above. I can well remember the feeling of dread that came over me lest the rope should slip or his arm give way under the strain, and he should come thundering down on the top of me; but he got out all right, and a moment later I followed. Most marvellously no bones had been broken, but how anyone could have fallen as he did without being instantaneously killed will always remain a mystery. He must have partially jammed some considerable distance higher up than the point where I found him, for he had a rucksack on his back, and this perhaps acted as a brake, as the walls of the crevasse closed in lower down. We were both of us nearly frozen and wet to the skin, for ice-cold water was slowly dripping the whole time onto us; and in my desire to be as little encumbered as possible, I had gone down into the crevasse very scantily clad in a flannel shirt and knickerbockers.'

"A rapid descent to the head of the icefall quickly restored circulation, and that night over the campfire the whole experience was gone over again, Thompson emphatically giving it as his opinion that, whatever scientific exploration or observation in future might be necessary on the summits of the Rocky Mountains, investigations made alone, 60 feet below the surface of the ice, in an inverted position, were extremely dangerous and even unworthy of record."

Appendix c

HINTS ON OUTFIT

A SHORT LIST OF ARTICLES of apparel and other incidentals, necessary or advantageous for mountain climbing, may be of help to some to whom more or less alpine conditions are new.

I. Personal wear.

A good stout suit. Knickerbockers preferred by most. (The latter must be strong, as forests and crags are very hard on soft materials.)

Puttees or leggings. For snow and forest.

Stout boots, with plenty of nails in soles.

Hat with good brim. Cap with earpieces useful to carry along if high ascents are undertaken.

Gloves or mitts. Woollen preferred.

Sweater. For high altitudes.

Smoked glasses. Essential for snow and ice.

II. Equipment. Necessary.

Rope. Strong but light manilla, about half-inch diameter. (If a guide is taken, he will supply rope.)

Ice axe. (This can be obtained at Canadian Pacific Railway hotels, but it is better to have a private one if much is to be done.)

Knife.

String. (For emergencies.)

Knapsack. (Unless guide can carry all needed.)

III. Equipment. Optional.

Camera or Kodak.

Field glasses.

Compass.

Aneroid.

Clinometer. (On high ascents in all but well-known territory.)

Sextant. (Ditto.)

IV. Provisions.

Bread (and butter, if possible).

Cheese.

Meat. Canned or otherwise.

Water or cold tea. (Gourd or canteen is best for carrying water.)

V. Useful luxuries.

Chocolate.

Jam.

Dried fruit. (Prunes or raisins.)

APPENDIX D

A LIST OF "FIRST ASCENTS"

(OF SOME PEAKS IN THE ROCKY MOUNTAINS
UPWARDS OF 10,000 FEET)

THESE RECORDS HAVE BEEN COMPILED from the most authentic sources possible. Chief amongst these are the valuable records of the magazine *Appalachia*, edited by Professor C.E. Fay and published for the Appalachian Mountain Club by Houghton, Mifflin and Co., at Cambridge, Mass., U.S.A. The works of Mr. W.D. Wilcox and Messrs. H.E.M. Stutfield and J.N. Collie have also supplied data for ascents made by these climbers.

The altitudes have been taken as far as possible from the most recently issued maps and publications of the Dominion Land Survey. Otherwise the best authorities available have been consulted.

The list is arranged according to precedence of altitude and includes 40 peaks. The names of amateurs are given in alphabetical order, irrespective of leadership. The names of Swiss guides are printed in italics.

MT. COLUMBIA,	12,500 ft.	July 19, 1902.	J. Outram,
	C. Kaufmann.		
MT. FORBES,	12,100 ft.	Aug. 10, 1902.	J.N. Collie,
	J. Outram, H.E.M. Stutfield, G.M. Weed,		
	H. Woolley, *C. Kaufmann, H. Kaufmann.*		
MT. LYELL,	11,950 ft.	July 24, 1902.	J. Outram,
	C. Kaufmann.		

MT. ATHABASCA,	11,900 ft.	Aug. 18, 1898.	J.N. Collie,
	H. Woolley.		
MT. ASSINIBOINE,	11,860 ft.	Sept. 3, 1901.	J. Outram,
	C. *Bohren, C. Häsler.*		
MT. BRYCE,	11,750 ft.	Aug. 21, 1902.	J. Outram,
	C. *Kaufmann.*		
MT. GOODSIR,	11,671 ft.	July 16, 1903.	C.E. Fay,
	H.C. Parker, C. *Häsler, C. Kaufmann.*		
MT. ALEXANDRA,	11,650 ft.	Aug. 23, 1902.	J. Outram,
	C. *Kaufmann.*		
THE DOME,	11,650 ft.	Aug. 21, 1898.	J.N. Collie,
	H.E.M. Stutfield, H. Woolley.		
MT. TEMPLE,	11,637 ft.	Aug. 18, 1894.	S.E.S. Allen,
	L.F. Frissell, W.D. Wilcox.		
DIADEM PEAK,	11,500 ft.	Aug. 26, 1898.	J.N. Collie,
	H.E.M. Stutfield, H. Woolley.		
MT. VICTORIA,	11,400 ft.	Aug. 5, 1897.	J.N. Collie,
	C.E. Fay, A. Michael, *P. Sarbach.*		
MT. HUNGABEE,	11,305 ft.	July 21, 1903.	H.C. Parker,
	C. *Kaufmann, H. Kaufmann.*		
MT. MURCHISON,	11,300 ft.	July 29, 1902.	J.N. Collie,
	H.E.M. Stutfield, G.M. Weed, C. *Kaufmann.*		
MT. LEFROY,	11,290 ft.	Aug. 3, 1897.	J.N. Collie,
	H.B. Dixon, C.E. Fay, A. Michael, C.L. Noyes,		
	H.C. Parker, C.S. Thompson, J.R. Vanderlip,		
	P. Sarbach.		
MT. HECTOR,	11,205 ft.	July 30, 1895.	P.S. Abbot,
	C.E. Fay, C.S. Thompson.		
CONSOLATION PEAK,	11,200 ft.	Aug. 19, 1902.	J. Outram,
	C. *Kaufmann.*		

MT. VICTORIA (N. PEAK), 11,150 ft.   Aug. 24, 1900.   J. Outram,
W. Outram, J.H. Scattergood, —*Clark*, —*Zurfluh*.

MT. WILSON,   11,000 ft.   Aug. 26, 1902.   J. Outram,
C. Kaufmann.

MT. DELTAFORM,   10,945 ft.   Sept. 1, 1903.   A. Eggers,
H.C. Parker, *C. Kaufmann, H. Kaufmann*.

MT. FRESHFIELD,   10,900 ft.   Aug. 4, 1902.   J.N. Collie,
J. Outram, H.E.M. Stutfield, G.M. Weed,
C. Kaufmann, H. Kaufmann.

MT. BALFOUR,   10,875 ft.   Aug. 11, 1898.   C.L. Noyes,
C.S. Thompson, G.M. Weed.

HOWSE PEAK,   10,800 ft.   Aug. 14, 1902.   J.N. Collie,
H.E.M. Stutfield, G.M. Weed, H. Woolley,
H. Kaufmann.

MT. CHANCELLOR,   10,780 ft.   July 30, 1901.   J. Outram,
J.H. Scattergood, G.M. Weed, *C. Häsler*.

MT. VAUX,   10,741 ft.   July 16, 1901.   C.E. Fay,
J. Outram, J.H. Scattergood, *C. Häsler*.

MT. SARBACH,   10,700 ft.   Aug. 25, 1897.   G.P. Baker,
J.N. Collie, *P. Sarbach*.

MT. HABEL,   10,600 ft.   Aug. 15, 1901.   J. Outram,
E. Whymper, *C. Kaufmann*, C. Klucker,
J. Pollinger.

MT. STEPHEN,   10,523 ft.   Sept. 9, 1887.   J.J. McArthur
and another.

MT. BIDDLE,   10,500 ft.   Sept. 3, 1903.   A. Eggers,
H.C. Parker, *C. Kaufmann, H. Kaufmann*.

MT. COLLIE,   10,500 ft.   Aug. 19, 1901.   J. Outram,
E. Whymper, *C. Kaufmann*, C. Klucker,
F. Pollinger.

Mt. Neptuak,	10,500 ft.	Sept. 2, 1902,	J.N. Collie,
	H.E.M. Stutfield, C.M. Weed, H. Woolley,		
	H. *Kaufmann*.		
Mt. Thompson,	10,500 ft.	Sept. 6, 1898.	J.N. Collie,
	H.E.M. Stutfield, H. Woolley.		
Mt. Gordon,	10,400 ft.	Aug. 10, 1897.	G.P. Baker,
	J.N. Collie, H.B. Dixon, C.E. Fay, A. Michael,		
	C.L. Noyes, H.C. Parker, C.S. Thompson,		
	P. *Sarbach*.		
Mt. Chaba,	10,300 ft.	July 31, 1901.	J. Habel and
	two others.		
Cathedral Mountain,	10,284 ft.	Aug. 26, 1901.	J. Outram,
	J. *Bossoney*, C. *Klucker*.		
Mt. Aberdeen,	10,250 ft.	Aug. 17, 1894.	S.E.S. Allen,
	L.F. Frissell, W.D. Wilcox.		
Mt. Kaufmann,	10,200 ft.	July 30, 1902.	J. Outram,
	C. *Kaufmann*.		
The President,	10,200 ft.	Aug. 9, 1901.	J. Outram,
	C. *Kaufmann*, J. *Pollinger*.		
Turret Peak,	10,200 ft.	Aug. 19, 1902.	J. Outram,
	C. *Kaufmann*.		
Cathedral Spires,	10,100 ft.	Sept. 5, 1900.	J. Outram,
	W. Outram, C. *Häsler*.		

ENDNOTES

1   The entire block of a mountain, including buttresses and spurs.

2   It is interesting to note that Dr. Hector (now Sir James) revisited some of the scenes of his early explorations in 1904, 47 years after his first expedition.

3   A notch or pass. A large number of technical mountaineering terms are taken from the French.

4   "Climbs and Exploration in the Canadian Rockies," p. 220.

5   "The Rockies of Canada," p. 89.

6   "Ridge."

7   W.D. Wilcox in "The Rockies of Canada," p. 109.

8   Fissures in a glacier.

9   "Hid." A trappers' term.

10 "Gully."

11 Overhanging shelves of snow.

12 According to the D.L.S. figures, giving 11,637 feet to Mt. Temple, and 11,600 to Mt. Goodsir. The latter figure corresponds with our party's estimate of the altitude of Mt. Goodsir, when we ascended within 150 feet of the summit; but Professors Fay and Parker, who climbed to the top in 1903, have claimed an elevation for that peak of nearly 12,000 feet, though the former in a very recent article (February, 1905) puts the height at 11,671 feet.

13 First Ascent of Mt. Victoria," *Appalachia*, vol. IX, p.5.

14 *Appalachia*, vol. VIII, p. 139.

15 *Appalachia*, vol. X, p. 298.

16 The upper part of a snow-covered glacier.

17 See also Appendix B, p. 283, for serious accident on Mt. Gordon.

18 The large fissures occurring at the point where a glacier breaks from the mountainside.

19 "The Rockies of Canada," p. 40.

20 *Appalachia*, vol. VIII, p. 140.

21 Professor Fay, in *Appalachia*, Vol IX, p 9.

22 "The Rockies of Canada," p. 46.

23 "Beautiful," an Indian word.

24 "The Rockies of Canada," p 199.

25 *Appalachia*, vol. X, p 295.

26 *Appalachia*, vol. X, p. 291.

27 W.D. Wilcox, "The Rockies of Canada," p. 244.

28 D. L. S. Report for the year 1887.

29 D. L. S. Report for the year 1892.

30 Professor Fay's description cannot be improved on. He says: "From one-half an inch to an inch above the surface rose thin laminæ of shale, perhaps a millimetre in thickness, and from one-eighth to one-third of an inch apart, of varying lengths yet none of many inches, giving with their light and shade a general effect of dry grass, and breaking down under our footsteps."

31 "Takakkaw," an Indian word signifying "it is wonderful."

32 Here, one morning, we espied 17 or 18 mountain goats browsing upon the southern slopes.

33 *Appalachia*, vol. IX, p. 22.

34 In the light of subsequent investigations it is probable that our altitude was at least two hundred feet greater.

35 *Appalachia*, vol. X, p. 288.

36 But see note 12.

37 *Verbum sapienti sat est:* "a word to the wise is sufficient."

38 *Appalachia*, vol. VIII, p. 1.

39 *Appalachia*, vol. IX, p. 28.

40 Musical direction meaning to "repeat from the head," from the beginning.

41 The only record of its being ascended is that of Messrs. Nichols, Noyes and Thompson, in August, 1898, when they went as far as Vulture Col, and, being unable to see a prospect of descending thence to Hector Lake, made their exit by the Bow Glacier.

42 It may be observed that Dr. Hector in a subsequent note expresses a doubt as to the accuracy of his former estimate of its altitude. From a close study of Dr. Hector's narrative and his outline drawing of the peak, the doubt has been very strongly borne in upon my mind as to whether he did not make some error of identification on one of his trips, and get his contour and estimated elevation from an observation of Mt. Forbes.

43 "Climbs and Exploration in the Canadian Rockies," p. 138.

44 "Climbs and Exploration in the Canadian Rockies," p. 251

45 Climbs and Exploration in the Canadian Rockies," p. 286.

46 Free from snow.

47 In view of the size and geographical importance of the river and valley, I would urge the adoption of some more convenient and euphonious name than the cumbrous present designation of "The West Branch of the North Fork of the North Saskatchewan!"

48 "Climbs and Exploration in the Canadian Rockies," p. 106.

49 See p. 239

50 A study of Dr. Hector's map and published notes with reference to the naming of Mt. Lyell by him in 1858, and observations made in the neighbourhood from all points of the compass, lead me to the conclusion that the peak intended by the great pioneer explorer is undoubtedly the triple mountain at the head of the grand icefield which sweeps down to Glacier Lake. Following Dr. Hector's footsteps, notes in hand, this deduction appears inevitable, but, strange to say, in the position assigned to Mt. Lyell on his map, some distance to the east of the accepted mountain of that name and almost exactly north of Mt. Forbes, rises a considerable peak, which stood out very prominently in the view from that summit and from other lofty altitudes, though it is doubtful whether it is visible from any of the lower elevations visited by Dr. Hector.

51 "Climbs and Exploration in the Canadian Rockies," p. 107.

52 "Climbs and Exploration in the Canadian Rockies," p. 117.

53 My estimate of height was made by observations from two aneroids, one a Watkin mountain barometer, checked for weather variations by records kept throughout the day in camp, about 12 miles distant, and by the Government meteorologist at Banff, 100 miles away. The elevation of the camp was estimated by a long series of dead reckonings by aneroid, hence the mean of 12,661 feet, obtained from the barometers, has been roughly arrived at, and I have preferred to give a round figure of 12,500. In a note of trigonometrical estimates of some of the highest peaks in the Rockies, made by Mr. A.O. Wheeler, of the Dominion Land Survey, as the result of azimuths taken from

various stations occupied by him on the summits of peaks in the Selkirks, the altitude of Mt. Columbia is given as 12,740 feet, the mean of four observations with a range of 261 feet.

54 Unless the glacier should receive the same name as that given to the West Branch Valley—perhaps the most suitable solution—or that of Alexandra from the dominating peak.

55 The same suggestion is made as to the name of the pass.

56 Many of the glaciers in the Rockies and Selkirks are remarkable for the red hue of the névé, acres of their surface being brilliant with ruddy particles, which, I have been informed, are animalculæ. This was perhaps the most extensive and highly coloured of the several I have seen.

57 "It is solved by walking."

58 "Climbs and Exploration in the Canadian Rockies," p. 126.

59 Ibid., p. 128.

FURTHER READING

Please turn the page for descriptions of some related titles from Rocky Mountain Books.

Mountain Classics Collection #1

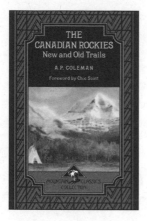

The Canadian Rockies:
New and Old Trails

by A.P. Coleman
foreword by Chic Scott

"There is a cleanness and virginity, an exquisite loneliness, about many of the Rocky Mountain peaks and valleys that has a peculiar charm. There is the feeling of having made a new discovery, of having caught Nature unawares at her work of creation."

—Arthur Philemon Coleman

Arthur Philemon Coleman was a passionate Canadian and one of the first to truly discover the beauty and majesty of this country's mountain ranges as an explorer, geologist and mountaineer. In 1884, before the railway traversed the Rocky and Columbia mountains, Coleman headed west on the first of what would be eight mountaineering expeditions, making his way on foot and pack horse, with Native guides and without, over passes in Alberta and British Columbia.

First published in 1911, this is the first book in the Rocky Mountain Books' Mountain Classics Collection. This new edition gives modern-day readers a glimpse of the early days of mountaineering in the Canadian West. It features a foreword by award-winning mountain historian Chic Scott.

ISBN 13: 978-1-894765-76-3
ISBN 10: 1-894765-76-1
5.5" x 8.5", 224 pages, softcover, $19.95 CDN

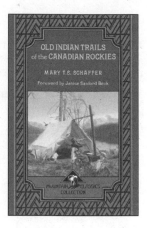

OLD INDIAN TRAILS OF THE CANADIAN ROCKIES

by Mary T.S. Schäffer
foreword by Janice Sanford Beck

"We seemed to have reached that horizon, and the limit of all endurance, to sit with folded hands and listen calmly to the stories of the hills we so longed to see, the hills which had lured and beckoned us for years before this long list of men had ever set foot in the country."
—Mary T.S. Schäffer

Mary T.S. Schäffer was an avid explorer and one of the first non-Native women to venture into the heart of the Canadian Rocky Mountains, where few women—or men—had gone before.

First published in 1911, *Old Indian Trails of the Canadian Rockies* is Schäffer's story of her adventures in the traditionally male-dominated world of climbing and exploration. It also sheds light on Native and non-Native relations in the early part of the 20th century. Full of daring adventure and romantic depictions of camp life, set against the grand backdrop of Canada's mountain landscapes, the book introduces readers to various characters from the annals of Canadian mountaineering history, including Arthur Philemon Coleman, Billy Warren, Sid Unwin, Bill Peyto and Jimmy Simpson.

Old Indian Trails of the Canadian Rockies, the second volume in the Mountain Classics Collection, is certain to entertain and enlighten 21st-century readers, historians, hikers and climbers.

ISBN: 978-1-894765-77-0
5.5" x 8.5", 192 pages, softcover, $19.95 CDN

No Ordinary Woman
The Story of Mary Schäffer Warren

by Janice Sanford Beck

Artist, photographer, writer, world traveller and, above all, explorer, Mary Schäffer Warren overcame the limited expectations of women at the turn of the nineteenth century in order to follow her dreams.

Mary Sharples, born into a wealthy Quaker family in Pennsylvania, was a precocious child who excelled at school yet "did not know how to make a bed at the tender age of 18." She was much more interested in the arts and in travelling. A trip across Canada in 1889 proved the turning point in Mary's life. Not only did she meet her future husband—doctor and botanist Charles Schäffer—she also fell hopelessly in love with the Canadian mountains.

After Charles' death, Mary embarked on a series of explorations into the Canadian Rockies at a time when it was not thought proper for a woman to do so. Her most famous trips of 1907 and 1908 resulted in the rediscovery of Maligne Lake and the highly regarded book *Old Indian Trails of the Canadian Rockies*. Mary eventually settled in Banff and there married her handsome young guide, Billy Warren.

Mary Schäffer Warren died in 1937, but her story lives on, a continuous inspiration to modern young people and women in particular.

ISBN: 978-0-921102-82-3
5.5" x 8.5", 224 pages , softcover, $24.95 CDN

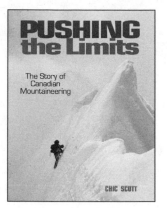

PUSHING THE LIMITS
The Story of Canadian Mountaineering

by Chic Scott

Recipient of the Banff Mountain Book Festival's Canadian Rockies Award

"A book to be read and digested, then sampled, then read and dipped into often. A fine achievement for this dedicated author."

　　　　—Bruce Fairley, *Canadian Alpine Journal*

This important book recounts Canada's 200-year mountaineering history. Through the use of stories and pictures, Chic Scott documents the evolution of climbing in Canada. He introduces us to the early mountain pioneers and the modern-day climbing athletes; he takes us to the crags and the gyms, from the west coast to Québec, and from the Yukon to the Rockies.

But most importantly, Scott showcases Canadian climbers—the routes that challenged them, the peaks that inspired them, their insatiable desire to climber harder, to push the limits.

ISBN 10: 1-921102-59-3
8.5" x 11", 440 pages , hardcover, $59.95 CDN